ON TRIAL

BY JACK BATTEN

for Virginia
Christmas 90
Best wishes.
Bay

Macmillan of Canada
A Division of Canada Publishing Corporation
Toronto, Ontario, Canada

For my sister, Betsy Bertram

Canadian Cataloguing in Publication Data

Batten, Jack, date.
  On trial

ISBN 0–7715–9920–X

1. Trials — Canada. I. Title.

KE225.B38   1988   347.71'07   C88–094028–X
KF220.B38   1988

Design: Don Fernley

Macmillan of Canada
A Division of Canada Publishing Corporation
Toronto, Ontario, Canada

Printed in Canada

CONTENTS

ACKNOWLEDGMENTS

As you'll gather in reading this book, many of the lawyers involved in the three cases I've written about were extraordinarily open and accommodating in recalling for me their adventures in and out of court. So were several of the people who were even more intimately and painfully caught up in the cases as plaintiffs and defendants. In each of the three cases, there was one person in particular who went to enormous lengths in helping me: Linda Nascher in the Hagood Hardy case, Wayne MacKay in the Luke Elwood case, and Harry Walsh in the Doug Palmer case. It was George Jonas and Guy Kay who introduced me to the Palmer case. And it was Anne Holloway who suggested the idea for the book and guided it through the editing process. Linda McKnight filled every notion of an author's ideal publisher. The Ontario Arts Council generously granted funds that helped cover much of the expense of travel and research. Ann Kemp came up with material on the Palmer case that was golden, and in Vancouver, the team of Garry, Julie, Julian, and Laurence, as they have been so often in the past, were wonderful hosts and companions. And Majorie Harris, as she has for twenty-two years, gave her love and encouragement. To everyone, I am tremendously grateful.

PREFACE

I used to think the best place to go for some drama and a few laughs, a hit of tension, and a tear or two was a movie theatre. Now I'm not so sure. From my experience of the past ten years, the best place may be a Canadian courtroom.

I started hanging around courtrooms and writing about what goes on inside them for a book called *Lawyers*, which was published in 1980. Three more books about the legal profession followed, and this one, *On Trial*, makes the fifth in the series. And for all of the books I've spent hundreds of hours sitting in courtrooms across the country taking in the action. Admittedly, "action" isn't always the accurate noun to describe court proceedings, not when counsel and judge bog down in legal debate that only insiders can truly appreciate. But for most of the time, action is the absolutely exact word.

It's mainly intellectual action. It's a matter of wit and mental games. It pits lawyer against lawyer in battles where the stakes are measured in many crucial ways, in money won or lost, in freedom or imprisonment, in reputations sacrificed or vindicated. There's an element of sport in it — as long as you're not too intimately involved in the result — and all the emotions come into play too. The action can even get a trifle physical, as it did in the exhilarating moment in a Provincial Court in Toronto when an accused man stunned me and everyone else, including the policemen on guard, by leaping out of the prisoners' box and charging through the courtroom in what turned out to be, after a hair-raising struggle, a futile break for freedom.

The intellectual action I'm taking about springs from the very nature of the system that operates in Canadian courts. It's called the adversarial system. Two opponents bang away at each other, and when they're finished, a referee chooses the winner. The referee is, of course, the judge, with assistance in some criminal cases from a jury. In a civil lawsuit, the two opponents are labelled plaintiff and defendant, and in a criminal case, it's the crown on one side and the accused on the other. In both kinds of case, civil and criminal, the parties rarely speak for themselves, except from the witness stand. Someone else speaks for them — lawyers. These are courtroom lawyers — defence counsel, crown attorneys, civil-litigation specialists — and they handle the verbal thrust-and-parry in court. That's how the system works, the adversarial system, and for me, it produces excitement of a remarkably high order.

In this book, I've chosen to write about three Canadian cases from recent years that especially fascinate me. Geographically, they represent diversity, one case each from Vancouver, Toronto, and Halifax. In legal terms, one is criminal and the other two are civil. One case, centring on the well-known Canadian musician and composer Hagood Hardy, offers the strange machinations of the first, and so far only, music-plagiarism case in Canada. Another, the Luke Elwood case, is a heart-breaker that brings the Charter of Rights into compelling play. And the third, a multi-million-dollar drug case from Vancouver, is full of stuff that you may have thought turned up only on *L.A. Law* — a recanting witness, a gang that couldn't shoot straight, behind-the-scenes legal manipulations, and moments of low comedy.

I've used some techniques in telling the wild and wonderful stories of these three cases that are more common to the silver screen than to the usual accounts of proceedings in court. I've moved much of the action out of the courtroom and re-created it in scenes on the street, in bars, in lawyers' offices, and, in one instance, on a Vancouver sidewalk where one man tried to gun down another. These scenes aren't the product of my imagination. They're based on careful reading of long trial transcripts and on extensive interviews with lawyers and others who were participants in the events or observers of them, or were otherwise privy to what went on. By employing this approach, I think I've made the impact of the cases even more powerful and brought the drama — and the occasional laugh — closer to the audience.

Just like in the movies.

HOMECOMING

Hagood Hardy had a headache.

It hurt so much that back at his lawyer's office during the noon break from the trial in the Toronto Courthouse up the street, the only way he could find relief was by lying on the office floor and staring at the ceiling while the lawyers sat around a table up above him munching sandwiches and talking strategy. The headache got worse. Hardy had to check out of the trial — *his* trial, the trial where *he* was the defendant — and into St. Michael's Hospital. Doctors told him the cause of the headache reached back to an accident he'd had a few months earlier in the winter of 1982. He'd bumped his head, not seriously he thought at the time, against a golf cart on a course in Florida where he was on vacation. He had a blood clot on his brain. The freakish accident accounted for the origins of the headache, but something much more recent was exacerbating the pain. It was the trial, a contest in the courtroom that threatened two of the things in Hardy's life that he most valued, his music and his honesty.

Hardy was so offended and outraged, so damned mad, that his head ached, and he thought the agony might never go away.

Until the headache, until the trial, Hardy had lived as close

1

as one gets to a charmed life. His background was steeped in honourable Canadian content. On his father's side, there were a County Court judge, a senator, and other figures prominent in the history of Brantford, Ontario. On his mother's side, there were ancestors immortalized in the name of the hamlet they helped to found, Hagood Corners, Alberta. Hardy grew up in comfortable circumstances in Oakville, a repository of established money just west of Toronto. For his secondary schooling, he was boarded at Trinity College School in Port Hope, Ontario, and in 1955 he progressed effortlessly to the University of Toronto, where he took a degree in political science and economics. When he married in 1959, it was to Martha Robert, a woman of patrician beauty and the daughter of a socially well-fixed family from the old Toronto enclave of Rosedale.

Parallel to these splendid pieces of fortune — family, education, good marriage — maybe at times taking precedence to them, Hardy had music to warm and spur him. The connection began in the traditional way with a kid's weekly piano lessons from nice ladies, Miss Lawrence and Mrs. Scott in Hardy's case, who taught in their parlours on the other side of town. Hardy absorbed seven years of lessons, and after them, apart from very short courses in composition from Gordon Delamont, the esteemed Toronto jazz composer, and from John Weinzweig, the esteemed Toronto classical composer, he had no other formal instruction. Perhaps he didn't need instruction. Hardy was a natural. He breathed in music the way the rest of the population takes in air.

His first bands came in the Oakville days, the Swing Slingers and the Mad Hatters, making music that the other kids could dance to. From the beginning, Hardy was usually the leader, less often the sideman. That was especially the case after he discovered the vibraphone in the mid-1950s. It's an eccentric instrument, three octaves of big fat keys that the player strikes with mallets, sending melodies and improvisations spinning into the air on the impetus of a small electric motor. "It's not what you call a necessary instrument," Hardy says. "But when Henry Mancini wrote parts for it into the background music to the *Peter Gunn* TV series, people started to notice it." A tiny handful of jazz musicians made ingenious music and their own reputations on the vibraphone — Milt Jackson, Terry Gibbs, Gary Burton — and Hardy set himself to do the same. Jazz was his prime musical love, and though he won plenty of applause from aficionados in clubs and concerts around Toronto, New York City was the town where a jazzman had to be measured. In January 1961, married and the father of a daughter, the first of four kids, Hardy lit out for the Apple.

While he waited for his New York musicians' union card to come through, he took day jobs. He ran the Addressograph machine at the Willard Alexander Agency, and when the big blizzard of '61 hit Manhattan, he shovelled snow for the Department of Sanitation. One February night, after a day at the end of a shovel, he dropped by the Five Spot, a cutting-edge jazz club where an alto saxophonist named Gigi Gryce was leading a small band. The band, daring and experimental, included a vibraphone in its instrumental makeup, but that night the vibraphonist, snowed in somewhere, hadn't put in an appearance. Gryce hired Hardy on the spot, and on the night that the gig at the Five Spot ended a month later, a flutist named Herbie Mann happened to be in the audience. Mann liked what he heard from the vibes player and offered Hardy a place in his group. The job began the following night and lasted a year and a half.

The work with Gryce and Mann, both respected jazzmen, gave Hardy hip prestige. But by 1963, with his family expanding, Hardy's greater need was for money and stability. He found it in Martin Denny's group. The music brought musical challenges of a different sort. "Lush sounds," Hardy describes Denny's music. "Exotic stuff, very moody, very emotional. You know — bird-calls." What came with the aviary songs was a salary that tripled the sum Hardy earned

3

from Herbie Mann and a chance for his family to settle awhile in Hawaii, where Denny made his headquarters.

Hardy's next employment shift in the summer of 1964 consolidated his status as a jazz musician of impeccable credentials. He joined George Shearing, a mightily gifted pianist, a civilized gentleman, and a demanding teacher. It's said among jazz musicians that six months with George Shearing is the learning equivalent of three years at the Juilliard School of Music. Hardy played alongside Shearing for two and a half years.

"Here's an example of what George would do to the rest of the guys in the quintet," Hardy remembers. "He'd get a request in a club for, say, 'Green Dolphin Street'. Well, that's a pretty familiar tune. Routine almost. But for interest's sake, George'd call out to us, take it in G-flat. *G-flat*?! It's an absolutely unheard-of key. But George was forcing us to dig into the music and understand all the possibilities."

Work with Shearing — six weeks on the road followed by two months off — was enlightening, and home life for the Hardys in Canoga Park in Southern California was blissful. That lasted until the kids began to grow up, and Hagood and Martha checked out the local schools. "Drug-dealing in the corridors," Hardy says. "Even at public school." He gave his notice to Shearing, and the family shipped home to safe, sane Toronto.

Hardy found plenty to occupy him around the old home town. Sometimes he worked as a solo pianist in supper clubs, more often he played with his new trio — vibes, bass, and drums — in upscale cocktail lounges. Stop 33 became his principal scene of musical operations, a handsome, spacious room on the top of the tony Sutton Place Hotel that offered a dramatic night-time view of the lit-up Toronto. In the spring of 1969, Hardy turned more adventurous and formed a bigger group, The Montage — bass, drums, the leader on piano and vibes, and two young women singers who had voices of startling range and élan. Hardy's idea was to perform contemporary songs in a style that mixed jazz and Latin rhythms. The Montage suffered early struggles; on its first date, at a club in Rochester, New York, called the Living Room, management paid Hardy in one-dollar bills and endorsed welfare cheques. But the group rapidly coaxed to itself a large and enthusiastic audience — as long as it confined its activities to dates beyond the Canadian borders.

"It was total frustration as far as nationalism was concerned," Hardy recalled the period. "We used to go away on weekends, play two concerts in Ohio or a date in Vegas, and come back with a few thousand dollars. But I couldn't get bookings up here. We toured Europe, played the American supper-club circuit, did shows with Bob Hope. But Canada? Forget it, except for a couple of hotels and a club in Toronto."

The Toronto club was conspicuously not Stop 33. Hardy had expected to use the room as The Montage's home base. After all, he'd put the place on the entertainment map, the first and longest-running musician to work in it. And perhaps even more to the point in the matter of loyalty, before Stop 33 opened, when it was in the design and renovation stage, Hardy had been summoned as a non-paid consultant on acoustics and décor. It was in at least a small sense *his* club. He performed at the staff Christmas parties. Thus, though The Montage had played Stop 33 during its early months as a group, when Sutton Place management handed Hardy a contract in the summer of 1970 for a measly one thousand dollars a week, which represented a five-hundred-dollar cut from The Montage's first appearances, he was so put off that he vowed never again to set foot in the place. He meant as performer *and* as patron. That declaration of anger in July 1970 turned out to have an unexpected significance almost twelve years later in April 1982 when Hardy faced his painful day in court.

The Montage stayed in successful and mostly non-Canadian business until early 1974, when Hardy closed down the group. By then, he felt he'd explored most of its musical possibilities. By then, the days and nights on the road away from home were beginning to fray his energies. And by then, he'd discovered himself to be particularly adept at another branch of music. It was a funny little corner of the industry. But it was spectacularly rewarding in dollars and cents.

Jingles.

That's the generic term to describe the bursts of melody that fit behind commercials on radio and television. It's the music, taking inspiration from breakfast cereals and laxatives and Detroit's finest, that hustles products. For some commercials, the music's role is mainly mood-setting sounds; in others, a quick jolt of melody is called for. In all, for messages that last in time frames calculated in seconds, brevity is of the essence.

When Hardy stumbled onto the jingles field in the late 1960s, the music of the pop charts and the music of commercials were beginning to interact. In the United States, one richly paid but obscure composer turned out jingles with titles like "Join the Pepsi Generation" and "You Deserve a Break Today". The composer decided to use his bent for catchy melodies on longer songs, which he recorded and performed. The songs hit the charts and his concerts sold out. The singer-composer's name was Barry Manilow, and, performing songs that didn't sound all that different from his jingles, he continued to be just as richly paid as in his jingles days. But not at all obscure.

"I don't downgrade jingles," Hagood Hardy said, speaking in the late 1970s when he'd been writing them for almost a decade. "I go by something Sonny Rollins once said — Sonny Rollins, the great tenor saxophonist. He said you can play every night of the week in a jazz club and you're lucky if you come out with eight bars that sound really original and satisfying. Well, okay, I'll get my satisfaction from writing, and jingles make a perfectly legitimate form. You've only got thirty or sixty seconds, depending on the length of the commercial, and in that time you have to be concise, distinctive, and deliver something that has a beginning, middle, and end. That's unique in *any* kind of music."

Though jingles had never occurred to Hardy as a possibility in his own music picture until advertising agencies approached him, his background equipped him for the field. So what if he lacked the Barry Manilow pop touch — Hardy had other equally valuable attributes. As a jazz musician, improvising solos every night on the job, he explored the art of instant melody. As a member of Martin Denny's ensemble, he developed a facility for moody musical moments. Along the way, he'd composed the odd song for the odd occasion — *Exotica Suite* for Denny, a love ballad for a movie called *Dirty Tricks* with Elliott Gould and Kate Jackson — and when the ad guys came knocking on his door, he was ready to enter the jingles biz.

Versatility was Hardy's long suit. He wrote music to order: a sprightly serenade for Acadia cars, a theme reminiscent of the music from *2001* for Pontiac Astra, a bouncy flute melody for Froot Loops cereal, something jazzy for Datsun, something rooty-toot for CP Rail. When GMC trucks needed music, Hardy delivered a big band of brass and rhythm surging through a mini-suite of orchestral effects. "Gravel-pit music," Hardy called it. He concocted a tune made up largely of hushes and spaces with a bongo pinging around the edges to summon up "the morning sounds of Rice Krispies". And for a celebration of General Tire, he spun out a country number that a folk-singer wrapped his nasal twang around.

"If anybody told me he recognized my stuff," Hardy said, "I'd be dead in the industry. The idea is to come up with a different — but appropriate — sound every time out."

Toward the end of July 1972, the Leo Burnett Advertising Agency summoned Hardy to a meeting. Burnett was launching a new campaign for its prized client, Salada Tea, and the thrust of the television spots, the ad people told Hardy, was to project something homespun but classy. They showed Hardy

7

a storyboard for the first projected commercial. A storyboard is a series of drawings that act as a primitive outline of the images that eventually reach the TV screen in fleshed-out form with actors, sets, words, and music. For the tea commercial, the storyboard illustrated a simple little tale: handsome young couple piling into a taxi, driving through a luscious down-east landscape to a chocolate-box house where an older couple welcome them over cups of hot Salada Tea. What Burnett expected of Hardy was twenty seconds of music, enough for a sixteen-bar theme that would, as Peter Anastasoff, the Burnett producer on the Salada account, put it, "convey a warm, loving, family, togetherness situation."

At home, Hardy sat down at the spinnet piano in his workroom on the second floor of the house where he, Martha, and the kids lived in the Moore Park section of Toronto and began to noodle. The process needed a few days. He thought and tried out ideas on the spinnet. Fairly soon he got something that appealed to him. He played it through a few times, changing bars, nudging notes, rewriting, and when he was very sure of the tune, he recorded it on his Sony 55. It was just piano playing the sixteen-bar melody.

As was his custom, Hardy ran the tape for his wife. Martha is the first to hear every note of music that Hardy writes. She liked the Salada theme. More than liked it — she was crazy about it. So was Peter Anastasoff at Leo Burnett. The music that Martha Hardy and Peter Anastasoff heard was sweetly lyrical, not saccharine, just romantic enough, warm, and curiously the kind of music that manages to linger in the mind for a day or two.

Hardy's theme went into the finished Salada commercial, the one with the cab and the old folks and the tea-party in the chocolate-box house. In fact, it went into three Salada commercials. All three set up homey situations. All acquired names from the agency people that reflected their content: "Taxi" and "Birthday" and "Church". And all three got exceptionally heavy TV play, though in different time periods for each of the three commercials, between January 1973 and June 1975. The commercials caught the attention of the market that Burnett was trying to reach, and that made Salada Tea a very happy client.

Much of the viewer response was to the music behind the pictures. The watchers by their TV sets were also listeners, and they wanted to know where they could purchase a recording of the lovely Salada song. They wrote to Salada and to Leo Burnett in sufficient numbers to pique everyone's interest in further possibilities for the song. Everyone's interest except Hardy's.

"I hate to go back to old work," he says. "I hate to rewrite."

But eventually, persuaded by the notion of all those fans who were apparently waiting with their money for a record, he set out to expand the sixteen bars. For the commercial, he'd written an eight-bar theme that was essentially repeated in the second eight bars. For the recorded version, he added another eight bars that contained a different theme — the "bridge" in musical parlance — and then returned to the original theme over the concluding sixteen bars. The result, with an introduction, more repetition, and an ending, provided the musical material for a conventional three-minute pop song, and Hardy recorded it with himself playing solo piano against a string background with a dash of flute for seasoning. Hardy now had, as they say in the record industry, product in hand. What he didn't have was a title for his song. Martha Hardy filled in that last gap.

"The Homecoming" she called the song.

"It wasn't too difficult," she says. "I got it from the looks on the faces of the old people in the commercial with the taxi."

Hardy formed a record label, Isis, and released "The Homecoming" as a single in the fall of 1974. Operating on his own, it turned out, was a big mistake. Hardy knew nothing about a crucial side of the record business: sales and promotion. "I think I sold two boxes of the thing to Sam the

9

Record Man at Christmas," he says. "That was about it." The record wasn't reaching the people who'd been enchanted by the tea commercial. Hardy took "The Homecoming" to the major record companies. A&M, Polydor, and GRT turned it down flat. WEA didn't bother to listen to it. And nobody at Canadian Capitol returned Hardy's calls.

"Everybody figured the music was too far out of the mainstream of what was happening in pop music," Hardy says. "I didn't blame them. I thought so too."

Tom Williams and Al Mair didn't think so. The two men were a couple of sharp operators who ran a small, aggressive company called Attic Records. Attic's specialty was folk music, but Williams and Mair thought they heard something very interesting when Hardy played them his tape of "The Homecoming".

"We heard a hit," Mair says. "You have to understand the way the Top 10 worked. A romantic vocal wasn't going to crack it, not a Perry Como or an Andy Williams. But every so often an instrumental in that style came in from nowhere. 'Love Is Blue'. 'Strangers on the Shore'. Theme from *Love Story*. Theme from *The Godfather*. Lot of movie music did the job. And we thought 'The Homecoming' would go the same route."

Attic wanted to market the song both as a single and as the centrepiece of an album. To fill out the album, Hardy recorded ten more ballads in the same lush vein he'd used in "The Homecoming", piano and string orchestra and acres of luxurious sound. Four of the additional tunes were familiar standards, and the other six were Hardy's own velvety compositions. One of them, "Jennifer's Song", came in an earlier version with a vocal by Hardy's younger daughter, Jennifer, who often sang on her father's jingles. And another, "Wintertime", was equipped with lyrics written by Hardy's stockbroker father-in-law, Paul Robert, a man whose affection for jazz and for a well-turned phrase made him a graceful lyricist. And, oh yes, the dreamy photograph that decorated the

10

jacket of the album *The Homecoming*, a name, you remember, which Martha Hardy conceived, was taken by Hardy. It was a family enterprise.

Attic released single and album in the summer of 1975, and the team of Tom Williams and Al Mair devised their promotional attack. It had three prongs. First, phone calls to program directors and disc jockeys at pop radio stations across the country. "There's nothing mysterious about selling records," Mair says. "You just hack away until you've got people to see the advantages." Second, displays of "Homecoming" posters and album covers in record stores. "We made customers think Hardy." And, third, Hardy autograph sessions in places like Eaton's, Simpsons, and The Bay. "Hagood was good at the autographing because he's such a straight-ahead person," Mair recalls.

The following January, the results began to come in. "The Homecoming" had sold fifty thousand copies as a single and eighty thousand as an album. And that was in Canada alone. When "The Homecoming" invaded the American market, distributed by Capitol Records, it soared to sales of a half-million for both single and album by the spring of 1976. Hardy's song, beginning life as a humble tea commercial, emerged an unqualified pop hit, a gentle pause in the clatter of rock and roll.

At the same time, through the mid-1970s, Hardy was pushing his own work as a composer far beyond the thirty seconds of a jingle or the three minutes of a pop song. He wrote longer works, scores for movies, background music for TV dramas, the accompaniment to documentaries. For a CBC-TV special that Malcolm Muggeridge prepared on the life and literature of Feodor Dostoevsky, Hardy produced twenty-nine minutes of music that caught the dark, dense, brooding tone of the images on the screen. Versatility, even over the long haul, was still the tip on Hardy.

The immediate effect of "The Homecoming" on Hardy's flourishing career, apart from fattening his bank account, was to draw him back into on-stage performance. Hardy's idea — and the idea of the two entrepreneurs over at Attic Records — was to offer audiences the chance to hear in concert the music they got on *The Homecoming* album. To do a Barry Manilow *sans* vocals.

Hardy didn't skimp on details. For concert presentation, he put together an orchestra that would fill the most formidable stage — eighteen strings, two French horns, oboe, flute, and a solid jazz rhythm section — and he had himself booked into the best halls across Canada and the United States. Hardy was back on the road. So, this time around, was his wife; Martha, proving that when it came to versatility, Hagood didn't hold a monopoly in the Hardy family, went along to handle the lighting in the cross-country concert halls.

Those halls, as it developed, were sell-outs when the Hardy ensemble arrived in town. The audiences that bought the album — "an older crowd," Al Mair says, "who didn't want music that preached at them" — bought the concerts. The music was of course the prime draw, but Hardy's on-stage persona helped to sell the act. He radiated a comfortable old-shoe attractiveness with his neatly arranged features, tightly curled dark hair, a figure running mildly to bulge, and the winsome smile that seemed to belong on a little kid rather than on a man who'd earned much of his living in bars. Between numbers, when he spoke to the folks in the seats, he was witty and cheerfully instructive. Hardy may have been a pro at work, but he came across as more like everybody's favourite high-school history teacher.

Hardy's work stayed in high gear over the rest of the 1970s. He composed. He performed. He recorded more albums. And he toured. Much of the impetus for the public side of his career, the concerts and tours, came from the success of "The Homecoming". No one, least of all Hardy, questioned that truth. In a real sense, the tune was Hardy's signature.

Frank Sinatra had "My Way". Tony Bennett had "I Left My Heart in San Francisco". And Hagood Hardy had "The Homecoming". They belonged together, man and song.

And then Hardy received a letter dated September 13, 1980, that tried to separate him from "The Homecoming". The letter didn't arrive as a total shock to Hardy. Four years earlier, he'd caught rumours that someone out there, someone he'd never heard of, was claiming to be the real composer of "The Homecoming". Hardy was indignant. He talked to Ralph McCreath, his friend and lawyer. Maybe he'd sue this guy. But after a while the whole thing drifted away. Hardy was busy. The claimant, whoever he was, was obviously a nut, and Hardy let the silly fuss recede, and got on with the rest of his very active life. The letter of September 13, 1980, however, made the rumours into reality and brought back all of Hardy's indignation.

The letter came from a lawyer named Brian Wheatley, and it said that Wheatley's client, a man named Ivan Gondos, was the one, the true, the only, the original composer of the piece of music that Hardy called "The Homecoming". Gondos called it "Variations on a Theme in A Minor", a piece that he wrote, Gondos said, long before Hardy composed "The Homecoming". Gondos was accusing Hardy of lifting "The Homecoming" from "Variations", and what Gondos wanted was primarily recognition of himself as the first writer of the melody in question and secondly recompense in cash. His claims were spelled out in more detail a few weeks later, on November 17, 1980, when Wheatley commenced an action on behalf of Gondos in the Supreme Court of Ontario. The action alleged that, with "The Homecoming", Hardy had infringed the copyright which Gondos held in his composition "Variations on a Theme in A Minor". As compensation, the lawsuit asked that Hardy pay Gondos one hundred thousand dollars.

"I felt unclean," Hardy said many years later, looking back

on the days after he was served in the action. "I knew I hadn't stolen anybody's music, but just being accused of it in public made me feel dirty."

It was the beginning of a twenty-two-month ordeal for Hardy, a period in which questions were raised about his veracity and talent, the start of a long stretch of time that gave Hardy a giant headache.

Ivan Gondos — or Louis Julian Ivan Gondos, to give him his full name, or Louis Ivanfai Gondos, Louis Gallant Gondos, Gallant Gondos, and Ivan Fai Gondos, as he variously billed himself in professional circles — didn't lead nearly so charmed a life as Hagood Hardy.

Gondos was born on July 11, 1934 — making him a couple of years older than Hardy — in the town of Kaposvar in the southwest corner of Hungary. He emigrated to Canada with his parents when he was two. After a few years in Hamilton, Ontario, the family moved to Toronto, first to the west end, then closer to the centre of the city. Ivan Gondos's father was a working man without much time for leisure, but there was plenty of music in the Gondos house. The father sang Hungarian and Gypsy folk songs, and the mother played an ancient instrument called the cymbalum, a kind of Magyar dulcimer, a boxy stringed instrument that the player struck with mallets. Little Ivan developed into a musical prodigy. He went to Central Technical School for his secondary education, but dropped out before Grade 12 to concentrate on the piano and the organ. His studies, he was later to say, took him to Professor Bela Borzorninyi at the Royal Conservatory of Music in Toronto, where Gondos busied himself at learning the mysteries of performance and composition. Music consumed the young Gondos.

When it came time to earn a living, he began with non-musical jobs. He apprenticed as a film editor at the CBC and worked in a toy factory. But inevitably music won out, and

Gondos launched himself in his early twenties on a career of teaching and performing. He gave lessons on both piano and organ, at first in arrangements with the Heintzman Piano Company and the Allen Organ Company and later out of his own home. As a performer, he found his niche in cocktail lounges. He thought of himself as a romantic interpreter of songs, a musician who preferred the classics and served up classical interpretations of popular ballads. His approach — "Stella by Starlight" à la Chopin — blended nicely into the atmosphere of chic bars where men wore suits, women dressed to kill, and everybody conversed in whispers. The Park Plaza Hotel, the bar at Winston's Restaurant, Le Cabaret, La Coterie, Café de la Paix, and briefly, but, as it later developed, significantly, Stop 33 at the Sutton Place Hotel — Gondos worked all the rooms in the late 1960s and early '70s, and felt right at home.

The date at Winston's was especially serendipitous for him because it was while he was booked into the place, a favourite Establishment hangout, that a man named Bill Waterhouse heard the Gondos piano stylings. Waterhouse ran Deerhurst Inn, a year-round resort in the Muskoka area about one hundred miles north of Toronto, and he thought Gondos's brand of music would lend a properly high-toned touch during Deerhurst's dinner hour and on through coffee and brandy until the last Deerhurst guest faded to bed. Waterhouse hired Gondos, and Gondos packed up his family — wife and six children — and headed north. The job at Deerhurst, beginning in 1972, continued through the rest of the decade, the longest — and last — engagement of Gondos's career.

Gondos cut a sauve figure at the Deerhurst piano, which, incidentally, was his own instrument. He had a face like the pianist-actor Dudley Moore's, handsome in a puckish way. He had Dudley Moore hair, too, grown in a thick, dark circle around his head. Where Gondos separated from Moore, who is diminutive at best, was in size; he was large, six feet two,

15

two hundred pounds, and very impressive. Gondos's speech patterns and accent were touched by Middle Europe. He was removed from Kaposvar by thousands of miles and dozens of years, but he hadn't surrendered his Hungarian sound or sensibility. It was part of his appeal — Ivan Gondos, the continental stylist of the keyboard.

As a composer, Gondos was, by his own estimate, prolific.

"How many songs have you written?" a lawyer asked him during the proceedings in which Gondos sued Hagood Hardy.

"Oh, a couple of thousand," Gondos answered airily.

His song-writing came in many forms. Some compositions — "Astronaut's Prayer", "April Legend Opus 23", "The Only World I Knew" — reflected what he called his "romantic style". Others — "Bicycles" and "Bachcycle" — were examples of his "baroque style". With a man named John Smy, Gondos wrote a kind of musical comedy called *Merry Go Round* that had a dozen or so songs with titles like "International Morse Love Song" and "Moonlight on Lake Louise". Gondos wrote love ballads — "No Candles Left to Burn" was a favourite of his — and longer pieces, among them a work called *Children's Suite*, which was to figure prominently in his lawsuit against Hardy.

Gondos was a tireless concocter of tunes, but no matter what style he wrote in, no matter what form his songs took, there were two points that were absolutely clear about the Gondos oeuvre. One was that he faithfully registered all of his songs, or almost all, with BMI. And the other was that, with a couple of exceptions, not many people ever *heard* Gondos's compositions — not "Astronaut's Prayer", not "Bachcycle", not "International Morse Love Song" or the other ditties from *Merry Go Round*, not a single note of most of the "couple of thousand" songs.

BMI stood for Broadcast Music Incorporated (its name was changed in the late 1970s to Pro Canada), and it was a non-profit society that operated for the benefit of, among others,

16

song-writers. On behalf of its members, BMI monitored the number of times that a composer's songs were performed in nightclubs, at concerts, and, by recording, on radio stations. It collected payments from the people who played or sang the songs and from the places where the songs were played or sung, and it passed on the payments to the composers. BMI, in brief, was in the royalty business. Hagood Hardy, for example, registered "The Homecoming" with BMI in 1975 and collected royalties amounting to tens of thousands of dollars for the use that other musicians and radio stations made of the song. Ivan Gondos was naturally anxious to get in on the payment end of composing, and he joined BMI in 1965. Thereafter, as "Moonlight on Lake Louise" and the other compositions emerged from his creative processes, he duly filed all of them — with one notable exception — on the BMI register. Alas, it appeared that no one, apart from Gondos himself, performed his songs, no other pianist or singer or instrumentalist, and the total of Gondos's payments from BMI added up to zip. BMI issued no royalty cheques to Ivan Gondos.

For all his prolific ways — and this is the second point about Gondos's music — he had somehow missed the popular touch. He recorded a few of his songs on three albums. They were called *Muskoka Reflections*, *Shoresands and Driftwood*, and *Ivan Plays Favorites*. But the albums were home-made affairs, recorded under Gondos's own supervision, and no record company or distributor picked them up. Gondos handled them himself, sometimes giving the albums away at Deerhurst as a promotion item, sometimes peddling them for six dollars apiece. Otherwise, Gondos's work didn't move, and it was plain that his songs were not the material of the Top 10 or even the Top 10,000.

But, as Gondos was to claim, there was one enormous exception, one song of his that was a proven popular hit of terrific proportions. According to Gondos, the hit number found life as part of his ambitious long work, *Children's*

17

Suite. Gondos said he began composing the suite when he was a young man, barely out of his teens, and that he continued to add to it, revise and improve it, over two and a half decades. It was made up of several sections, "Little Snowflake", "Baroque Serenade", "Ode to Lucky" (a piece in memoriam to the Gondos dog, written immediately after her death). And among the sections that comprised *Children's Suite*, the section written first, as early as the mid-1950s, was a composition that Gondos called "Variations on a Theme in A Minor". It was this song, "Variations", that Gondos knew to be a hit because he heard it on the radio many, many times in the mid-1970s — except that on the radio, the song was called "The Homecoming" and the composer's credit went to Hagood Hardy.

Gondos said he started to write "Variations on a Theme in A Minor" in 1956. In its completed form, though precisely *when* it was completed became a large issue at the trial, the song began with a one-bar introduction followed by a statement of the main theme which lasted to the end of the tenth bar. Then came three variations on the main theme. The first variation, which seemed quite distinct from the main theme, covered bars eleven to eighteen inclusive; the second variation, which picked up on the main theme, began at bar nineteen and lasted for seven bars; and the third variation, which was also an elaboration of the main theme, stretched over the composition's concluding sixteen bars. Gondos said that everything in the piece except the first variation sounded like the music he heard in "The Homecoming" and that the third variation was almost note for note the music that Hardy wrote.

Gondos's contention was that "Variations on a Theme in A Minor" hadn't been hidden away in a trunk somewhere. It had been right out in the open for years. He played it at his cocktail-bar jobs and at Deerhurst Inn. He played it every night. It was his theme song, he said, and everybody identified him, Gondos, with the melody. His only conclusion was

18

that, in some way or other, Hardy had stolen his music from him and given it a new and different and richer life under the title of "The Homecoming".

Gondos had many stories to explain how this terrible state of affairs must have come about. This is one of the stories:

In September 1970, Gondos was booked to play over the cocktail hour, 5:30 to 8 p.m., at Stop 33 on top of the Sutton Place Hotel. The engagement lasted three weeks, from Monday, September 7, to Saturday, September 26. On the second-last night of the job, Friday the twenty-fifth, during the last set, approaching eight o'clock, Gondos played "Variations on a Theme in A Minor" as his second-last number. Gondos finished the set, and as he was leaving the room, on the way to the door, a man at one of the tables stopped him.

"Excuse me," the man said. "What was the number you just played, the second-last tune of the set?"

"Ah," Gondos said. "That's one of mine. It's a classic. I call it 'Variations on a Theme in A Minor'."

"Very nice," the man said. "It's a very nice tune."

At the table, as Gondos told the story, there were three people, the man who spoke to him, another man, and a black woman.

Gondos chatted with the three for a couple of minutes and continued on his way out of the room.

A waiter touched his arm.

"Know who that was?" the waiter said.

"What're you talking about?" Gondos said. "Who was who?"

"The man you were just talking to over there," the waiter said.

"Oh, him," Gondos said. "Just a customer. I don't know him."

"He's a musician like you, always plays up here," the waiter said. "Hagood Hardy."

"That's nice," Gondos said and left Stop 33.

One night several months later, according to Gondos's story, he paid a visit to the Cav-A-Bob, a nightclub on Victoria Street in downtown Toronto. His intention was to hear Clem Hambourg, who was playing intermission piano at the club. Hambourg, in his seventies at the time of the Cav-A-Bob job, was a legendary figure among Toronto musicians. He played an eccentric brand of classical piano, but he was better known as the proprietor in the 1950s and early 1960s of the House of Hambourg. It was a rambling, elegant old residence on Bloor Street near Avenue Road that functioned as the headquarters for modern jazz in Toronto. In the basement, Hambourg ran a nightclub where musicians performed for their fans; on the first and second floors, there were practice rooms and rehearsal studios; and on the top floor, Hambourg rented rooms to the musicians who performed and practised on the lower floors. What Ivan Gondos didn't know was than Hagood Hardy had lived and worked at the House of Hambourg during his years at the University of Toronto. Something else of more immediate importance that Gondos was unaware of before he stopped by the Cav-A-Bob was that the club's featured group that night, the band during whose intermission Clem Hambourg played, was none other than Hagood Hardy's Montage.

But, Gondos later said, before he left the Cav-A-Bob, he had twigged to the Hardy name and general appearance. Ah yes, he thought, this was the fellow who admired "Variations on a Theme in A Minor" on the Friday night in September 1970 when I played it as the second-last tune on the last set at Stop 33.

Hagood Hardy was fixed in Gondos's mind.

Here is another story that Ivan Gondos told:

On a Saturday night in August 1974, Gondos taped a set of his piano stylings at Deerhurst Inn. A professor from York

University named Derek Best helped him with the technical details, and Gondos later had the tape made into a record album that he called *Ivan Plays Favorites*. The album caught the flavour of a typical Gondos live performance, seventeen tunes interspersed with introductions and comments from the maestro himself. Of the seventeen tunes, fifteen were standards or current pop tunes — "Fly Me to the Moon", the theme from *The Godfather*, "The Girl from Ipanema" — and the other two were Gondos's own compositions.

Which two?

"No Candles Left to Burn" and, inescapably, "Variations on a Theme in A Minor".

This recorded version of "Variations", curiously enough, was much shorter than the version Gondos said he wrote. On *Ivan Plays Favorites*, the song had a theme and one variation rather than the theme and three variations of the written composition. And, what's more, the variation on the record was the first, the one that covered bars eleven through eighteen and was much different from the principal theme, and not the third variation, the one that Gondos was to insist that Hardy borrowed almost note for note in writing "The Homecoming". In one other curiosity, Gondos's composition had a couple of different names on *Ivan Plays Favorites*: it was referred to as "Variations on a Theme" on the jacket to the recording, and as "Theme and Variation" on the record label.

When the Gondos-Hardy litigation rolled around, Hagood Hardy's lawyer thought there was something decidedly suspect about this truncated and retitled rendition of "Variations".

By a coincidence, Gondos said, on the very Sunday after the Saturday evening in August 1974 when Professor Best helped him tape his set of seventeen tunes, Gondos was watching television, and for the first time he saw and heard the Salada

Tea commercial which used as background music Hagood Hardy's melody, the music that was to become "The Homecoming".

"I almost fell off my chair," Gondos described his reaction. "I heard *my* theme on television."

By yet another coincidence, according to Gondos, a little later in the summer of '74, two executives of Salada Tea — President Arnie Langbro and Vice-President Frank Dennis — checked into Deerhurst with their wives.

"We've got a very sweet commercial on television these days," Langbro said to Gondos one evening after the men had got acquainted with one another. "You heard the music on it? Lovely piano-playing."

"Have I *heard* it?" Gondos answered. "I've heard it a thousand times. I *wrote* it."

"Don't kid me," Langbro said. "Our ad agency had a top guy write that music. Hagood Hardy."

"Who's kidding?" Gondos said. "I'm telling you it's my music from years ago. Listen, I'll play it for you."

Gondos sat at the piano and tickled his way through "Variations on a Theme in A Minor".

"You see?" Gondos said to the Salada executives. "You didn't need to hire a Hagood Hardy. I had the music already."

What was the reaction of Langbro and Dennis?

"Incredulous" in Gondos's description.

Six years later, when Gondos learned during the lawsuit that word had reached Hardy early on about a claimant to the authorship of "The Homecoming", he surmised that it must have been the Salada people who filtered the news to Hardy. But at the time, in 1974, Hardy took no serious steps to investigate the claim. And as for Gondos, he started to grumble. He mentioned the striking similarity, the downright plagiaristic sameness, between his "Variations" and the tea-commercial music to his boss at Deerhurst, Bill Waterhouse. When the Salada jingle took popular form as "The Homecoming", Gondos stepped up his grumbles. In the summer of

1975 he made his complaint, illustrating it at the keyboard, to a guest at Deerhurst, a lawyer named Brian Wheatley, who seemed to know a lot about music. And in the summer of 1977 he did the same routine — complaint and illustration — for another guest, a leading Toronto jazz musician, composer, band-leader, and jingles-writer named Doug Riley. Gondos was griping to anyone who'd sit still for a few minutes. He was getting very sore about the whole business.

"Hagood travelled an awful distance on a few notes, when you think of it," Gondos said in the spring of 1981, trying to express how he felt in the mid-1970s. "I certainly didn't travel the distance he did. I'm still at Deerhurst. What Hagood did was travel on my steam."

Gondos said that, during the time of his general grumbles, he was also seeking legal advice. But with the lawyers, he said, the going was slow. Two firms that he consulted, he later explained, couldn't accept him as a client because they happened to have connections with Hardy. Another lawyer told Gondos he'd need to pay twenty thousand dollars out front before anyone would take the case. Gondos had nothing close to twenty grand, and things on the legal front bogged down.

One lawyer whom Gondos consulted, however, took a key step on Gondos's behalf. On March 14, 1979, the lawyer, Douglas Jarvis, filed "Variations on a Theme in A Minor" with the copyright registry in Ottawa. This step, carried out under the federal Copyright Act, ensured that Gondos held the copyright in his composition. In effect, he owned "Variations", and if it could be shown that anyone else copied, borrowed, or pilfered from the song without Gondos's permission, Gondos could sue the copier, borrower, or pilferer for infringement of his copyright. Unlike registry with BMI, filing under the Copyright Act was not a money-earning move; it was a protective measure.

But, speaking of BMI, what of it and "Variations on a Theme in A Minor"? Curiously — *very* curiously in the later view of Hagood Hardy's lawyer — Gondos took no steps to register "Variations" with BMI. He registered his other songs. He registered the tunes from *Merry Go Round*. He registered "Lovers' Prayer" and "Believe My Heart" and "When the Sky Is Red" and his other compositions from the album *Shoresands and Driftwood*. He registered "No Candles Left to Burn", one of his own two songs that appeared on the album *Ivan Plays Favorites*. But he didn't register the second of the two songs, "Variations", a composition he said he'd begun work on way back in the mid-fifties. It wasn't until April 1980, again under the advice of the lawyer Douglas Jarvis, that Gondos got around to approaching BMI (or Pro Canada, as it had by then been renamed) with "Variations" along with the other sections of his *Children's Suite*.

Including Douglas Jarvis, Gondos thought he consulted six lawyers about pursuing a claim against Hagood Hardy before he arrived in the offices of the man who'd visited Deerhurst in the summer of 1975. He was Brian Wheatley, a lawyer who spent much of his pre-law youth as a money-earning musician. And it was Wheatley who finally took the steps that enabled Gondos to test the truth of his claims in a court of law.

Surprisingly — no, *astoundingly* — Hagood Hardy wasn't the only composer Gondos charged with lifting music from "Variations on a Theme in A Minor". Someone else, he said, had done a similar heist, and Gondos was on to the thief. Or, rather, thieves, since Gondos alleged that this steal was a team job. He said three men, Rudy Toth, his younger brother Jerry Toth, and Rudy's son Chris, had taken different roles in converting part of "Variations" into a song that was credited to Rudy and Jerry and that first appeared in 1970 on a record album featuring a group called the Jerry Toth Singers. The Toth song was titled "Moment of Love", but, in Gondos's contention, it was a direct copy of the first variation in his

24

composition, the one covering bars eleven through eighteen.

The Toth brothers enjoyed reputations as industrious and respected members of the Toronto commercial-music community. Rudy was the older by a year; he was stocky, Jerry was slight, Rudy was dark and voluble, Jerry blond and soft-spoken, and both had easy, open natures. Rudy played keyboard instruments, Jerry played reeds. They worked in studio bands for CBC-TV shows, wrote and performed on jingles sessions, and played in dance and concert orchestras. Jerry was also a skilled jazz musician. Alto saxophone was his usual instrument, and he got a silky tone out of it that made him especially effective on ballads. He was a sideman with the Boss Brass, arguably Canada's most polished and powerful big jazz band, and he led his own small groups on occasional dates in jazz clubs. Jerry had impressive music credits, and so did brother Rudy.

In mid-1970, the record division of the CBC commissioned Jerry to put together an album of bright and romantic vocal pieces. Since the album was to stick strictly to Canadian content, Jerry asked his Toronto musician pals to contribute material. Rob McConnell, the Boss Brass leader, chipped in with a dulcet number called "How I Think of You", Jerry used his own charming ballad "Let's Go to the Country", and Doug Riley, the same musician with whom Ivan Gondos was later to lodge his complaint at Deerhurst, wrote something more lusty, "Travellin' Down to Make-It Town". Altogether, Jerry needed a dozen tunes for the album, and he turned to his brother for one contribution. Rudy fiddled away with pencil and music paper, doing much of it during a business trip in late fall from Toronto to Winnipeg by plane. He brought the results of the fiddling to Jerry, and the two of them jiggered the tune into a slightly different shape and equipped it with a title, "Moment of Love", and with a set of innocuous lyrics:

The love affair of love

We have just begun
Now it's all undone
Love is gone
The moment of love is gone.

Jerry took his dozen tunes into the recording studio and, using a small orchestra and four women vocalists, came out with music that was sprightly and crisp, just the ticket for background sounds to a cheerfully romantic occasion. The album, titled *Moment of Love*, was distributed by Warner Brothers Records and scored a modest success. It sold about two thousand copies, nothing in the class of, say, Hagood Hardy's *Homecoming*, but Jerry Toth was pleased enough with the results, another paying job in a commercial musician's life.

And as a bonus from the date, five years later, Jerry included the song "Moment of Love" on an instrumental album called *The Classic Jerry Toth*, which he cut in 1975. He used a full orchestra of thirty-three instruments on the album. It was glossy, big-concept stuff, and Jerry arranged all the numbers — twelve of them — conducted the orchestra, and produced the recording session in the studio. The "classic" in the album title got a generous interpretation; the represented composers ranged from Rachmaninoff and Satie to John Lennon and Paul McCartney, all the way to Jerry and Rudy Toth and their "Moment of Love". In this version of the song, without lyrics or vocalists, Rudy played the theme on piano while strings and woodwinds and brass swirled around him. The album was distributed by United Artists, and it received plenty of radio play, much more than the vocal album from 1970. Over the following ten years, Jerry thought he personally earned "a few thousand dollars" out of the album, and "Moment of Love" figured prominently in the earnings. He and Rudy had registered the song in 1970 with CAPAC, another royalty-collecting agency that operated in the same manner as BMI, and though the instrumental version made the Toths only marginally richer than the vocal version had, they looked on their use of "Moment of Love" as a case of getting maximum mileage out of a serviceable little tune.

But to Ivan Gondos, "Moment of Love" represented yet another invasion of his musical territory. It was a second piece of thievery from "Variations on a Theme in A Minor", and Gondos told a story that, he reasoned, must explain how this treachery came about.

The story had three parts, and here, according to the word from Gondos, is the first part:

Many, many years earlier, in 1956, when Gondos was twenty years old and still living with his parents, his mother's cymbalum went on the blink. Repairs to the Hungarian stringed instrument called for a specialized craftsman. The craftsman who took care of the task was Carl Toth, the father of Rudy and Jerry, and through Carl, Ivan Gondos was introduced to Rudy Toth. Indeed, one afternoon Rudy was invited to the Gondos house to play some Liszt on the brand-new Steinway that Gondos's parents had presented to Ivan on his twenty-first birthday.

A few months later, a film-maker hired Gondos to compose the music score for a movie that told a story of escape from behind the Iron Curtain. Gondos's music, which he described as "heavy and European", included feature parts on the cymbalum and the clarinet, and as players, Gondos summoned his new young friend Rudy Toth and Rudy's brother Jerry. The Toths, according to Gondos, accepted the assignment, which lasted three days, and afterwards vanished from Gondos's immediate life. (So apparently did the movie, called *The Iron Fence*, which seems never to have reached a movie theatre.)

Many years went by, two decades, before the second part of the story that Gondos told of his association with the Toth brothers picked up. This is the second part:

In the summer of 1975, Gondos said he noticed that one

27

young employee at Deerhurst, a busboy, seemed particularly entranced with the Gondos piano style. The lad, a teenage student who was working for the summer at the inn, used to hang around listening intently to the music, and Gondos was curious to discover his youthful admirer's identity. He was Chris Toth, and it wasn't long before Gondos made the connection between Chris and his old buddy Rudy Toth. They were son and father. Gondos was aware that the Toth brothers had carved out a fairly prosperous place for themselves in the Toronto music world, but he hadn't crossed paths with them since *The Iron Fence*. Now another Toth had entered the Gondos orbit.

"Mr. Gondos," Chris said to Ivan one night, as this part of the story went, "I'd like to buy one of your albums."

"You want *Ivan Plays Favorites*?"

"Are they expensive?"

"No, no, just six dollars."

"My father'd be interested in hearing it," Chris said.

The night of the record purchase, Gondos drove Chris home. He'd done Chris the same favour three or four times before. Chris was staying at the family cottage, which was only two or three miles from Deerhurst, and on this night Chris invited Gondos to come in and say hello to his father. It was late, after midnight, but Rudy was still up, sitting in the living-room in his shorts and sipping a drink.

"Rudy, how the heck are you?" Gondos recalled himself as beginning the conversation.

"The years have been pretty good to you, Ivan," Toth answered.

"Not so bad."

"Playing up in this nice part of the country, steady work all year, that's great, Ivan."

"Well, you know, we've both come a long way since the day you played Liszt on my new Steinway," Gondos said. "You remember?"

"You want a drink?" Toth said.

He mixed Gondos a Scotch and soda, and the two passed the thirty minutes that Gondos stayed in relaxed conversation. The talk centred almost exclusively on the old days and, most particularly, touched not at all on "Moment of Love", a song that, in any event, Gondos hadn't yet heard.

The song came to his attention a year later, and that encounter — Gondos meets "Moment of Love" and is shocked — forms the third part of his story.

It seemed that in the summer of 1976, a regular guest at Deerhurst, a man named Vic Pfeiffer, had an intriguing conversation with Gondos.

"I heard a song on the radio the other day," Pfeiffer said. "It sounded just like you."

"Really?" Gondos said, thinking Pfeiffer was probably talking about "The Homecoming".

"You could've written it, that's how much it was like your music."

"You remember the name?"

"No, it went by so quick, I didn't catch the title," Pfeiffer said. "But I tell you what, if I hear it again, I'll tape it and play it for you. It could've been something you wrote."

The following weekend, Pfeiffer turned up at Deerhurst with a tape which he played for Gondos.

"You listen, Ivan," Pfeiffer said. "This is exactly your style."

What Pfeiffer played for Gondos, according to this part of the Gondos story, was "Moment of Love". It wasn't the original 1970 recording with the vocal group from the album called *Moment of Love*. It was the 1975 instrumental recording from the album called *The Classic Jerry Toth*.

"You're not fooling it's my style," Gondos said to Pfeiffer when the tape finished. "I *wrote* that piece."

"They called it 'Moment of Love' on the radio," Pfeiffer said.

"It's from my 'Variations'," Gondos said, getting more heated by the second. "You hear me play it all the time up

29

here. It's the first variation in the piece. You know, my theme song."

"Apparently it belongs to this fellow Toth," Pfeiffer said.

"No, no, not the Toths," Gondos said. "It's *mine*."

As he did with "The Homecoming", Gondos grumbled to friends and guests at Deerhurst, to Doug Riley and others, about this second raid on his music, though he never brought the matter to the attention of Rudy Toth, who had the cottage a few minutes away from Deerhurst. Gondos's theory was that Rudy had listened to the album *Ivan Plays Favorites*, which Chris Toth purchased on the night Gondos drove him home from Deerhurst, and had appropriated the first variation from the Gondos composition "Variations on a Theme in A Minor". Rudy dressed up the melody, retitled it "Moment of Love", passed it on to brother Jerry, who — presto — had a recording made that got played on the radio. My old friends the Toths, Gondos said, have played me for a sucker.

What the Gondos theory overlooked was that "Moment of Love" didn't appear first in the version that Gondos heard on Vic Pfeiffer's tape of the 1975 recording from *The Classic Jerry Toth*. It originated much earlier in the 1970 recording of the vocal album, *Moment of Love*. The song predated by five years Chris Toth's alleged purchase of *Ivan Plays Favorites* and Gondos's late-night conversation with Rudy Toth over Scotch and soda. If Rudy made a steal from Gondos, it didn't result from his listening to *Ivan Plays Favorites*. But at the time, Gondos was unaware of the earlier history of "Moment of Love", and besides, he was too busy taking his complaint from lawyer to lawyer until he finally retained Brian Wheatley.

On September 13, 1980, when Wheatley wrote a letter to Hagood Hardy explaining Gondos's claim to the music in "The Homecoming", he wrote a similar letter to the Toths — Rudy, Jerry, and Chris — explaining Gondos's claim to "Moment of Love". And on November 17, 1980, when

Wheatley commenced an action in the Supreme Court of Ontario on Gondos's behalf alleging infringement of copyright against Hardy, he began a similar action against the three Toths.

Everyone was headed for court.

Brian Wheatley was in his early forties when Ivan Gondos retained him in July 1979, though Wheatley's looks took a half-dozen years off his age. His face was round and unlined, and his hair was full, dark brown, and beautifully barbered. His body registered in the category between plump and husky, which was surprising, since his kinetic energy should by rights have burned him down to wraith size. He talked rapidly, not to mention pungently, and his body language spoke of action and argument, a guy with a metaphorical finger jabbing the other guy's chest. Wheatley was a naturally combative — and clever — counsel.

He grew up in Welland, a dowdy port town in the Niagara Peninsula, and from the beginning he took to music. He started on drums as a precocious eight-year-old, concentrated on piano long enough to pass his Grade 6 exams, and settled on clarinet and alto saxophone. At twelve he made his debut as a professional musician in a polka band, and through high school, working weekend gigs in dance bands around the Peninsula, he pulled down heady money for a teenager, an average of twelve hundred dollars a year. He stuck to the lucrative sideline during his years as an arts student at McMaster University in Hamilton. He played jazz and dance tunes with a big band, and one summer he hitched up with a six-piece group that supplied the entertainment on a boat from the Holland-America Line running trips across the Atlantic. Wheatley paid his early dues in the music business.

That ended in the early 1960s when he packed off to Osgoode Hall Law School in Toronto and got immersed in legal studies. He articled with Levinter, Grossberg, Shapiro & Dryden, the kingpin Toronto firm in personal-injury litigation. It's the branch of the law that mixes in the often murky law and vicious quarrels of automobile accidents and insurance liability, and in it, Wheatley found a profession. After his call to the bar, he joined a small partnership that specialized in the personal-injury field, and over the years, Wheatley built a reputation, acting about ninety per cent of the time for insurance companies, as a tenacious and knowledgeable courtroom lawyer.

Given his specialty, the Gondos case represented a departure for Wheatley, but he had his persuasive reasons for taking up Gondos's cause. Not all the reasons had to do with the law.

"To tell the truth, I felt a little sorry for the guy," Wheatley explains. "He'd spent four or five years being turned away from lawyers' doors, driving up and down the highway between Toronto and Deerhurst, getting awfully frustrated, and I thought he deserved a shot at having his claim taken seriously."

Then there was Wheatley's own liking for the man.

"Ivan was a nice guy," he says. "My wife and I met him the two or three times we stayed at Deerhurst, and I found him to be a humorous, pleasant man. Once he knew you, he'd show great affection, hugging and kisses on both cheeks and all that Hungarian stuff. He was very engaging."

Then, among other motivations for Wheatley, music naturally entered the picture.

"I knew that I knew enough about music to appreciate what might be going on in the case," he says. "And I knew enough about music to appreciate that Gondos was a talented guy. He did some remarkable things. When he was still a kid, in his twenties, he organized a sixty-piece orchestra of European immigrants who worked day jobs, violinists who were janitors, that kind of thing. Ivan whipped them into shape, conducted the orchestra, and they made some won-

32

derful music. I heard a tape of that orchestra, and I was impressed."

So Wheatley accepted Gondos as a client, but he attached a caveat.

"What I'm going to do first," he told Gondos at the first interview in Wheatley's office in July 1979, "is satisfy myself you've got a case."

"It's my song," Gondos said, sticking to his Johnny-one-note refrain. "Those people, they stole from me."

"That's what you say," Wheatley said. "But before I go issuing claims for money against Hardy and the Toths, I want to do my own research into your allegations."

"Money?" Gondos said. "That isn't important."

"Well, if you're right in your claims, money is something you may get," Wheatley said. "Maybe the court would order the other people to pay you from the royalties they earn on their songs, something along those lines."

"So, okay," Gondos said. "But the important thing is this, those guys should give me back my song. They should say, sorry, Ivan, you wrote 'Variations on a Theme in A Minor', and we took our songs from yours."

"No matter what, Ivan," Wheatley said, "they're not about to roll over that easily."

"No?"

"You know what you sound like, Ivan?" Wheatley said. "An innocent."

"Do your investigating," Gondos said. "You'll see about the music."

It took Wheatley, fully booked with his personal-injury practice, a year of part-time research to reach a conclusion about Gondos's predicament. In the year, Wheatley collected every piece of recorded Hardy and Toth music he could put his hands on. He listened to tapes of Gondos's playing and studied the Gondos collection of sheet music. He ransacked the libraries of Toronto's newspapers for clippings and advertisements that traced the careers of Hardy, the Toths, and

Gondos. He studied books on musicology. And, sitting at the grand piano in his own splendid home in Oakville, he played "Variations on a Theme in A Minor" in various keys and at several tempi.

"If I say so myself," Wheatley says, "it was *quite* an undertaking."

Gondos and his possible case never wandered far from Wheatley's focus. One bright late-summer Sunday he and his wife happened to be entertaining a visiting English solicitor to brunch at the Terra Cotta Inn, a graceful little spot in the countryside northwest of Toronto, when he spotted John Arena across the room. Well, well, Wheatley thought, John Arena of Winston's Restaurant, an old Ivan Gondos employer. He introduced himself to Arena and led him to a quiet Terra Cotta corner.

"I want you to listen to something," he said to Arena, and went into his musical act, humming eight bars of melody. Wheatley has a warm voice and a firm grasp on pitch.

"You recognize that?" he asked Arena.

"Of course," Arena said. "It's Ivan Gondos's Song."

"You certain?"

"He played it three, four times a night at my restaurant," Arena said. "I used to call it the Winston's Theme Song."

"Do you know it under any other name?"

"That song?"

"Has it got another name in your mind?"

"'The Homecoming'," Arena answered. "I always thought Ivan must have sold it to somebody else."

"That's one thing he didn't do."

"Well, I don't know about these matters."

"But," Wheatley said, "you're sure about the music?"

"I've got a pretty good ear from all the opera I listen to," Arena said. "Sure, I recognize Ivan Gondos's song."

By September of 1980, Wheatley decided he was on to something, well, *suspicious*.

"Coincidence is what I had," he says. "Too much of it."

He ticks off the matters he thought rang out-of-key clinks and clanks in his head.

"These people — I mean Gondos, Hardy, the Toths — were all playing around Toronto at the same time," Wheatley says. "This is the late 1960s, early 1970s, and we find Hardy working one room at the Park Plaza Hotel and a little later Gondos at another room in the Park Plaza. Gondos is playing La Coterie and Café de la Paix, and a few blocks away, same time, Hardy is at Sutton Place. That kind of connection kept recurring. The Toths worked different kinds of jobs, but they were also on the general scene at the same time. Musically speaking, everybody was in each other's pockets."

Next, there was the matter of musical styles.

"Ivan always wrote in the romantic vein," Wheatley says. "'Variations' wasn't a departure for him. It was his usual mode, and he had the tapes to prove it. With Hardy, I didn't find much in the way of romantic composing before he wrote 'The Homecoming'. I thought that was odd, and it was pretty much the same picture with the Toths as far as I could determine."

Another curiosity for Wheatley, given the nature of Gondos's claims, was the connection between Hardy and the Toth brothers.

"How could it be that two melodies, one for Hardy and one for Rudy Toth, came from the same piece of music, from Gondos's music?" Wheatley says. "That seemed strange to me. And I thought it got even stranger when I found all the links among the people involved. Hardy was in the jingles business. The Toths were in the jingles business. Hardy worked at a particular jazz club, George's Spaghetti House, and so did Jerry Toth. They were friends with one another. I make no accusations, but this struck me as an awful lot of coincidences."

Wheatley totted up his list of happenstances and suspicions and oddities, factored in his knowledge of copyright law, added the similarities of the three songs in question, and came out with a conclusion he regarded as unavoidable.

"I thought Ivan had enough to take to court," Wheatley says. "There was still plenty of work to do. Was Hardy really in Stop 33 the night of September 25, 1970, listening to Ivan play 'Variations on a Theme in A Minor'? That had to be established, and so did many other points. But I was satisfied Ivan had a case for trial."

To understand how a lawsuit in musical plagiarism works, the place to start is the federal Copyright Act. A copyright, it's instructive to know first off, functions differently from a patent. If someone, call him Smith, invents a device and registers it under the federal Patent Act, and if someone else, call him Jones, later conceives the same invention on his own, then Smith's patent prevents Jones from making commercial use of the second invention, even though Jones's creation was entirely independent of Smith's earlier act of invention. It's an automatic process of protection under the Patent Act. The Copyright Act, by contrast, doesn't pack the same instant impact. Suppose Smith writes a piece of music and registers it under the Copyright Act. Then suppose Jones composes a song that seems to bear a remarkable resemblance to Smith's earlier composition. Smith cannot invoke the Copyright Act to prevent Jones from earning a dollar out of the later song. Or, rather, Smith can't invoke an *automatic* provision of the Copyright Act. There is no such provision. Smith must somehow *prove* that Jones had copied or borrowed from Smith's earlier song before he can stop Jones from using the later song and recover damages for the transgression. How does Smith go about proving the theft? For an understanding of that exceptionally tricky task, the place to look is in the case law in plagiarism, in the interpretive decisions made by judges in all the lawsuits brought by all the Smiths against all the Joneses who may or may not have stolen music from the Smiths.

Plenty of plagiarism case law is available for guidance, but as the twinned lawsuits of *Gondos v. Hardy* and *Gondos v. Toth* cranked up for trial, none of it was Canadian. Canada had no reported cases of one composer suing another for theft of a song. The Gondos suits were about to make Canadian legal history, the first of their kind, and in the absence of home-grown authorities, it is the case law of other countries, especially of England and the United States, where song thievery apparently flourishes, that maps out the legal intricacies of musical plagiarism.

The foreign cases establish a couple of key principles.

The first is that, in order for a plaintiff to succeed against a defendant, for the composer of a song to argue successfully that another composer has copied the first composer's work, it isn't necessary that both songs be note-for-note identical. In the language of the cases, it's enough if the two songs are "strikingly similar" or "substantially similar", or if there is in the two songs something like "sufficient objective similarity". On these standards, the plaintiff stands a good chance of clearing the first hurdle in making his case.

Of course, where the two songs *are* utterly identical, then the copycat who is being sued is almost a sure loser. That was the fate of George Harrison, the Beatle. In 1970, he wrote a song that was based on the repetition of a simple and almost hypnotic three-note motif. Harrison called the song "My Sweet Lord", and on record it became a monster hit. Alas, a 1963 song called "He's So Fine", composed by a man named Lonnie Mack and made into a less monster hit by a group called the Chiffons, was based on the very same simple and almost hypnotic three-note motif. The holders of the copyright in "He's So Fine" sued Harrison in the New York U.S. District Court and won an easy decision in their favour.

But such note-for-note sameness isn't the norm, and the case law says it's enough if the plaintiff shows that the defendant's song repeats a substantial portion of the plaintiff's song and if the two songs therefore sound alike to the ordinary listener.

The second principle from the cases is that there must be a causal connection between the two songs. That is, the second song-writer, the alleged copycat, must be shown to have had access of some kind to the song composed by the complaining song-writer.

Access, according to the case law, is a slippery concept. It's difficult, practically impossible, for a plaintiff to prove that the defendant sat down in the secrecy of his den, music paper at hand, and copied the plaintiff's composition from a recording or from sheet music. That's access of the most conclusive sort, but evidence rarely, if ever, comes so clearcut. Thus, the case law holds that other, more circumstantial, more round-about ways of showing access may come into play. Maybe the plaintiff's song was often performed in clubs or on the radio in the city where the defendant, a regular frequenter of clubs and a constant listener to the radio, happened to live. Or perhaps the plaintiff, an amateur song-writer, actually mailed his song to the defendant, a professional in the business, and the plaintiff next heard the song when the defendant started passing off something very much like it as his own. Under those sets of circumstances, the courts might infer that the defendant had access to the plaintiff's song. There's also a small hint, nothing more, in American case law that the court might make the same inference if the two songs in question, the original and the alleged copy, were so incredibly similar that copying was the only possible explanation for the similarity.

The American case law developed an interesting variation on the whole vexing matter of access and copying. In the United States, the courts subscribed to a distinction between "conscious" and "unconscious" copying. Conscious copying was the obvious variety, the kind where the evidence showed that the defendant had a clear opportunity to listen to the plaintiff's song and deliberately borrow from it. Unconscious copying was much more subtle and psychological and put the defendant in the disheartening position of being guilty of innocently misappropriating someone else's composition.

The great American jurist Learned Hand was the fellow who developed the concept of unconscious copying. It came to him in a 1924 case where the defendant, the man accused of swiping another man's song, was Jerome Kern, the first giant of the American musical theatre, the composer of, among hundreds of other songs, "The Way You Look Tonight", "I Won't Dance", "Yesterday", and all the numbers from *Show Boat* and *Roberta*. Kern's problem in 1924 was that his song, a popular ditty called 'Kalua', bore an uncanny resemblance to an even more popular number of a year or so earlier called 'Dardanella'. At the trial, Kern testified that he wasn't conscious of plagiarizing from 'Dardanella', and Learned Hand believed him. Hand said he was bound to hold in favour of the complaining composer of 'Dardanella' — the two songs were just too similar and Kern was bound to have heard the earlier song, since it was so often played in clubs and on radio — but he fastened on to the key difference between conscious and unconscious copying.

"Everything registers somewhere in our memories," Hand wrote in his judgment, "and no one can tell what may evoke it. On the whole, my belief is that in composing 'Kalua', Mr. Kern must have followed, probably unconsciously, what he had certainly often heard only a short time before. I cannot see how else to account for a similarity which amounts to identity. So to hold, I need not reject his testimony that he was unaware of such a borrowing."

Later American judges, though not their English counterparts, picked up on Learned Hand's reasoning as a means of resolving difficult plagiarism cases. It was unconscious copying that nailed George Harrison in the "My Sweet Lord" suit. Like Jerome Kern years before, Harrison swore in court that he hadn't deliberately copied the earlier song, "He's So Fine". But the plaintiffs led evidence establishing that "He's So Fine" had reigned in 1963's Top 10 for twelve weeks in England, where Harrison lived and worked. Harrison, a musician, couldn't have avoided hearing the song.

"What happened?" U.S. District Court Judge Robert Owen asked in his judgment. "I concluded that Harrison, in seeking musical materials to clothe his thoughts, was working with various possibilities. As he tried this possibility and that, there came to the surface of his mind a particular combination that pleased him as being one that would be appealing to a prospective listener; in other words, that this combination of sounds would work. Why? Because his subconscious knew it had already worked in a song that his conscious mind did not remember. Having arrived at this pleasing combination of sounds, the recording was made and the song became an enormous success. Did Harrison deliberately use the music of 'He's So Fine'? I do not believe he did so deliberately. Nevertheless, it is clear that 'My Sweet Lord' is the very same song as 'He's So Fine' with different words, and Harrison had access to 'He's So Fine'."

Judgment was awarded against poor George.

Brian Wheatley, preparing his cases in *Gondos v. Hardy* and *Gondos v. Toth*, digested the case law, all the precedents and judgments from England and the United States about musical similarities and the various kinds of copying, and decided on his general lines of attack.

Against Hardy, he would argue that there was unconscious copying. Hardy must have heard Gondos playing "Variations on a Theme in A Minor" at nightclubs around Toronto, certainly at Stop 33 on the night of September 25, 1970, and unthinkingly absorbed the melody until he brought it back from the recesses of his mind in composing the Salada Tea commercial which later emerged as "The Homecoming".

Against the Toths, Wheatley would argue both conscious and unconscious copying. The unconscious arose out of the

Toths' hearing "Variations" during the years they and Gondos were working the Toronto club circuit, and the conscious copying was the result of Rudy Toth's acquisition of the Gondos record album with "Variations" on it in the summer of 1975 (though, to be sure, the fact that Rudy wrote "Moment of Love" in 1970 seemed to present an insurmountable obstacle to proof of conscious copying).

And against both Hardy and the Toths, Wheatley would argue, though this point was based on very thin and undeveloped American precedent, that the similarity of their songs to the earlier Gondos song was so close, more than "striking" or "substantial", that copying had to be inferred as the only logical explanation.

Wheatley may or may not have taken into consideration one other possible element that the courts tossed around in the case law of musical plagiarism. That was the notion of commonplace, and it said that, in the world of music, there are many clichés which dozens of composers, hundreds of them, adapt to their own particular needs. If two songs sound alike, it may be because they also sound like many other songs, all of which employ the same musical devices.

Once again, it was Learned Hand who put his judicial finger on this possibility. In a 1940 case, an argument over a pair of forgettable tunes, Hand, a judge who had a direct and often salty way of expressing himself, defined the matter of musical commonplace this way: "It must be remembered that, while there are an enormous number of possible permutations of the musical notes of the scale, only a few are pleasing; and much fewer still suit the infantile demands of the popular ear. Recurrence is not therefore an inevitable badge of plagiarism."

In fact, in later American cases, courts found instances where the songs that were the subject of the lawsuits had antecedents far back in musical history. Wilma Ferguson ran into that problem in 1977 when she sued John Williams. Wilma was a Texas housewife who wrote a song in 1953 that she called "Jeannie Michele". She mailed the sheet music to Guy Lombardo and Dinah Shore. Guy and Dinah mailed it back to Wilma. "Jeannie Michele" was never published, recorded, or performed. John Williams was a musician with a long track record as a composer of movie music (the *Star Wars* theme was his) and as a conductor (he succeeded Arthur Fiedler at the Boston Pops). In 1973, Wilma Ferguson heard Williams's theme song to a NBC-TV show called "A Time to Love" and insisted it was her "Jeannie Michele". Wilma sued, and in the subsequent trial, it came out in evidence that the only similarity between the two pieces of music was a recurring three-note sequence which was also found in the works of Johann Sebastian Bach. The court dismissed Wilma Ferguson's claim, and in his judgment, Texas Circuit Court Judge Alvin Goldberg wrote, "It is not enough to place two works back to back if both trace their ancestries back to Bach."

Would commonplace become an issue in the Ivan Gondos cases? Were the songs of Gondos, Hardy, and the Toth family coincidental variations on the same ancient musical clichés?

Only the court would decide.

Rudy Toth took the legal documents that Brian Wheatley served on him in the late fall of 1980 to his lawyer, a man named Alfred Shaul, who practised alone in the northeast corner of Toronto. These were the documents claiming damages against Rudy, Jerry, and Chris Toth for stealing the music to "Moment of Love" from Ivan Gondos. A lawsuit under the Copyright Act was not up Shaul's alley, but he knew Peter Steinmetz, a lawyer who specialized in entertainment law. Steinmetz was with Cassels, Brock & Blackwell, an old, large, and very reputable firm in the Continental Building in downtown Toronto. Rudy went to Steinmetz, who led him across the hall to one of the stars of the Cassels, Brock litigation department, Ken Cancellara.

"I've never had a client on a first interview who was more emotional than Rudy," Cancellara said many years later. "He was almost impossible to control."

Cancellera is a short, muscular man with posture defined by a plumb-line. His face suggests Charles Aznavour's in *Shoot the Piano Player*, tough but compassionate. Ken Cancellara is a simpatico guy, and he needed all his understanding when Rudy Toth presented his problem.

"I can't believe what's happening," Rudy said in Cancellara's office. "This is stupid and insulting and not true and a thousand other things."

"You'll have to tell me the story," Cancellara said. "Look, you want some coffee? You have to go slow and explain it to me."

"No coffee," Rudy said. "First off, Ivan Gondos, I don't remember hearing of anybody named Ivan Gondos."

"It says in these documents you took his song."

"I know a lot of musicians," Rudy said. "Him, he doesn't ring bells."

At this point in the lawsuit, Rudy — and Cancellara — were unaware of Gondos's tale about his relationship with the Toth family, the meeting over the cymbalum repairs, the work together on *The Iron Fence*, the midnight Scotch and soda at Rudy's cottage.

"I sound excited to you?" Rudy said to Cancellera. "I'll tell you one reason why. This guy's suing me for money I made out of 'Moment of Love', which he says I stole from him? Right? Well, guess what I made from the song? *Practically nothing*! A couple thousand, and he's suing!"

"So even if Gondos wins," Cancellara said, "he's not going to collect much money in damages."

"Well, he's not gonna win," Rudy said. "I don't have to copy songs from anybody. That's my business. I compose songs."

"It's economically useless for him to sue you," Cancellara said. "That's the point I'm making. The damages would be measured by how much you earned out of the song, and you say that's not a whole lot."

"Look, what would it cost to fight this guy in court?" Rudy asked. "How much for me and Jerry and my son altogether?"

"That depends on the plaintiff, this man Gondos," Cancellara answered. "It could be thousands."

"How many thousands?"

"Forty, fifty, sixty," Cancellara said. "The case goes to trial and maybe Gondos calls twenty witnesses, that'd mean we could be in court a long time. Two and a half, three weeks. That'd be expensive. As much as seventy thousand even."

"That's ridiculous."

Cancellara said, "What's ridiculous is it doesn't make any sense for you to spend that kind of money paying a lawyer when the amount at stake is only the couple of thousand you earned by writing the song."

Rudy said, "Something else's at stake here."

"What?"

"My reputation."

"That's true."

"From the money angle, what 'Moment of Love' earned me, maybe the whole deal is stupid," Rudy said. "But this guy's saying I cheat at my music. He says I steal. That's untrue, and not only that, it's also going to look bad to other people. I think we don't have a choice, Jerry and me, we have to fight this Gondos. Whoever he is."

Unlike the Toths, Hagood Hardy stood to lose a great deal of money if Gondos's allegations stood up in court. "The Homecoming" made tens of thousands of dollars, and Gondos could be looking at a big chunk of cash. But, like the Toths, it was reputation that Hardy was more concerned about. He was as outraged as Rudy Toth that someone would accuse him of stealing another man's music, and that's the way he put it to his lawyer friend, Ralphy McCreath. Either way, money or reputation, McCreath said to Hardy, this is very serious litigation, and he dispatched Hardy to see J. Edgar Sexton.

Ed Sexton had no musical training — neither did Ken Cancellara — but he knew a little copyright law because he acted for CAPAC on some matters. In fact, Sexton was adept in many areas of the law. Combines cases. Commercial arguments. Personal-injury claims. Fights over estates. Sexton was a litigation lawyer who took on cases of infinite variety. He handled lawsuits for Lloyd's of London, and when New Brunswick tycoon K. C. Irving's interests were dragged into court, Sexton was K.C.'s counsel of first choice. He was a courtroom practitioner in the John Robinette tradition of generalists — whatever case came along in whatever field, if it offered a chance to argue new or particularly intriguing law, Sexton was game. That attitude made Hagood Hardy and his problem — ah, *plagiarism*, never had one of those — welcome in Ed Sexton's office.

The office was at Osler, Hoskin & Harcourt. The firm, on five floors in First Canadian Place in the heart of the city, was a century old and had more than 150 lawyers in 1980, qualifying it somewhere in the top five in size in Canada. Sexton ran the litigation department, and still does today. He's a tall, lean, dark-haired man in his late forties, and he seems to be tireless. "I work best under pressure," he says. The catch is that you can't tell when he's feeling the pressure. Ed Sexton is unflappable.

At first Sexton didn't know that Hagood Hardy's predicament was shared by the Toths. Brian Wheatley had brought two quite separate actions, one against Hardy and the other against Rudy, Jerry, and Chris, and at the early stages they weren't linked. But soon enough Sexton and Ken Cancellara found out about their overlapping concerns.

"I learned there was a case against Hardy when I went to see Brian Wheatley," Cancellara says. "And that turned on a few lights in my head. I couldn't understand why Brian was suing my people, who made no money out of their song. But Brian played a tape for me of 'Variations on a Theme in A Minor'. He said, see, there's 'Moment of Love' and, listen, there's 'The Homecoming'. I couldn't make out one from the other. I really haven't got an ear for music. But the point I sorted out pretty fast was that Brian was saying there was a mishmash of two songs in 'Variations', which meant he had to go against us both. If he just sued Hardy, he might have to explain why he didn't sue the Toths as well. It was a strategic thing. He needed to have both alleged copiers embroiled."

That isn't exactly the way Wheatley describes his reasons for suing the Toths.

"The point I had to keep repeating is that money never mattered that much to Ivan," Wheatley says. "If there was one thing that was constant with him, it was that he wanted recognition, not necessarily money, and that was the reason I started an action against the Toths. It was to get Ivan acknowledgment from everybody, Hardy and the Toths, that he composed the music we were all quarrelling over."

Whatever the explanation, as soon as Sexton and Cancellara discovered they were in the same interest, they pooled ideas and modes of defence. They shared expert witnesses who examined the three pieces of music for similarities and differences, and attempted to sort out who wrote what, or, more essentially, who wrote what *when*. And Sexton and Cancellara co-operated in plotting their attacks on the plaintiff. For both, Ivan Gondos had to be discredited or unmasked as a liar or somehow destroyed.

The first major step in the lawsuit took place on Monday, February 23, 1981, when Brian Wheatley conducted his examination for discovery of Hagood Hardy. A discovery is a proceeding in which, before trial, the lawyer on one side of a case is permitted to examine the party on the other side and ask questions that help to narrow the issues in the case. The questioning, which is done under oath and is transcribed by a reporter, usually proceeds in the office of a court official called a Special Examiner. Ed Sexton and Ken Cancellara were entitled to "take discovery" of Gondos, as the legal phrase puts it, and Wheatley could examine Hardy and the Toths. He went first with Hardy, and during his questioning, which lasted most of a day, he touched on such matters as Hardy's early career, the circumstances under which he wrote the Salada Tea commercial, its expansion to "The Homecoming", and Hardy's whereabouts through the month of September 1970. On the last point, in Wheatley's questioning, he was careful not to tip his hand that it was the early evening of September 25 that most interested him. There was no sense at this stage, he reasoned, to alert the other side to the significance of the date. It was better to make them scramble later for evidence that pinpointed where Hardy was on the twenty-fifth.

"Now specifically, Mr. Hardy," Wheatley asked, though he wasn't being precisely specific, "did you in September 1970 go to Stop 33 of Sutton Place to listen to any performer playing piano in the 5:30-to-8-p.m. time slot?"

In answer, Hardy told the story of his anger at Sutton Place management for dropping the fee for The Montage in the summer of 1970 and his resolve never again to cross the place's threshold as either performer or customer.

Then Hardy added a general all-purpose reason for avoiding Stop 33.

"This may sound odd to you," he said to Wheatley. "It seems odd to my musician friends. But I am not a fan of music. I use music as a means of personal expression, and that's why I went into it in 1958 and that's what intrigued me about it. But I was not really interested then nor am I now in other people's expression. That's not to say other people's expression is bad or not worth listening to, but it doesn't play a role in my reason for being a musician. When I'm not

47

playing or performing, I don't listen to music. CKO and the CBC are my stations on the radio in the car even today."

Wheatley asked no more questions on the subject.

Ivan Gondos had cancer of the lung.

He'd been feeling ill for several weeks, and after the doctors at Princess Margaret Hospital, the Toronto institution that deals with cancer patients, put him through a series of tests, the answer came back in the late winter of 1981. Gondos had the disease.

"But that hardly slowed him down," Brian Wheatley says. "He kept on working, kept on playing the piano, and he just said to everybody he'd be the guy to beat cancer."

Gondos clipped newspaper and magazine articles that told of patients who recovered their health after struggles with cancer. He read the articles so often he had them memorized, and he resolved to follow the example of the people he read about. He insisted that life go on as usual, and that included his lawsuits against Hagood Hardy and the Toth family.

But the preliminaries to the case moved slowly through the spring of '81, and on May 25, Wheatley flew to England on one of his regular trips to confer with British insurance people for whom he handled litigation in Canada. When he got back to Toronto on June 10, it was to the news that his client's health was sliding.

"What sort of time are we talking about?" Wheatley asked Gondos's doctor at the Princess Margaret. "We've got a lawsuit in the works, and Ivan's pushing me to get it on for trial."

"A trial?" The doctor, a man named Quirt, seemed surprised. "Well, at the very least, I'd suggest you proceed awfully darned fast or you won't have anyone to take to court."

"Ivan's that bad?"

"The cancer's spreading," Dr. Quirt said. "Mr. Gondos has lost a lot of weight, and we've got him on morphine."

"How much has he got?" Wheatley asked. "Days? Weeks? What?"

"He may not see the end of the summer."

Wheatley pressed his hurry-up button.

He went to the Ontario Supreme Court and got an order consolidating *Gondos v. Hardy* and *Gondos v. Toth* into one action. The order meant that the cases would be tried together.

He conducted his discovery of Jerry, Rudy, and Chris Toth and learned their side of the story, particularly the Toth version of the ways in which "Moment of Love" was conceived, polished, and recorded.

And he hustled Ed Sexton and Ken Cancellara into holding their discovery of Gondos.

Gondos's condition meant that the discovery had to take place under circumstances that weren't exactly customary. Gondos was too weak to sit up for long periods. He was sometimes woozy from his regular shots of morphine. And fluids were passing through his system so rapidly that he could never be far from a bathroom.

"What choice did I have?" Wheatley says. "I arranged for the discovery to take place in a hotel room."

On the morning of Wednesday, June 17, the three lawyers, a court reporter, a nurse, and Gondos's wife Carole Anne met in a room at the Westin Hotel, two blocks south of the Courthouse in downtown Toronto. They gathered around a bed where Gondos lay — sick, weak, forty pounds under his normal weight, but ready to put up a fight for the song he claimed was his.

The atmosphere at the discovery was, putting it mildly, tense. The outrage of all the parties to the case — Gondos, Hardy, and the Toths — was beginning to filter through to their lawyers, and the call to rush into the discovery put extra pressure on Sexton and Cancellara. In the hotel room, wired in angst and anger, the feelings among the counsel during the two days that the discovery lasted broke through in testy exchanges.

At one point, Cancellara, having just heard for the first time Gondos's story about his midnight visit to Rudy Toth's cottage, asked whether, at the time of the visit, Gondos was aware of the existence of the "Moment of Love" recording.

"He certainly answered that before," Wheatley broke in. "He said he found out about the recording in the summer of 1976 and he was at the cottage in 1975. That's a tricky question."

"Not at all," Cancellara said.

"It *is* a tricky question," Wheatley snapped, "and you are making me mad with it."

"I could care less whether you're angry," Cancellara fired back.

"The next question," Wheatley directed.

"I could care less whether you're angry," Cancellara repeated. "And I want an answer to my question."

"You have got my objection," Wheatley said.

"Well, you should not interrupt," Cancellara said, "and you should let the examination go on —"

"Don't lecture me, young man," Wheatley interrupted.

"Sir," Cancellara said in a louder voice, "I am not lecturing you."

"I hope not," Wheatley said, just as loud.

"You might show the courtesy I expect from you," Cancellara said.

"Likewise," Wheatley said. "Let's get on with it."

In the spaces between the skirmishes, Cancellara and Sexton drew out Gondos's story. It wasn't an especially difficult task. No matter how ill he was, Gondos seemed eager to answer questions. Lying on the bed, he wanted nothing more than to pour out the injustice he said he'd been carrying around all those years. When he answered a question from

Sexton or Cancellara, he talked in galloping rushes.

"Could you speak a little bit slower, Mr. Gondos?" Cancellara asked early in the discovery. "I have a hard time following you."

"I have a hard time breathing," Gondos said. "I am sorry."

Was Gondos working on the sympathy factor? Cancellara and Sexton thought it might be possible. They could hardly blame the man — he *was* dying before their eyes — but they had a duty to their clients, and they pressed Gondos for answers. Relentlessly, they got from him the whole story, all about the history of "Variations on a Theme in A Minor", the encounter at Stop 33 on the evening of September 25, 1970 (the date was now out in the open), Gondos's early associations with the Toth brothers, Chris Toth's purchase of *Ivan Plays Favorites*, and Gondos's delivery of Chris and the record album to Rudy Toth's cottage.

And along the way, in the course of the questioning, Sexton and Cancellara dug out a few nuggets of testimony that seemed pure gold.

"Aside from the album you sold Chris Toth in 1975," Cancellara asked Gondos, "what other knowledge do you have about any access that any of the defendants had to your composition 'Variations'?"

"Nothing exactly," Gondos answered.

Well, Cancellara thought, if Rudy Toth wrote "Moment of Love" five years before Chris allegedly bought *Ivan Plays Favorites*, and if Gondos knew of no other way that the Toths might have come across "Variations", then Brian Wheatley was going to have a tough time proving the key ingredient of the Toths' access to the Gondos song.

The discovery of Gondos finished on the afternoon of June 18, and when Sexton and Cancellara left the room in the Westin Hotel, they had, for the first time, a good idea of the case they'd have to meet in court.

The next day, Friday the nineteenth, Wheatley went back to the Ontario Supreme Court and got an order from Mr. Justice Richard Holland directing that the first part of the trial in the consolidated case of *Gondos v. Hardy and Toth* begin on the following Monday morning.

None of the lawyers, not Wheatley, nor Sexton, nor Cancellara, was ready for a full-scale trial. They had witnesses to prepare, evidence to round up, law to master. It'd be weeks before they had everything set to go to court. But Wheatley wanted to get the trial on just long enough to take Ivan Gondos's testimony. He argued that, given the man's dicey state of health, it was essential to place his testimony on the record. Then, whether he survived or not, the rest of the trial could proceed when all parties were ready. Mr. Justice Holland agreed with Wheatley and granted an order placing the case down for partial trial on Monday, June 22.

Over the weekend, a Supreme Court judge had to be assigned to the case, and the man who got the call was Mr. Justice Douglas Carruthers, a tall, trim, sandy-haired man in his early fifties and a member of the bench since August 18, 1977. Carruthers was already tied up in a trial at the Toronto Courthouse, but he agreed to put it on hold while he looked into this fascinating Gondos business. It was a typical Carruthers move. He had a reputation among litigation lawyers as a judge who liked to nose around in cases that promised something off-beat. Carruthers was an activist in all things; away from the bench, he jogged, lifted weights, and played killer tennis, and on the bench, he emphasized speed and efficiency and didn't suffer plodding counsel gladly.

Carruthers had another qualification that made him a nice fit with the Gondos case. Like Wheatley, unlike Sexton and Cancellara — and unknown to all three — he understood a thing or two about music. Carruthers didn't have Wheatley's formal or practical experience, but he'd been honing his ear on jazz from the time he was a kid. For twelve years, beginning when he was eleven, he had worked as an usher at the Club Kingsway, a night spot in Toronto's west end that booked touring American bands. "With jazz," Carruthers says, "I go way back." He still collects records, pays regular visits to the clubs, and now and again he sits down at the drums and does his imitation of the late Buddy Rich.

Also over the weekend, the Toths started remembering.

"Here's what I got from Gondos at the discovery," Ken Cancellara said to Rudy, Jerry, and Rudy's son Chris. And he told them about *The Iron Fence* and about Gondos's visit to Rudy's cottage.

"*That* guy," Rudy said. "His mother was the lady with the cymbalum."

"The insane movie," Jerry said. "I know who you're talking about now."

"So you *did* meet Ivan Gondos," Cancellara said.

"The guy I think it is," Rudy said, "he asked me to play the cymbalum on the music track for this movie about people getting out of Hungary. Years ago it was, the 1950s some time."

"Right," Jerry said. "Rudy brought me in with a bunch of other musicians to do the job. But we couldn't get off the ground with the music."

"Practically unplayable," Rudy said.

"Okay, Rudy," Cancellara said. "Gondos says he came to your cottage late one night. Midnight, he says, in the summer of 1975."

"I remember him at the cottage once," Rudy said. "But it wasn't any midnight. What year'd you say?"

"Gondos says definitely 1975," Cancellara said.

"I don't know," Rudy said. "It might've been."

"He says it was the summer Chris was working at Deerhurst," Cancellara said. "A busboy."

Chris Toth spoke up.

"I was a porter," he said. "Not a busboy."

"He says you bought an album from him," Cancellara said to Chris. "*Ivan Plays Favorites*."

"No way," Chris said. "I didn't buy any album."

"And he drove you home from Deerhurst this night," Cancellara said. "And you took him in to meet your father."

"Wait a *second*," Chris said. "I was never in a car with this man in my life. I didn't really know him, apart from he was the piano-player in the lounge. I was just a porter."

"If I remember right," Rudy said, "Gondos came by the cottage on a weekend. He had a kid with him, a couple of his kids, and he said he wanted to get acquainted again. Something like that."

"What about the record album?" Cancellara asked.

"What record album?"

"*Ivan Plays Favorites*."

"Never heard of it."

"His song's on it," Cancellara said. "'Variations on a Theme in A Minor'."

"What Gondos wanted," Rudy said, "was for me to come over to Deerhurst and listen to him play."

"What'd you say?" Cancellara asked.

"I said nope," Rudy answered. "The reason we go up to the cottage is to get away from everything. I'm around music all the time in the city."

"You've never heard the music of Ivan Gondos at any time in any form?" Cancellara said. "That's what you're telling me?"

Rudy said, "Not since the stuff he wrote for the movie twenty-five years ago."

Jerry said, "I never played such crazy music."

Ken Cancellara decided that Ivan Gondos was a liar. The fabrications, in Cancellara's opinion, went beyond such items as Gondos's claim that he sold a record to Chris Toth. They went beyond even the Gondos assertion that the Toths had stolen "Moment of Love" from him. On the contrary, Cancellara thought, it was more likely Gondos who stole from the Toths. His reasoning went that Gondos hadn't written all of "Variations on a Theme in A Minor" back in 1956, as he insisted he had, but had written at least part of it, the part that was similar to "Moment of Love", much later, *after* he heard the Toth piece. Gondos copied "Moment of Love". That conclusion led Cancellara to two decisions: one, he'd counter-claim against Gondos on behalf of the Toths for plagiarizing their song, and, two, when Gondos gave his testimony, Cancellara would attack him on cross-examination as a liar.

Ed Sexton arrived at approximately the same conclusion. He wasn't prepared to accuse Gondos of borrowing from "The Homecoming", not yet anyway, but his strategy on cross-examination, like Cancellara's, was to shake Gondos's credibility. After the discovery, Sexton thought Gondos had showed himself to be vulnerable to several lines of questioning. The alleged meeting at Stop 33 on September 25, 1970, was one area where Gondos and Hardy met head-on — Gondos swore the meeting happened, Hardy said he wasn't near the place that night — and Sexton felt he could make yards by grilling Gondos on the subject. In fact, he'd give Gondos such a ride that maybe a few pieces of truth would come loose.

At two-thirty on the afternoon of Monday, June 22, all the people involved in *Gondos v. Hardy and Toth*, except Hagood Hardy and the Toths, assembled in a two-room suite on the thirty-second floor of the Westin Hotel. It was almost certainly the first time in Canadian judicial history that a court case was about to be held in a hotel room.

Brian Wheatley was in charge of reserving the suite and organizing it to resemble premises where trials normally took place. He designated the bedroom as the quarters where Mr. Justice Carruthers retired during recesses, and he arranged the furniture in the sitting-room to approximate the kind of court setting that his lordship was accustomed to. The judge's dais was a desk pushed into one corner of the room, and the court reporter and the registrar grouped themselves to the immediate right of the desk. In front of Carruthers, almost within touching distance if he reached out, were two other desks which the three lawyers sat behind. Back of them, two people from Ed Sexton's office squeezed together on a narrow sofa; they were Brian Morgan, an Osler, Hoskin lawyer, and Linda Nascher, the firm's litigation law clerk, and their job was to take notes of Gondos's testimony and handle other chores for Sexton.

Against the wall to Carruthers' far right, Gondos lay on a single bed that faced lengthwise into the rest of the room. Gondos's wife, Carole Anne, sat on a chair at his bedside, and so did a nurse who kept herself available to feed pain-killers to Gondos. For judicial flavour, two court ushers ranged around the room, and Carruthers ordered that the door to the corridor should stay open. That made the proceedings officially public, since anyone would have access to the "courtroom". But nobody dropped in during the three days that Carruthers conducted the trial, and the only time he directed the ushers to close the door was on Tuesday afternoon when a bunch of conventioneers got too frisky in the corridor.

"The whole set-up was incredibly bizarre," Ed Sexton says, no doubt understating the scene in the suite on the thirty-second floor.

Wheatley needed all of Monday afternoon and most of Tuesday morning to conduct the examination-in-chief that elicited Gondos's story. Compared to his performance at discovery the previous week, Gondos seemed downright peppy. He groaned in apparent pain from time to time and the nurse had to do her pain-killing duties, but Gondos showed even more spirit and talked in even more rapid spurts than he had on June 17 and 18.

"No question the man was dying," Wheatley says. "But somehow the fact that the trial was really under way gave him a shot of adrenalin."

Under Wheatley's guidance, Gondos unfolded once again his story. How he was trained as a musician from a young age. How his career took shape. How, among hundreds of other pieces of music, he came to compose "Variations on a Theme in A Minor". How, on two fleeting but meaningful occasions, he ran across Hagood Hardy, once at Stop 33 and again a few months later when he saw Hardy with The Montage at the Toronto club called the Cav-A-Bob. How he had social and musical dealings with the Toth family. And how he wanted to get back the two songs he said were stolen from him.

"All right now," Wheatley said to Gondos during the examination-in-chief, "you have just said you composed 'Variations on a Theme in A Minor' in 1956. Do you have a copy of the 1956 piece of that music?"

"It's been lost," Gondos answered.

Sexton and Cancellara sat up in their seats.

No original manuscript of the music!?

But Wheatley produced and Gondos identified another manuscript of "Variations". It was written out on large-sized music paper, eighteen inches by fourteen, and it covered four pages. "Little Snowflakes", one of the pieces from Gondos's *Children's Suite*, took up the first page, and "Variations", another section of the suite, stretched over pages two, three, and four. The music manuscript was dated "10/11/62". November 10, 1962. Gondos said that was the date when he wrote out this version of "Variations".

Wheatley produced and Gondos identified another written copy of "Variations". According to Gondos, this was a Xerox of the 1962 manuscript. The Xerox covered two pages, back and front. "Little Snowflakes" was on the front of the opening page, the first part of "Variations" on the back, and the second and third parts of "Variations" took up the front and back of page two. Gondos said the Xerox was made some time in 1965 for a piano student of his named Roy Robson. Robson hung on to it for fifteen years and brought it to Gondos after his old teacher began the action against Hardy and the Toths. Or so Gondos testified.

"You play this," he said, "and you hear all the music."

Ken Cancellara felt queasy as he watched Gondos testify.

"I couldn't cope with it at first," he says. "I kept saying to myself, why is this guy, who's undoubtedly lying anyway, spending some of the last days of his life in a hotel room while two lawyers wait to cross-examine him? I could think of a lot of things I'd rather do if my days were numbered like his were."

Cancellara worried about his cross-examination of Gondos. Could he really attack this dying man as he planned to? Accuse the poor guy of lying and dissembling? Cancellara took his worries to Sexton, who wasn't enjoying the spectacle in the hotel suite either and was having his own doubts about grilling Gondos.

"How do we approach this guy on cross-examination?" Cancellara said.

"Well, that's the problem, isn't it," Sexton said. "Do we treat him the way we would an ordinary witness?"

"If it's any help," Cancellara said, "that's what Doug Carruthers seems to be doing."

"He's firm, all right," Sexton agreed.

"If Carruthers is feeling the emotions of this thing, the

man dying and the rest," Cancellara said, "he's keeping it under control."

"The point is, I can see all *kinds* of discrepancies in Gondos's testimony," Sexton said. "We have to make him explain them if he can."

"Right."

"That isn't pleasant to do to a witness who's healthy," Sexton said. "With Gondos, it's going to be extremely unpleasant."

"Well," Cancellara said, "we hammer the guy."

"Yeah," Sexton said. "Why else are we here?"

Sexton began his cross-examination of Ivan Gondos just before the noon recess on Tuesday, the twenty-third.

"When did you say you wrote 'Variations on a Theme in A Minor'?" he asked Gondos.

"Originally?" Gondos said.

"You can only write something once," Mr. Justice Carruthers broke in. "After that, aren't you copying it?"

"Well," Gondos said, "I am developing it."

"When did you originally write it?" Sexton started again.

"1956," Gondos answered. "I started working on my suite, and I believe that one was done in 1962."

"Well," Sexton said, "I was interested in — "

"1960," Gondos interrupted.

"The first time you put 'Variations on a Theme in A Minor' on paper was 1960?" Sexton asked.

"I am very bad on organization," Gondos said.

Carruthers broke in again.

"You've just said," he said to Gondos, "that you first wrote 'Variations on a Theme in A Minor' in 1960. Was it 1960 or some other date?"

"1960," Gondos said. "I will let it stand."

"I don't want anything to stand," Carruthers said. "The

question really is a significant one, and it is, again, when did you first put pen to paper in the act of writing down that which you call 'Variations on a Theme in A Minor'?"

"1960," Gondos said.

"All right," Carruthers said. "The answer is 1960."

"At discovery last week," Sexton said to Gondos, "I think you said you wrote 'Variations' in 1956."

"I wrote it in 1956," Gondos said. "Yes. Originally."

"Now which is it?" Sexton said. "Did you write it in 1956 or 1960?"

"1956," Gondos said.

"I see," Sexton said.

"I was heavily sedated last week because I was just entering a new treatment," Gondos said.

"Now you say it was 1956?" Sexton asked.

"Definitely," Gondos said.

Then Sexton began to zero in on the point behind this line of questions, the point, that is, apart from demonstrating Gondos's seeming confusion over when he really wrote the composition.

"Did you write it on a piece of paper?" Sexton asked.

"Yes," Gondos answered. "But it was lost when I moved to Huntsville."

"That was 1972?"

"Yes."

Sexton referred Gondos to the manuscript of "Variations" that was dated November 10, 1962.

"When did you write that?" he asked Gondos.

"1962."

"But," Sexton said, pouncing on the space that Gondos seemed to have left, "you already had one written from 1956. Why write it again?"

"Well, it's like the story about Haydn," Gondos said. "He dropped his music off the table and he was too lazy to pick it up. So he wrote it out again. I perhaps misplaced it. I wrote it out again, maybe for a student. It doesn't take long."

60

Sexton wasn't amused by the little story about Haydn.

"When you wrote it out in 1962," he asked Gondos, "did you have the 1956 document in front of you?"

"I might have."

"Perhaps you can try again to answer my question," Sexton said. "What is your best recollection as to why you didn't use the 1956 document when you wrote the 1962 document?"

"Probably because I didn't have a duplicating machine," Gondos answered. "So I had to write it."

Sexton had the feeling that Gondos's glib answers may have been testing Doug Carruthers' credulity.

Sexton used forty-five minutes of his cross-examination to review with Gondos the reasons why it wasn't until April 1980 that he attempted to register "Variations on a Theme in A Minor" with BMI, the royalty-collecting agency. Sexton reminded Gondos that he joined BMI in 1965, and that, on joining, he listed a number of his compositions for which he would seek royalties. "Variations", supposedly written in 1956, wasn't on the list.

"Why?" Sexton asked.

"It was part of *Children's Suite*," Gondos answered. "And it was incomplete."

Sexton later tried the question again.

"Why," he asked, "did you register many of your songs with BMI and not 'Variations'?"

"One of the reasons I didn't register everything I wrote," Gondos answered this time, "was because I don't presume myself to be a genius that everything I write is going to be preserved for posterity. I wrote 1500, and of those, 36 are played. Chopin wrote hundreds and destroyed everything, and 126 are played."

Sexton moved to the record album, *Ivan Plays Favorites*, which included a version of "Variations".

"If your record album was bought at Deerhurst and played on a radio station," Sexton said, "and if you'd registered 'Variations' with BMI, you would have got royalties."

"I don't care about that," Gondos answered.

"You don't care about royalties?"

"No."

"Mr. Gondos," Sexton said, holding the record album in his hand and pointing to the songs on it, "you apparently thought it was important enough when you made this record to put those little initials BMI after 'No Candles Left to Burn', the other song on the album you wrote."

"It was co-written with my wife," Gondos said. "You'd put these initials after the song too if you almost had a divorce over the number."

"When did you write 'No Candles Left to Burn'?" Sexton asked.

"In 1970."

"You reported to BMI that you wrote it?"

"I think so."

"So," Sexton said, "of the only two numbers on the album that you composed, you registered with BMI one, 'No Candles Left to Burn', and not the other, 'Variations'."

"It wasn't completed," Gondos said.

Sexton returned to his point that "Variations" wasn't filed with BMI until April 1980, and Gondos repeated his explanation that the composition wasn't in final form until that date.

"What puzzles me in hearing you say that," Sexton said, "is that more than a year before, you apparently thought it was complete enough to file with the copyright office in Ottawa under the name 'Variations on a Theme in A Minor'."

"It probably had something to do with I was running from pillar to post," Gondos said. "I was trying to get myself protected, and there was a suggestion from my lawyer at the time."

"Your lawyer told you to do it?" Sexton asked.

"Yes."

Sexton hadn't finished exploring Gondos's relationship with "Variations on a Theme in A Minor".

"Mr. Gondos," he asked, "did you indicate that this composition was used by you as a sort of theme song?"

"That's correct."

"What does that mean?"

"It's my signature," Gondos answered. "I open with it and close with it."

"The performance on your record, the tape of the live performance at Deerhurst Inn," Sexton asked. "That would be the sort of performance where you would open and close with 'Variations'?"

"Yes."

"You used it as a theme song?"

"Oh, it isn't used as a theme on the album," Gondos said, backtracking in a hurry. "You can only put so much on a record."

"And when you signed off that performance," Sexton asked, "didn't you say that the song 'I'll Be Seeing You' was your theme?"

"I use various numbers."

"Didn't you say you invariably used 'Variations' as your theme?"

"It isn't entirely my choice," Gondos said. "I do requests."

"Let's listen to the record," Sexton said. "*Ivan Plays Favorites.*"

There was a record-player in the hotel suite, a machine that Sexton's secretary, acting on an emergency call from her boss, had bought earlier in the day at Simpsons and delivered to the Westin. The secretary, either rushed or keen to save on budget, chose a player made by Fisher Price, the toy company. When Sexton put *Ivan Plays Favorites* on the machine,

63

the sound emerged tinny and strained. Carruthers frowned, Cancellara grinned, Sexton shrugged. Still, the sound was distinct enough to make out the sequence at the end of the record: "The Girl from Ipanema", then Gondos's voice, then "I'll Be Seeing You".

"Mr. Gondos," Sexton said when the last strangled notes died away, "that was your voice just before 'I'll Be Seeing You'?"

"Yes."

"And you said you were going to play your theme?"

"Yes."

"So I take it you were in error when you said you invariably played 'Variations'?"

"I play eleven thousand pieces," Gondos said. "It just happened to be another piece that night."

Sexton knew from Hagood Hardy that Hardy had never run into Gondos at Stop 33, not on September 25, 1970, not ever. And now Sexton picked at Gondos for the flaws in his story about what Sexton was certain had been a phantom event.

"On this evening in September 1970," Sexton asked, "did you play 'Variations on a Theme in A Minor'?"

"That was my second-last piece that night."

"What was your last piece?"

"'I Will Wait for You' or 'Autumn Leaves', one or the other," Gondos answered. "I didn't plan. I just finished the evening and went home."

"What was the third-last piece?"

"I don't know."

"That was a Friday evening?"

"Friday evening."

"What was your second-last piece on Thursday evening?"

"I don't know."

"How about Wednesday evening?"

"I don't know."

"Do you know your second-last piece on any evening?"

"I don't have a program," Gondos said. "I just play according to the crowd."

"But you clearly remember one Friday night when it was your second-last piece?"

"Yes," Gondos said. "I was asked about it."

"What hours were you playing at Sutton Place?"

"Five to eight or five-thirty to eight."

"And what time were you called over to the table?"

"When I was leaving," Gondos said. "At the close of my engagement for the evening."

"And then where did you go?"

"I was going through the door to go home."

"You can't recall whether you would have been going to play somewhere else?"

"No," Gondos said. "My equipment was there, my organ. I play them together, organ and piano."

Sexton picked up a document from the table in front of him. It was a contract between Gondos and the Park Plaza Hotel, and it covered a period of weeks ending September 26, 1970, when Gondos played in a cocktail lounge at the hotel each evening from 9 p.m. to 1 a.m.

"Can you identify the signature on this contract?" Sexton asked.

"That's mine," Gondos answered.

"So you were in error when you told me you went home after the performance?"

"I don't remember," Gondos said. "But I suppose I was in error."

Sexton took Gondos back to Stop 33 on the night of September 25.

"You say you went over to somebody's table?" Sexton said. "How many men were at it?"

"Two men and a black girl."

"Would you describe the men?"

"The chap I talked to," Gondos said, "he had hair, he wasn't bald, and it looked like Hagood Hardy other than the fact the hair was straighter, quite straight."

"What colour was the hair?"

"It was dark in there," Gondos answered. "It wasn't blond. Brown."

"Long hair or short hair?"

"Normal for a musician, I guess."

"Four inches long? Three inches long?"

"Maybe three or four inches long."

"And what would the man's height be?"

"He is sitting."

"What would be his approximate weight?"

"Oh, normal. One fifty, one sixty. He didn't stand up."

"Did he have glasses on?"

"Not at the time."

"And," Sexton asked, "would you describe the other gentleman to me?"

"I can't," Gondos said. "I didn't look. I had sweat in my eyes. My face was swelled up."

Face swelled up? What was *that* all about? Sexton didn't bother pursuing it. He moved ahead to Gondos's visit to the Cav-A-Bob.

"Will you describe Hagood Hardy's looks on that occasion?" he asked Gondos.

"He was jumping around a lot," Gondos said. "I can't describe his looks."

"Jumping around a lot?"

"He was going from piano to vibraphone."

"But you can't describe his looks?"

"He was thirty feet from me."

"How were you able to tell it it was the same man you say you saw at Sutton Place?"

"It's just that I remember the name," Gondos answered.

"Nobody else is called Hagood."

"Was it his name rather than his appearance that caught your attention?"

"I could see it was the same man, other than the fact his hair was different," Gondos said. "It was tousled."

"And who was playing in his group?"

"I don't know," Gondos said. "They were making so much noise I was going crazy."

"You didn't enjoy the playing?"

"They gave me a terrific headache."

From his research, Sexton had an idea there was something out of whack about Gondos's account of seeing the Salada Tea commercial for the first time on the Sunday in August 1974 after he'd recorded *Ivan Plays Favorites* the previous night. The time — August of '74 — and the nature of the commercial's visuals were the items that Sexton wanted to get straight.

He began this phase of his cross-examination by playing for Gondos the three different Salada commercials — "Taxi", "Birthday", and "Church" — on a video cassette machine that was hooked up to the television set in the hotel sitting-room. The video machine wasn't a Fisher Price product.

Sexton asked Gondos, "Is one of these commercials the one you saw the day following the taping of your record album?"

"I've seen them so many times," Gondos said. "Possibly."

"Perhaps I can help you," Sexton said. "Do you recall, on your examination for discovery, telling me that the commercial you saw had a stained-glass window in it?"

"I recollect the church."

"Yes," Sexton said. "And the third commercial on this tape had a church in it. Did you see that?"

"Yes."

"And it showed windows the way churches have," Sexton coaxed. "Did you see those?"

"Yes."

"And do you believe that the third commercial is the one you saw following the taping of your record?"

"I have seen the commercials so many times."

"Well, do you *believe* it is the one you saw?"

"It has been a while," Gondos said. "Yes. I think it's close. I wish I could answer you better."

"I take it you mean it is closer than the other two commercials."

"Yes."

"And would your best recollection be that you believe that would be the commercial you saw after the taping?"

"Yeah," Gondos said. "I think so."

Sexton stored away the admission for future reference.

While the commercials and the music that went with them were fresh in Gondos's mind, Sexton cinched one fact for the court record.

"I'm showing you the 1962 sheet music for 'Variations on a Theme in A Minor'," Sexton said to Gondos. "I also have here a green pen, a pen with green ink, and what I'm going to ask you to do is mark the part which you say was on the commercials. Can you do that?"

"Certainly," Gondos said.

Brian Wheatley wasn't as confident as Gondos about Sexton's intention and interrupted with a question of clarification.

Mr. Justice Carruthers took care of the clarifying.

"The witness," he said, "has given evidence that there were sixteen bars of 'Variations on a Theme in A Minor' contained in each of the three commercials we watched. Mr. Sexton is taking the 1962 sheet music and saying, give me the sixteen bars from the music you just heard in the commercials."

Sexton nodded in agreement.

"Do we have a clipboard?" Carruthers asked. "Something for the witness to write on? Anybody bring a clipboard?"

Linda Nascher, Sexton's litigation law clerk, produced a clipboard from her seat on the sofa, and the court registrar carried it, the sheet music, and the green pen to Gondos on his bed.

"All right," Carruthers said, acting the role of play-by-play announcer as Gondos made his marks on the sheet music. "The witness has now placed on the sheet music two vertical lines marking the beginning and end of the sixteen-bar passage."

Gondos's green lines identified the last sixteen bars of "Variations on a Theme in A Minor", all of variation three, as the music he heard in the Salada Tea commercial.

These sixteen bars, he was saying, represented the music that Hagood Hardy copied for the commercial and, by extension, for "The Homecoming".

"That answer your question, Mr. Sexton?" Carruthers asked.

"Thank you," Sexton said.

Sexton knew that Gondos had been inconsistent, maybe worse, in his description of his educational background. He decided to tackle Gondos on the subject, anticipating that Gondos's answers might give another shove to his credibility, which, in Sexton's view, was already tottering. He began by getting Gondos to concede that he had dropped out of high school before Grade 12 and that, while Gondos said he had studied with Professor Bela Borzorninyi at the Royal Conservatory of Music, he hadn't been granted the final certificate, an ATCM.

"I am showing you your application to BMI," Sexton said to Gondos. "I am showing you paragraph five of the application which says, 'Educational Background, Academic & Musical'. Do you see the words 'Senior Mat'? Does that mean matriculation?"

"Yes."

"Is that your writing?"

"Yes."

"And do you see the words in brackets below that, 'Gr. XIII'?"

"Yes."

"And do you see 'Tor. Conservatory of Music ATCM?' "

"Yes."

"And did you write all that?"

"Yes."

"And none of it is true, is it?"

"I had the level," Gondos said. "No, I didn't have the paper."

"You were willing to use the initials after your name, ATCM, because you felt you were entitled to it, isn't that it?"

"Well, I didn't," Gondos started. Then, "This is . . ." And he started again. "It doesn't say by penalty of death. It was just a form I filled out and I didn't think it was very important."

"And did you assume as well that you were entitled to say you had your Grade 13?"

"It's the only time I used it," Gondos said. "I don't even understand this. It isn't even important on that paper."

"Did you feel, as regards those things, the Grade 13 and the ATCM, that really you deserved those things?"

"Yes."

"And you also feel you deserve recognition for writing 'Variations on a Theme in A Minor', don't you?"

"Yes."

"Those," Sexton said to Mr. Justice Carruthers, "are my questions."

Sexton was relieved that his cross-examination was over.

"It was one of the hardest things I've ever done in my life," he said years later.

Nevertheless, Sexton was so masterful and thorough in his questioning of Gondos that Ken Cancellara needed only an hour to pick over loose ends in his own cross-examination. He took Gondos once again through his often-told story of the connections with the Toth family. Cancellara got back to a theme he'd explored at discovery — he wanted to know how Gondos imagined that the Toths, especially Rudy, came across "Variations on a Theme in A Minor". Gondos kept fixing on Chris Toth's purchase of the record album in the summer of 1975 as the key event in the theft, but since Rudy wrote "Moment of Love" in 1970, and since, anyway, Chris said he never bought the album, Cancellara was looking for other ideas that Gondos might have of the Toths' access to "Variations".

He asked, "Mr. Gondos, have you performed 'Variations on a Theme in A Minor' on television?"

"No."

"And have you performed it on radio?"

"No. I haven't personally. No."

"Well, have you *heard* anyone perform it on radio?"

"What are you asking about? The record?"

"I am asking about 'Variations on a Theme in A Minor'."

"Well, I've heard . . . but there again, it's hearsay. I haven't heard it personally. No."

"You haven't heard it personally?"

"No."

"And I take it," Cancellara asked, "you wouldn't have any particulars of its air play?"

"No."

Cancellara thought that was good enough, and he wound up his cross-examination.

The time was 1:01 p.m. on Wednesday, June 24.

"We'll adjourn *sine die*," Mr. Justice Carruthers said to the counsel, meaning that the case was put over to an undetermined future time. "I'll have to meet with you to pick a date when you want to conclude the trial."

The lawyers went back to their offices. Carruthers walked two blocks north to the Courthouse to check on the trial he'd adjourned while he presided in the suite at the Westin. And Ivan Gondos took a taxi to the Princess Margaret Hospital.

Seventeen days later, on July 11, 1981, Gondos died.

Later in the summer, Brian Wheatley met with Carole Anne Gondos, Ivan's widow. She was an elegant, remarkably self-possessed woman.

"I want the case to continue," she told Wheatley.

"Well, you're entitled to have that happen," Wheatley said. "As the representative of Ivan's estate, you have the capacity to get on with the rest of the trial."

"Ivan took it to his death-bed," Carole Anne Gondos said.

"He did," Wheatley said. "But, think about it, this isn't going to be easy."

"It's my obligation," Mrs. Gondos said.

"Yes?"

"To Ivan's memory."

Wheatley didn't tell Carole Anne Gondos that he'd be fighting the case with one arm tied behind his back. When the trial resumed, he wouldn't have a client to rely on. Wheatley had hoped that, during Gondos's testimony in the hotel room, he could have called on him to illustrate his musical points at a piano. Showing rather than describing, Wheatley thought, would have worked a more persuasive impact on Mr. Justice Carruthers. But Gondos's failing health canned that bright idea. Now, at the rest of the trial,

Wheatley wouldn't be able to make use of Gondos's piano-playing or his memory or his advice. And, what's more — a second arm tied behind his back — Wheatley would be operating on a bare minimum of funds. Gondos had little in the way of savings. His widow had even less. Though Wheatley has never talked or complained about money, he undoubtedly conducted the Gondos case at bargain-basement fees.

"Okay," he said to Carole Anne Gondos, "let's get the trial back on the rails."

The first date when all the legal people could make their schedules coincide — Wheatley, Cancellara, Sexton, and, most necessarily, Carruthers — was mid-April 1982.

In the months before the trial, the lawyers scouted out their witnesses and tuned up for court.

Brian Wheatley gathered eleven witnesses who would say they'd heard Ivan Gondos play "Variations" at different times in different places through the 1960s. And he had one expert witness, Dr. Paul McIntyre of the University of Windsor School of Music, who would describe the amazing similarities that "The Homecoming" and "Moment of Love" bore to different sections of "Variations on a Theme in A Minor".

Ken Cancellara concentrated on two groups of witnesses. The first was made up of the three Toths, Rudy, Jerry, and Chris, and the second comprised music experts who would point out differences and anomalies among the three songs. Cancellara and Ed Sexton shared the expert witnesses.

Sexton's witnesses, apart from Hagood Hardy and the music experts, came to him as a result of smooth and inventive detective work. Sexton recognized — so did Cancellara — that this was a case that would ultimately turn on credibility. Who would Carruthers believe? The Gondos side? Or the Hardy-Toth side? In Sexton's view, the defence had already gone a long way in demonstrating that Gondos was an outrageous liar. During the Gondos cross-examination, out of the man's own mouth, Sexton thought Gondos had shown himself to be a fraud. Why did Gondos lie? Maybe it was the cancer that affected his capacity for truth. Maybe it went back further, to Gondos's disappointment that he hadn't become a concert pianist or won bravos for his compositions or just somehow got *famous*. Maybe the damned case was all about regret. However you cut the motivations, Sexton's thinking went, Gondos had skirted the truth when he testified in the hotel sitting-room, and Sexton assigned two of his people at Osler, Hoskin to run down the real story. Or stories.

Chris Morgan — no relation to Brian Morgan, the Osler lawyer who assisted Sexton at the Gondos testimony — was in his year of articles at Osler, Hoskin & Harcourt, the year when law students take practical training in a firm before their call to the bar. Morgan went through the usual articling rotation, three months in Osler, Hoskin's tax department, three in labour, three in real estate, and, in the spring of 1982, three in litigation, where Ed Sexton hauled him into the Gondos case. Chris Morgan was in his mid-twenties, tall, lean, blond, hard-working, and — Sexton liked this — equipped with a good set of nerves, kind of a Cool Hand Luke. Just the guy for detective work.

Linda Nascher already knew her way around the Gondos case. She was Osler, Hoskin's litigation law clerk, and she had been in on the Gondos sessions at the Westin Hotel, taking notes and organizing Sexton's files. She was a slim, dark woman in her mid-thirties, and she'd spent six years at her job, gathering evidence for cases, briefing witnesses, assisting in court, learning how to be patient and resourceful.

Morgan and Nascher set out to take apart and reassemble three parts of the Ivan Gondos case.

Gondos's education.

During his testimony, Gondos was caught in a little white lie when Sexton showed that he incorrectly wrote on his BMI application that he completed Grade 13 at high school and held an ATCM certificate from the Royal Conservatory of Music. The Sexton team speculated that Gondos might be masking even more of the truth about his music-training. Had he really studied at the Conservatory "up to Grade 8", as he said in answer to questions at discovery? Chris Morgan went to the Conservatory offices to find out and hit pay dirt in the person of June Stewart.

"She was your classic librarian type," Morgan says. "She knew the records cold."

Among other duties, June Stewart kept tabs on the examination records at the Conservatory, and she'd been doing it for twenty-five years. The progress of students through the Conservatory was marked in two ways: on a card-file system and in a collection of newspaper clippings that announced examination results. There was nothing sleek about the system — most of the file cards seemed to be stored in shoeboxes — but June Stewart had the records under control. And when Chris Morgan explained his mission, she asked only for a bit of time to handle the search.

Two days later, June Stewart telephoned Morgan.

"I've gone through the student file cards from 1919 to 1978," she said.

"Yes," Morgan said.

"I also read the newspaper clippings."

"Yes."

"As far as we're concerned," June Stewart said, "no one with the name of Gondos ever applied to the Conservatory or took an examination."

Morgan told June Stewart she would be needed as a witness at the trial.

"That'll be fine," she said.

The Roy Robson Xerox.

During his testimony, Gondos referred to a Xerox copy of the sheet music to the version of "Variations on a Theme in A Minor" that he said he wrote out on November 10, 1962. The Xerox, Gondos testified, was made in 1965 for a student of his named Roy Robson. Robson had returned the Xerox to Gondos in 1981 after the case began, and Brian Wheatley filed it as an exhibit in the case.

Linda Nascher thought there was something not quite right about the Xerox. The size was one thing. The copy, like the original, was outsized, eighteen inches by fourteen inches, and it was done on both sides of the paper. Nascher wondered whether a machine existed in 1965 that could handle an oversized, double-sided copying job. But that wasn't the only reason Nascher's warning bells went off. It was just the *look* of the copy that seemed wrong.

"The part that really made me ask questions," she says, "was that the Robson copy was what's called a dry copy. I worked in an office in 1965, and we didn't have dry copying. I don't think it'd been invented that early. We had wet copying, the kind where you took the paper off the machine and hung it up to dry. It's easy to tell the difference between wet and dry, and to me, the Robson was definitely dry."

Chris Morgan got the paper-chase assignment. He had an undergraduate degree in engineering and was expected to be able to grasp the technical minutiae of wet and dry copying. Nascher's intuition set the Sexton team on the trail, but Morgan had to pin down the science.

His research led him to a man named Peter Schopfer, who, by 1982, had been running a copy shop in mid-town Toronto for twenty-three years. Ask him a question about the copy business, and he had the answer.

"What type of copy is this?" Morgan asked, showing Schopfer the Robson document.

"Dry," Schopfer answered.

Linda Nascher was right.

"How can you tell?" Morgan asked Schopfer.

"There are three kinds of copy only," Schopfer said. He talked with a German or Austrian accent. "Dry, moist, photographic. It isn't photographic, this copy, because it isn't on photographic paper. It isn't moist because it hasn't got the coating you get with moist copies. It's dry."

Morgan was impressed.

"Next question," he said. "Who made this copy? The one I'm showing you from the court case?"

"Xerox."

"You can tell just like that?"

"See the way the black parts on here have faded in the middle?" Schopfer said. "These music notes, they would be all black on the original, but now they're faded at the centre, you see? That's Xerox. They always had that problem until Kodak came along and solved it."

Morgan was *really* impressed.

"One more question," he said to Schopfer. "Look at this copy, the Xerox, double-sided, and tell me if you could have made one like it in 1965."

"Not possible."

"Why not?"

"No machine copied two sides at once like that in 1965."

"When was the earliest a machine could do the job?"

"I got one in here, my shop, in 1975," Schopfer said. "Xerox brought it out, oh, I don't know, a couple years before that."

"So this copy I'm showing you couldn't have been made in the 1960s?"

"I've told you already," Schopfer said. "No."

Morgan was finished for the moment with Peter Schopfer but not with the Robson copy. Schopfer's information sent Morgan to the Xerox offices in Toronto, where he met a man named Ernie Sniedgzins, whose title at Xerox was Product

Support Manager. Sniedgzins was a whiz at the dry-copying process, and he confirmed everything that Schopfer had told Morgan.

"Model 3103," Sniedgzins said. "It was the first machine we made, first machine *anybody* made, that could do the kind of copying you're talking about, large-sized and double-sided."

"When did the 3103 come into Canada?" Morgan asked.

"That was 1974," Sniedgzins answered.

Then Morgan asked a question which drew a response from Sniedgzins that Morgan, to his ever-lasting good fortune, stored away in an accessible corner of his brain.

"How about this?" Morgan asked. "What if somebody, back in 1965, ran a piece of sheet music through an old Xerox machine and got a copy and then fed the copy through on the other side to get another piece of the sheet music on the back? Could that be done?"

"It'd be a lot of trouble," Sniedgzins said. "But, sure, that was a possibility in 1965."

Morgan showed Sniedgzins the Robson copy.

"Is that what might have happened here?" he asked.

"No, no, this is from the 3103 machine," Sniedgzins said.

"You're positive?"

"One way I know," Sniedgzins said, "is there aren't any track marks on this copy."

And he proceeded to educate Morgan, one professional to another, on the fine points of track marks. The trouble was, Sniedgzins said, that with the early Xerox machines in the 1960s, there was something imperfect about the seals that held in the dry ink. They allowed dust to leak out of the ink. The dust got on the rollers. And when the rollers pushed the paper out of the copier, they left little rows of black dots along the bottom of the copy paper. "Track marks" was the name people in the copy-machine industry gave to those rows of little black dots.

"Now you look at this copy," Sniedgzins said, referring to

the Robson document. "It's got no track marks, and that means it wasn't made in the 1960s."

Track marks.

Morgan would remember the term, but in the meantime he rejoiced in the information he'd uncovered. The Robson copy wasn't made, as Gondos claimed, in 1965. It was done much later, at least as late as 1974, and the implications of that fact were potentially immense. If the copy of the 1962 sheet music was the subject of a lie, then what about the original? Perhaps it wasn't written in 1962. There wasn't anything about the sheet music's paper that indicated it came from a date later than 1962, but if Gondos was lying about the copy, the chances were he was lying about the original. And, for another thing, to take a giant leap in speculation, the lies about the copying might imply that Gondos didn't write "Variations on a Theme in A Minor" until the mid-1970s. That would put his composition *after* Hagood Hardy's writing of "The Homecoming". So, was it Gondos who really copied from Hardy? Was the shoe on the other foot? Morgan didn't want to get too carried away with possibilities. For the moment, he contented himself with what he had for Sexton — a collection of facts that would put another hole in Gondos's credibility.

Morgan told Peter Schopfer and Ernie Sniedgzins that he'd be sending them subpoenas to appear as witnesses at the trial.

The Encounter at Stop 33.

Hardy said it never happened.

Where was he on the night of September 25, 1970?

"Working," Hardy said. "Or at home with Martha and the kids."

Well, which?

The team of Nascher and Morgan got on the investigation. Nascher handled the inside, Morgan the outside. She dug through Hardy's records; he roamed the bars looking for waiters and waitresses who had been on the evening shift at the top of the Sutton Place Hotel on September 25, 1970.

"On my part of the job," Morgan remembers, "I got to sample a lot of good Scotch."

He started his search, logically enough, at Stop 33 and found one waitress who joined the room's staff in 1967 and had been on the job for the following fifteen years. Her name was Margaret Murray. She couldn't remember what happened at Stop 33 on the night of September 25, 1970, but she was certain of a few facts. She didn't recognize Ivan Gondos from a photograph that Chris Morgan showed her, didn't recall "Variations on a Theme in A Minor" that Morgan played for her, and had never seen Hagood Hardy with anyone who resembled Gondos.

"Okay," Morgan asked, "is it possible Hardy could have been in here as a patron, just a guy having a drink, and you wouldn't have seen him?"

"That's not very likely," Margaret Murray said. "The thing about Hagood, he was the friendliest guy with everybody who worked here. If he came in for a drink, which, by the way, I've never heard of him doing, he would've spoken to me. Just to say hello. That's the kind of person he was."

Morgan tracked down another former Stop 33 waitress who was now working at Czechoslovakian Airlines, a third ex-waitress who had a job as a medical secretary, and a one-time Stop 33 maître d' who had moved to the same position at the World Trade Centre. Their stories matched up with Margaret Murray's. Gondos and "Variations" had made little or no impression, and for certain, none of the employees had ever noticed him in conversation with Hagood Hardy.

As evidence, the word of the four witnesses didn't qualify as a complete refutation of Gondos's insistence on the encounter at Stop 33. But *four* witnesses? Not bad, Morgan thought, enough to have strong persuasive value in court.

Meanwhile, back at Osler, Hoskin, Linda Nascher leafed

diligently through the work records that Hardy had brought to her, records that covered his career in the jingles business and his years on the road with The Montage. And, after a couple of hours of leafing, Nascher got her reward for diligence: invoices covering the afternoon and early evening of September 25, 1970. On that date, according to the invoices, Hardy was recording a jingle he wrote for Rice Krispies. Hushes and pauses and a bongo pinging around the edges to summon up "the morning sounds of Rice Krispies".

The recording session took place at the RCA studios on Mutual Street in mid-town Toronto, and it appeared that the session got under way at two in the afternoon. The invoices showed the studio was booked for three hours, then one more was tacked on, plus two more hours "out of time". What did all that mean, especially the part about "out of time"? Nascher traced the recording engineer who worked the Rice Krispies job. His name was George Semkiw, and he'd been the engineer at the RCA studios from 1966 to 1975. Semkiw's own records for the Rice Krispies jingle indicated the session had run from two in the afternoon to eight at night. "Out of time"? That meant the hours after six o'clock. The rates were bumped up for the hours you used the studio beyond six. Out of time.

"Would Hagood have been in the studio for the entire period?" Nascher asked.

"As far as I recall," Semkiw said. "On all the jobs I worked with him, he was the type who always stayed to the end."

"Until eight o'clock?"

"Much longer," Semkiw said. "After we finished recording, we'd be around another half-hour anyway to make copies of the music for the writers and the clients."

Nascher and Morgan thought they had a fix on Hardy's whereabouts for the night of September 25, 1970. It wasn't Stop 33.

On the morning of Monday, April 19, 1982, John Arena stepped to the witness stand in a courtroom on the third floor of the Toronto Courthouse, and after a ten-month delay, the trial in the case of *Gondos v. Hardy and Toth* resumed before Mr. Justice Douglas Carruthers.

Arena, a sleek, plump man in a dark three-piece suit, oozed assurance. In answer to Brian Wheatley's questions, he said that he was the proprietor of Winston's Restaurant and that he hired Ivan Gondos to play the piano in his establishment for several weeks in 1972.

Wheatley had brought a record-player to the courtroom, a shiny machine with crisp audio. He put *Ivan Plays Favorites* on the machine and asked Arena to listen to the version of "Variations" on the album.

"That's Ivan's song," Arena said. "He played it every night at my place. Many times every night. He played this song at the opening and at the closing. I called it the Winston's Theme. Very lovely."

The cavalcade of witnesses who would swear to the early origins of "Variations on a Theme in A Minor" had begun.

Gesta Abols, a lawyer, said he took piano lessons from Gondos way back in 1962 and '63, and he testified that, sometimes during the lessons, Gondos used to play this song, "Variations".

Abols was a bit of a snob about the composition.

"It wasn't something I expected from a concert pianist like Gondos," he said on the witness stand. "It was a piece of schmaltz. Like gold paint, you know, romantic, flowery, reflective of the Hungarian temperament."

But Abols was certain the song he heard in the Gondos house and in clubs where he later went to listen to Gondos was this very same "Variations on a Theme in A Minor".

So were other former Gondos students and friends.

"I heard it at Ivan's many times," a man named Arthur Frederico testified.

"How many times?" Wheatley asked.

"Thirty times," Frederico answered. "Forty."

"When was this?"

"I met Ivan in 1968," Frederico said. "It was in the late 1960s I heard the song."

Dorothy Frederico, Arthur's wife, backed up her husband.

"When I heard Ivan's music on the radio, I thought I must phone and congratulate him," she said on the witness stand. "But the announcer said it was 'The Homecoming' by Hagood Hardy. How could this be? I heard Ivan play it in 1968."

Alan Lowry, a man who did repair work on organs and pianos, testified that he met Gondos in 1965, and from the beginning of their long friendship, Gondos had always played the song he came to know as "Variations on a Theme in A Minor".

"I never heard a composer write the same kind of romantic music that Ivan wrote," Lowry said in court.

Arena, Abols, the Fredericos, Lowry, and three other witnesses called by Brian Wheatley based their testimony on the recording of "Variations" that appeared on *Ivan Plays Favorites*. Yes, they said, as Wheatley played the record for them in the courtroom, that's the song we remember. None of them referred to the sheet music that Gondos said he wrote on November 10, 1962. These eight witnesses didn't know about the written version of "Variations".

But three more Wheatley witnesses talked about the sheet music.

Sharon Pagliuso testified that Gondos actually gave her a copy of the written-out "Variations". Pagliuso was another Gondos piano student in the mid-1960s, and she said she came into possession of her music document in 1964.

"It was narrower and longer than the 1962 sheet music," she said. "And it was put together in accordion fashion with masking tape, but it was the same song."

83

Could she produce her copy of "Variations"?

"I don't know where it is now," Pagliuso testified. "But Ivan told me he wrote it the year before he gave it to me."

Marcello Febbo had even hotter testimony about the 1962 sheet music of "Variations".

"In 1962," Febbo said in answer to Wheatley's questions, "I sat beside Ivan while he wrote it out."

Febbo, a flamboyant fellow, was an artist who painted in a realist style, and his connection with Gondos went back many years. In spite of the long relationship between the two men, Wheatley was mildly surprised that Febbo testified so generously on Gondos's behalf. After all, Wheatley knew, Carole Anne Gondos had been married to Febbo before she married Gondos.

"When Ivan wrote it out," Febbo said in court, referring to the 1962 sheet music, "he wrote it from another rough copy of the music."

Then there was Roy Robson.

"I first met Ivan when I went to him for lessons on the organ in 1965," Robson testified. "Not long after that, probably in early 1966, he gave me a Xerox copy of his sheet music for 'Variations on a Theme in A Minor'."

Wheatley produced the Xerox which had been filed as an exhibit in the case when Gondos gave his testimony about the copy in June 1981, and Robson identified it as the document he received as a gift in 1966.

"I didn't see Ivan make the copy," Robson said. "I just imagined he was the one who had it Xeroxed, and I put it away in a drawer until I found it in 1980. Anyway, I know the music. Ivan always used to play it."

Ed Sexton took the lead in cross-examining Wheatley's witnesses. He had a tougher case to meet than Ken Cancellara, and his client, Hardy, had more at stake than Cancellara's clients, the Toths. So Sexton went first in questioning John

Arena and the others, and he persisted longer in his cross-examinations.

But with these witnesses, the ones who said they heard Gondos play "Variations" years before Hardy wrote "The Homecoming" and the others who swore they saw the sheet music to "Variations" in the 1960s, Sexton had a problem.

"It was one thing to go after Gondos as a liar, because he *did* lie," Sexton explains. "But it was a very different proposition to show that Arena and the rest were liars too. They had nothing to gain by lying. That meant what I had to do was show they were simply mistaken in the music they thought they heard."

To assist with that awkward task, Sexton used an aural aid. It was something that came out of a discussion with the three expert witnesses whom Sexton and Cancellara had recruited to testify for the defence. The three were Gus Ciamaga, the Dean of the Faculty of Music at the University of Toronto, and Jimmy Dale and the ubiquitous Doug Riley, two pianists and composers who were active on the Toronto jazz and commercial music scenes. In conversation, Dale pointed out a tune that was similar in melody to both "The Homecoming" and "Variations"; it was the theme song that a composer named Lalo Schifrin wrote for the 1968 movie *The Fox*. Sexton asked Dale to cut a tape of the song, just Dale and piano, and when he went to court, Sexton tucked the tape in his briefcase.

As each of Wheatley's witnesses stepped to the stand and identified "Variations" from *Ivan Plays Favorites* as the song they heard years earlier, Sexton asked them on his cross-examination to listen to the Dale tape. He didn't tell the witnesses the name of the tune they were listening to, and since all witnesses were excluded from the courtroom when they weren't testifying, none of them could benefit from an advance listen to the theme from *The Fox*. Sexton played the song and asked for the witnesses' reactions.

"Well," John Arena said, "the opening part resembles 'The

Homecoming', but, yes, I heard part of Ivan's song in there."

"That's the same piece we're talking about, 'Variations'," Arthur Frederico said with great certainty. "Maybe not exactly the same. But the melody is there, and that's Ivan himself playing the piano on that tape."

"It sounds like the music from Ivan's other album, *Shoresands and Driftwood*," Dorothy Frederico said at first. Then she changed her mind. "No, I think it's the same music as on *Ivan Plays Favorites*. It's 'Variations'. The way Ivan played it sounds just like this."

And so it went.

Sexton made yards in demonstrating that Wheatley's witnesses didn't possess infallible ears. And he picked up a few other useful tidbits in his cross-examination; for example, Alan Lowry, the organ and piano technician, testified that, as he remembered it, Gondos mentioned seeing the Salada Tea commercial in 1973, at least a year earlier than August 1974, which Gondos swore was when he first came across the commercial and its music. Sexton was reasonably satisfied with the results of the cross-examination — the displays of fallibility, the stray pieces of evidence. They were as much as he could expect. Certainly he knew that Wheatley's witnesses would never break down and admit that what they heard Gondos play in the 1960s *wasn't* the tune called "Variations on a Theme in A Minor".

Jimmy Dale's tape of the music from *The Fox* gave Sexton and Cancellara an idea.

"We thought maybe there were more songs that sounded like 'The Homecoming' and 'Moment of Love' and the relevant sections of 'Variations'," Sexton says. "If there were, we wanted to use them in cross-examination of one particular witness of Wheatley's."

The witness was the Wheatley expert, Dr. Paul McIntyre, Dean of the Music School at the University of Windsor.

Sexton and Cancellara knew that McIntyre would try to make the case for plagiarism in musical terms, fastening on to melodic similarities among the three songs. But if the defence could bring in yet more songs with the similarities, McIntyre's points might be weakened or confused.

The timing, though it was tight, favoured Sexton and Cancellara. Wheatley finished with all of his witnesses except McIntyre on Thursday afternoon, April 22, and Carruthers decided the court wouldn't sit on Friday. That gave the defence's experts, Jimmy Dale and Doug Riley, a long weekend, three days, to sort through their musical memories for more tunes like *The Fox*.

Everybody met late Sunday morning — Dale, Riley, Sexton, Cancellara. Sexton brought along his dishy wife Rosemary, and a couple of other musicians sat in. One was Tommy Ambrose, the jazz and ballad singer and a successful writer and performer of music for TV commercials. The meeting took place in an office over a restaurant that Ambrose owned on Church Street north of Maple Leaf Gardens. Ambrose named the restaurant after the business that rewarded him so handsomely. The restaurant was called Jingles.

Dale and Riley took turns at the piano, punching out spurts of melody. Ambrose searched through musical reference books. The gin flowed, and there were a couple of smokers in the room. The musicians talked among themselves in jazz lingo and musical shorthand. And Sexton thought the scene was teetering on chaos.

"I was just hanging on by my fingernails trying to understand what was going on," he says. "All I knew for sure was that I had to be in court next day cross-examining a key witness, and I began to wonder, the later it got, whether I'd have anything to take with me."

To Sexton's astonishment, in the midst of the gab and the gin and the smoke in the office over Jingles, Dale and Riley and the others produced a terrific tape. The music was played

87

by Dale and Riley alternating on piano, and the tape had on it six songs that resembled "The Homecoming" and five that sounded something like "Moment of Love".

"I'd have been happy with two or three songs," Sexton says. "But eleven altogether, that seemed amazing."

The six that suggested "The Homecoming" were these:

"Je ne songeais pas à Rose", a 1969 ballad written by a Belgian song-writer.

"What Was Good Enough for Me", an American tune written in 1967.

Lalo Schifrin's theme for *The Fox*.

A passage from *The Four Seasons* by Vivaldi, who lived from 1675 to 1741.

"Fly Me to the Moon", the 1954 American pop hit.

"Vurria", another pop tune from 1963.

The songs that seemed similar to "Moment of Love" were less well known: two French songs, "L'Amour c'est comme un jour" (1952) and "Bon anniversaire" (1963), and two American pop tunes, "As Years Go By" (1947) and "To Die of Love" (1971).

Sexton clutched his copy of the tape and drove home with his wife to think thoughts of cross-examination.

Dr. Paul McIntyre, a dark, precise, bearded man whose field of expertise was classical music and not the pop variety, testified for the entire day, Monday, April 26.

Wheatley asked him for his credentials as a musician and teacher. McIntyre answered, and then, Wheatley questioning, McIntyre explained the mission he'd carried out on behalf of the plaintiff.

He worked from the sheet music of "Variations on a Theme in A Minor" that Ivan Gondos dated November 10, 1962, and from the sheet music of Hagood Hardy's "The Homecoming".

He took the third variation of Gondos's composition, the

one that covered the final sixteen bars. This variation was written in the key of G Major. McIntyre transposed it down a fifth to C Major, and transcribed the notes on an enlarged sheet of music paper. There were twenty-six notes, and they made up the melody of Gondos's third variation.

McIntyre took the melody of "The Homecoming" as Hardy had written it, covering the first sixteen bars of the song following a short introduction. "The Homecoming" was in the key of C Major. McIntyre wrote the notes of the sixteen bars on the enlarged sheet of music paper below the notes to variation three of Gondos's song. There were also twenty-six notes in the melody of the Hardy song.

McIntyre compared the two melodic lines.

"What did you find?" Wheatley asked.

"Of the twenty-six notes in each of the two works," McIntyre answered, "the first twenty-five are identical."

"How are they identical?"

"They are identical as to pitch and as to duration or rhythmic structure," McIntyre said. "They are the same notes."

Wheatley asked, "What are the chances of this happening, of two songs being so alike, without one song having influenced the other?"

McIntyre answered, "The chances are infinitesimal, next to zero, one in the order of one hundred million."

Wheatley introduced the enlarged sheet of music paper that McIntyre had prepared as an exhibit in the case.

McIntyre wasn't finished.

He explained that he had done another comparison in which he matched up the first variation of the Gondos composition, bars eleven through eighteen, with the melody of "Moment of Love". There were twenty-two notes in both melodic lines, and McIntyre transcribed the two sets of notes, the Gondos over the Toth, on an enlarged sheet of music paper.

"What did you discover?" Wheatley asked.

"Of the twenty-two notes in each composition," McIntyre

answered, "I found eighteen to be identical in pitch and in duration."

Wheatley asked, "What are the chances of this happening, two songs being so alike, without one having influenced the other?"

"Infinitesimal," McIntyre said. "Next to zero. One in the order of one hundred million."

Wheatley introduced this chart of musical comparison as an exhibit in evidence.

Wheatley asked McIntyre if he drew any conclusion from his studies.

"I found what I felt to be musical plagiarism," McIntyre said.

Mr. Justice Carruthers interrupted.

"That's for me to decide," he said to McIntyre. "Your job is to point out the similarities in the pieces of music."

Sexton began his cross-examination of McIntyre by getting the witness to set a few matters straight. They were:

That the Gondos music which McIntyre used for his comparison, the third variation, did not appear on Gondos's 1974 recording of his song "Variations" from the album *Ivan Plays Favorites*.

That the 1962 sheet music of "Variations" travelled through an eclectic and perhaps puzzling series of keys: A Minor for the main theme, C Minor for the first and second variations, and G Major for the third.

And that, in particular, on the sheet music, when Gondos moved from the main theme to the first variation, he went from A Minor to C Minor, but when he made the same move on the recording, he remained in A Minor.

It took Sexton about forty-five minutes to clear the decks of these details, all of them tending to raise questions about the legitimacy of the origins of "Variations on a Theme in A

Minor", and when he was done, Sexton asked McIntyre a potent question.

"In doing your study," he asked, "did you try to find any other works that were similar to 'The Homecoming' and 'Variations'?"

McIntyre had an elaborate answer.

"My attempt," he said, "was to find melodies that might have influenced either of these composers to put down the melodies they put down. My primary source for that was a pair of books edited by Harold Barlow. Each book contains about ten thousand themes or tunes cross-indexed by pitch. I could find nothing that could reasonably be interpreted as, may I say, a common source."

Well, Ed Sexton thought, do *we* have a surprise for *you.*

At that point Sexton began his bid to cross-examine McIntyre on the tape that Jimmy Dale and Doug Riley had prepared at the previous day's session in the office over Jingles Restaurant. But Wheatley, recognizing what Sexton was up to, rose to object.

"My friend Mr. Sexton is getting into the field of common domain in music," he said to Carruthers. "I submit, my lord, he's not permitted to do that. He hasn't pleaded it as a defence in this action. He can't bring it up now."

"My lord, I'm merely trying to establish authorship," Sexton answered back. "I'll have two arguments on the point. One is that Ivan Gondos took his song from other songs, and it's therefore not original and can't be protected by copyright."

"What's the second argument?" Carruthers asked.

"That Gondos took his song, 'Variations', from the defendant Hardy's song, 'The Homecoming'," Sexton said.

There it was, out in the open in court — Sexton was saying, as Ken Cancellara had earlier said, that it wasn't Hardy, or the Toths, who had committed musical theft. It was Gondos.

91

"This defence," Wheatley argued, still trying to persuade Carruthers not to allow Sexton to use the Dale-Riley tape on McIntyre, "should have been specifically pleaded much earlier. Mr. Sexton can't raise common domain or whatever his point is at this late hour in the case."

"Oh, really, my lord, it's been an issue from day one of the trial," Sexton said. "The defence has continually cross-examined Mr. Wheatley's witnesses about one earlier work that resembled 'Variations' and 'The Homecoming'."

Carruthers made up his mind.

"Subject to further argument on the point," he said, "I'll accept this line of questioning by Mr. Sexton."

Sexton asked Chris Morgan, his student, to put the Dale-Riley tape on the machine in the courtroom and play the first tune. It was the 1969 ballad by the Belgian song-writer, "Je ne songeais pas à Rose".

"Do you recognize this piece?" Sexton asked McIntyre.

"No."

"Is it similar to either the Gondos or Hardy works?"

"It is similar to passages in both."

"Would you say," Sexton asked, "it's similar to the Gondos piece?"

"Yes."

"Strikingly similar?"

"Yes," McIntyre answered. "I'll stretch it to that."

"What about the Hardy work?" Sexton asked. "Is the piece you just heard strikingly similar to it?"

"Yes."

Sexton asked Morgan to play the second piece on the tape, the 1967 pop song called "What Was Good Enough for Me".

"Do you recognize this work?" Sexton asked McIntyre.

"No."

"Is it strikingly similar to both the Gondos and Hardy works?"

"Yes."

McIntyre had no trouble identifying the third piece on the

tape, Lalo Schifrin's theme from *The Fox*. Sexton had played it for the other witnesses, and Wheatley had tipped off McIntyre about its name and composer. McIntyre made one goof. He called the composer "Lionel Schifrin".

"Is this song strikingly similar to the Gondos and Hardy pieces?" Sexton asked.

McIntyre, maybe picking up confidence, had his reservations.

He said, "The similarities are less pronounced than in the first two selections."

Sexton played the fourth tune. It was the excerpt from Vivaldi's *The Four Seasons*.

"Do you recognize this work?" Sexton asked.

"No," McIntyre answered.

"Is it strikingly similar to the Gondos and Hardy songs?"

"Not strikingly," McIntyre answered. "Not even similar. It's more like a variation of the Gondos and Hardy pieces. All of them have one common element, and that's the chord progression."

Sexton tried another angle.

"Would a layman find this piece strikingly similar to the Gondos and Hardy songs?" he asked.

McIntyre dug in.

"I hope not," he said.

Sexton switched directions.

"Well, if someone *heard* the selection you just listened to," he asked, "could he progress to a point where he'd write what Gondos wrote in 'Variations on a Theme in A Minor'?"

"Yes," McIntyre said, bending at last. "That could happen."

Good enough, Sexton thought.

McIntyre agreed that the fifth and sixth songs on the tape, "Fly Me to the Moon" and "Vurria", neither of which he recognized, were similar, though not strikingly so, to the Gondos and Hardy pieces. And after a few more questions, Sexton wound up his cross-examination.

What had he accomplished?

Maybe he'd made Dr. McIntyre look a trifle silly. But that was only an incidental benefit to the defence. More positively, Sexton had got McIntyre, Wheatley's own witness, to concede that there were other melodies out there — who knew how many or how far back they went in musical history? — that a lay listener or even a trained listener like McIntyre himself could not differentiate from "Variations" or from "The Homecoming". In a sense, the point that Sexton made operated as a double-edged sword: if Gondos's song wasn't original, then neither was Hardy's. Hagood Hardy wouldn't care for that suggestion. He regarded "The Homecoming" as an entirely fresh composition, uninfluenced by anything that had been written earlier by any other composer, not even Vivaldi. But Sexton would risk Hardy's hurt feelings if he thought he could help to win the case by scoring a point off Dr. McIntyre, and the point was that, if Gondos's song wasn't original, he had no grounds under copyright law, no grounds of any sort, for claiming that Hardy had stolen his composition.

Sexton would continue to press the argument that Gondos was demonstrably not a person to be believed, and that it was more likely he had borrowed from Hardy than the other way around. But through his cross-examination of McIntyre, Sexton had pushed Carruthers to ponder the mysteries of originality in the songs that were the subjects of the trial. And Sexton was willing to bet that if, in the end, the case turned on the question of originality — is *any* of these songs original? — Carruthers would have to come down on the side of the defendants.

Ken Cancellara wasn't as successful as Sexton in his cross-examination of Dr. McIntyre. When Cancellara played the five tunes from the Dale-Riley tape that were supposed to resemble "Moment of Love", and the first variation of the

Gondos composition, McIntyre refused to bite. None of the melody lines in the five songs, he said on the witness stand, sounded similar to either the Toth tune or "Variations". The most he granted was that one song, "Bon anniversaire", had a chord progression that was "strikingly similar" to the chord progressions in the Gondos and Toth songs. Cancellara was hoping for more, but he thought, what the heck, at least Carruthers would be thinking about this similarity angle.

On Tuesday, April 27, the day after McIntyre testified, the defence began to present its case to Carruthers. Ed Sexton had witnesses who would wipe away Ivan Gondos's stories and credibility. Ken Cancellara would let all of the Toths give their own accounts of "Moment of Love" and its creation. And the two lawyers would share the expertise of Gus Ciamaga, Jimmy Dale, and Doug Riley.

June Stewart testified. She was the librarian at the Royal Conservatory of Music, and in answer to Sexton's questions, she said that from 1919 to 1978 there was no sign of a student named Ivan Gondos at the Conservatory.

Brian Wheatley tried out Ms. Stewart on cross-examination.

"What name were you given?" he asked. "Gondos?"

"Yes," June Stewart answered. "Gondos."

"What about Gondosh?" Wheatley asked. "Did you look under that name?"

"Oh, well, I used Gondos as a *base* name," Ms. Stewart answered. "Anything that started off like that, I looked for and found nothing."

Wheatley refused to quit.

"Do you know of a Professor Bela Borzorninyi?" he asked, invoking the name of the teacher whom Gondos said he studied under at the Conservatory.

"Borzorninyi?" June Stewart said. "That doesn't ring a bell."

Sexton called three waitresses and one maître d' who worked at Stop 33 on the night of September 25, 1970. All testified that they hadn't seen Hagood Hardy in conversation with Ivan Gondos. Not that night. Not any night. George Semkiw, the recording engineer, testified that, as far as he recalled, on the evening in question, September 25, 1970, Hardy was over at the RCA studio cutting a jingle for Rice Krispies.

Peter Lighthall was the financial clerk-expediter at the Leo Burnett Advertising Agency.

"You were involved in the Salada Tea commercial?" Sexton asked Lighthall.

"Yes."

"In the production and the later handling of the tapes?"

"Yes."

Sexton played the three Salada commercials for Lighthall on the video machine that had been set up in the courtroom. First, the commercial called "Taxi", then "Birthday", and finally "Church". Lighthall identified them, and Sexton asked him when each of the commercials appeared on television.

"'Taxi' and 'Birthday' both started running on January 7, 1973," Lighthall said. "'Taxi' stayed on air until June 1975 and 'Birthday' till March of '75."

"And 'Church'?" Sexton asked.

"It first appeared on April 29, 1973," Lighthall said, "and it went off in July 1974."

Which seemed once again to make a liar out of Gondos, who said he saw the "Church" commercial, the first time he ever came across Hardy's Salada Tea music, on a Sunday in August 1974, a date that was fixed in his mind, he said, because it came the day after he taped *Ivan Plays Favorites* at Deerhurst Inn.

Peter Schopfer and Ernie Sniedgzins did their brief but effective numbers. They were the copy experts whom Chris Morgan dug up: Schopfer, the proprietor of a copy shop, and Sniedgzins, the Xerox employee. And they explained why the Xerox of the 1962 sheet music that Gondos and Roy Robson claimed to have been made in 1965 or '66 couldn't have been done earlier than the mid-1970s.

Sexton asked Sniedgzins, "When was the first time a machine in Canada was capable of making a copy like this, on both sides and large-sized?"

He showed Sniedgzins the Robson copy.

"Well, that would be a model 3103 machine," Sniedgzins said. "It was introduced to Canada in 1974."

The three Toths — Rudy, Jerry, and Chris — were not happy witnesses. Rudy and Jerry resented the need for them to be in a courtroom answering the claim against them that they regarded as so outrageously fraudulent. And all three Toths were baffled by Chris's involvement as a defendant. He was a kid who'd never met Gondos, let alone played a role in stealing a song from the guy.

The two senior Toths, replaying to Ken Cancellara's questions, explained the history of "Moment of Love" and got on record for the first time in court the key fact that the song dated back to 1970. And all three Toths testified in rebuttal to Gondos's tale about the alleged events of a night in the summer of 1975 when Gondos supposedly drove Chris and a copy of *Ivan Plays Favorites* to Rudy's cottage. None of it, the Toths swore, ever happened.

"No," Chris Toth said on the witness stand, "I never bought that album."

"Did you hear Ivan Gondos play the composition 'Variations on a Theme in A Minor' at Deerhurst Inn?" Cancellara asked.

"No. Never."

"Or any place else?"

"I didn't hear the song until this case came up."

"If you had heard it," Cancellara asked, trying to close off every possibility, "could you have transcribed what you heard on to paper?"

"I don't have that kind of musical talent," Chris answered.

After the Toths testified, Mr. Justice Carruthers had a question for Brian Wheatley.

"Are you going to remove Chris Toth as a defendant?" he asked.

"No, my lord," Wheatley answered.

"Mr. Wheatley, let me put it this way," Carruthers said. "The action against Chris Toth can't succeed."

Carruthers meant that, clearly, Chris had no part in stealing Gondos's song, particularly since "Moment of Love", as Carruthers now understood, predated the events of the summer night in 1975, if they ever occurred, by five years.

"We'll leave him on the list of defendants," Wheatley said to Carruthers.

"Unrelenting," Ken Cancellara said years after the trial ended. "Brian was that way from beginning to end. The situation with Chris was typical. There was no case against Chris, but Brian wouldn't withdraw. He forced Chris to stay to the end. That suggested one of two things to me. Either Brian had tremendous conviction that events were as Gondos testified or Brian got involved as more than just a lawyer. Maybe he got caught up in the whole music side of the case. Whatever, he was unrelenting."

Dr. Gustav Ciamaga, tall and silver-haired, was the first of the defence's expert witnesses to take the stand. He testified longer than the other two, Jimmy Dale and Doug Riley, taking up most of Wednesday, April 28, and he led off by conducting a short seminar on the evolution of the popular song. Ciamaga had the background for such instruction. True, he was an academic and a teacher of classical music, the Dean of the Faculty of Music at the University of Toronto, but he'd earned his way in the pop world, composing songs and film scores, writing arrangements of George Gershwin music for a choral group called the Gershwin Singers, doing collaborative work with Phil Nimmons, the celebrated Canadian jazz clarinetist and composer. Ciamaga's practical experience gave him an edge over the plaintiff's expert, Paul McIntyre, who was almost exclusively conversant with classical music. And Ciamaga had another advantage in court — shortly after eleven o'clock on the morning of the twenty-eighth, as he was just launching into his seminar, a piano was delivered to the courtroom. Sexton had arranged for the instrument, something that Ciamaga — and Dale and Riley — could sit at and play and use to make musical points more vivid.

"Pardon my arthritic fingers," Gus Ciamaga said to Mr. Justice Carruthers as he rippled a few warm-up scales.

Carruthers looked as pleased as a kid with a new toy. *Another* piece of theatre in his courtroom.

Ciamaga said a major difference between classical music and pop music that everyone should keep in mind was that, in classical music, the melody drives the harmony, but in pop music, it's the reverse, harmony coming first and pushing the melody. That, Ciamaga said, makes pop music a simpler form for the composer, since the toughest job in creating music is to conceive fresh melodies.

"With popular music," Ciamaga testified, "the harmony generates melody in close to a semi-automatic way. You begin with one harmony and proceed to the second, the third, and so on, according to a sort of natural cyclical sequence, and that sequence almost implies the melody."

From this basic truth, Ciamaga went on, two other truths

99

become immediately apparent.

One is that, in analysing a pop song, melody cannot be separated from harmony. But that, Ciamaga pointed out, is exactly what Paul McIntyre had done in his expert testimony.

"Dr. McIntyre's analysis of the songs at issue was very incomplete," Ciamaga said. "He dealt with only one aspect of the music — the melody."

The second truth is that, to no one's surprise, certainly not to Ciamaga's, pop music abounds in clichés and repeated devices. The form has such creative simplicity, harmony driving melody in predetermined sequences, that pop composers keep arriving at melodic patterns that repeat earlier melodic patterns. It isn't a case of one composer copying another. It's a matter of numbers.

"In the first fifty years of the twentieth century," Ciamaga testified, "there were approximately five hundred thousand popular songs copyrighted. I find it hard to believe that all five hundred thousand were original. In fact, in this repertory, there were very few original works."

Sexton said to Ciamaga, "Dr. McIntyre told the court that in the case of the Gondos and Hardy songs, they are so alike that it was a one-hundred-million-to-one chance they could have been composed without one song influencing the other."

"I heard Dr. McIntyre say that," Ciamaga said. "And I don't agree with his statistic."

Sexton asked, "Is it possible that Gondos and Hardy could have written the two works without reference to one another?"

"I believe that," Ciamaga answered. "It's possible for two composers in two places to deal with compositional materials in a similar way so that the melodies between the two works are similar and the harmonies are similar too."

Ciamaga was taking the defence further down the path

that Sexton had explored when he played the Dale-Riley tape in cross-examining Dr. McIntyre. Hardy and Gondos, working entirely independently of each other, may have come up with essentially the same melody. Hardy wouldn't be crazy about such an inference. But, Sexton thought, by developing the point for Carruthers, he could win the case.

When Sexton finished his exploration of melodic similarity with Ciamaga, he guided the witness into a look at the bona fides of Gondos's composition. Ciamaga said he'd studied the 1962 sheet music of "Variations" and listened to the 1974 recording from *Ivan Plays Favorites*, and he spotted plenty of trouble.

"The anomalies seemed to leap off the page," Ciamaga said.

He offered examples, beginning with the first variation in Gondos's composition, the one that was similar to "Moment of Love".

"Gondos stated his main theme in A Minor," Ciamaga said. "Then he chose for some inexplicable reason to move to C Minor for his first variation. I find that extremely puzzling. It isn't a variation, that first one, in the commonly accepted definition. I asked myself why the composition went from A Minor to C Minor so abruptly, and, staring at it, the impression I got was of two different compositions. It was as if variation one was wrenched into the compostion from somewhere outside."

Ciamaga said he felt even more baffled when he turned to the third variation, the one exactly like "The Homecoming".

"The music for the left hand in variation three doesn't seem to belong to the same composer who wrote the music for the left hand in the main theme," Ciamaga said. "The main theme has bland block chords, but in the third variation, it's an elegant left-hand part."

"Yes?" Sexton said, begging for more of the stuff that seemed to label Gondos as a fraud.

"Variation three is altogether more sophisticated music," Ciamaga answered back. "That was troublesome to me."

"How so?"

"Well, I suppose the point is that the entire Gondos piece seems like a scissors job," Ciamaga said. "It's a very patchwork piece of music."

"Is it your opinion," Sexton asked, recognizing that Ciamaga was in position to answer the question that got to the heart of the case, "that Mr. Hardy would have copied music from Mr. Gondos?"

Ciamaga said, "I find it hard to believe that a musician of professional stature like Mr. Hardy would go to such an amateur source."

When Ken Cancellara questioned Ciamaga, he firmed up one point.

"If the first variation were taken out of the version of Mr. Gondos's composition in the 1962 sheet music," Cancellara asked, "would it detract from the theme and other variations?"

"One would never miss the first variation," Ciamaga answered. "It just isn't an integral part of the composition."

The conclusion in Cancellara's mind, and, he hoped, in Carruthers', was that Gondos must have hijacked "Moment of Love" and jammed it into his own composition, that patchwork thing, as the first variation.

Jimmy Dale followed Dr. Ciamaga to the witness stand and to the courtroom piano. He was a short, round, poker-faced man who'd done everything in his musical life from conducting the orchestra on the 1970s Sonny and Cher TV show to playing piano in the 1980s Boss Brass, and in his testimony he made it explicit that he, too, had all kinds of reservations about "Variations on a Theme in A Minor".

"I don't regard it as one piece of music," Dale said in the courtroom.

"Why do you say that?" Sexton asked.

"Well, just look how abruptly it changes when it gets to the third variation," Dale said, echoing Ciamaga. "It uses about four or five sophisticated elements that never appeared earlier in the composition. The third variation's got passing melodies in the left hand, ninth chords, subtle harmonic techniques. The musicianship is far higher than in the rest of the piece, which makes me think, in my opinion, that whoever wrote the third variation didn't write the first ten bars of this Gondos composition."

The implication of Dale's testimony couldn't have been clearer — if anyone was stealing from someone else, Gondos was the leading candidate for thief.

From there, Sexton went happily on to explore one other angle with Dale, and he got into it by asking Dale to listen to the first six tunes on the tape that he and Doug Riley put together the previous Sunday.

"The songs on the tape," Sexton asked after the last piano note of "Vurria" died away, "do they compare harmonically with the Gondos piece?"

Dale answered, "They're similar, the songs on the tape and Gondos's song."

"And with 'The Homecoming'?"

"It's also harmonically similar to the tunes on the tape," Dale said.

"What about melodically?" Sexton asked. "Do the tunes on the tape have melodies that are similar or even strikingly similar to the Gondos and Hardy works?"

"It varies," Dale said. "The first two tunes on the tape, I'd call them strikingly similar to the melody in 'Variations' and 'Homecoming'. The other four, well, they're *quite* similar."

"Suppose a composer heard the fourth selection, the

Vivaldi," Sexton asked. "Would you say he could, having heard it, go out and write the Gondos and Hardy pieces?"

"Obviously he could," Dale answered. "The thing we're dealing with here is something called in music a common root movement. It's the way chords move in a song, and the common root movement in the songs we're talking about isn't unique."

"You heard Dr. Ciamaga speak of musical clichés?"

"That's what I was just referring to when I brought up common root movement," Dale said. "The songs on the tape and the other two pieces, the Hardy and Gondos, all of them repeat the same musical clichés."

Now Sexton had two experts on record with testimony about the possibility that none of the composers, not Gondos, not Hardy, had written an entirely original piece of music.

Of the defence's three experts, Doug Riley was the most blunt.

"It's been tampered with," he said in his testimony, speaking of "Variations on a Theme in A Minor". "I've got a lot of doubts about its authenticity."

Riley, dark, smooth, olive-skinned, had a hip manner. He'd composed tunes for a wide range of musicians that took in the soul singer Ray Charles and the jazz flutist Moe Koffman. He played piano in a style that blended jazz, gospel, and blues, and he was so generously talented that he had staked out a place in the jingles business. Riley possessed an overload of energy, seemingly at ease only when he sat at a piano, and his sartorial habits always called for a stylish hat, usually the kind of chic chapeau that Ernest Hemingway might have worn on safari. Riley's appearance in court marked one of the rare times anyone could remember seeing him without something on his head.

He spent four hours testifying. It might have been shorter

except he insisted on illustrating his answers with lengthy examples at the keyboard. Sexton didn't mind. Neither did Carruthers, the jazz fan.

Sexton asked Riley, "Could you play for us 'Variations on a Theme in A Minor'?"

"I don't know if I can play it as written," Riley said, looking at Gondos's 1962 sheet music.

He started on the main theme, the first bars of "Variations".

Tinkle. Clash. Thump.

"I don't know whether it's playable," Riley said.

"Could you indicate the places you say it's impossible to play?" Sexton asked.

"Bars two and three," Riley said, talking over his own playing. "I can't get my hands on his notes. The hands'd have to be a lot bigger than mine, and I can play a ten."

Riley meant he could span a tenth chord, a stretch of notes that covers more than an octave.

"What about the third variation?" Sexton asked.

"The styles change drastically when you get to it," Riley said, stroking the keys. "Lot of passing ninth chords in here. Very nice music."

Riley used an adjective that occurred to both Ciamaga and Dale.

"Very sophisticated compared to what went before," Riley said. "It gets all of a sudden quite musical after the stuff in the main theme."

Sexton knew that Riley, unlike the other two defence experts, had an in-close experience with Gondos, and he brought it up as a way to dig out more of Riley's views on the music.

"You've met Ivan Gondos?" Sexton asked.

"In the summer of 1977 at Deerhurst Inn," Riley answered. "He asked to be introduced to me in the lounge, and he told me he felt Hagood Hardy and Rudy Toth both borrowed his music. The next set, when he went back to the piano, he played his piece to show me what he was talking about."

"What was your reaction?" Sexton asked.

"The first thing I recall very specifically," Riley said, "he never went to major."

"Maybe you should explain that."

"In this sheet music right in front of me for Gondos's song," Riley said, playing along as he talked, "he starts out in a minor key and then in the third variation —hear this? — he goes to G Major. Okay, he didn't do that when he played for me at Deerhurst. He stayed in minor. Never went to major. And that's strange for the same composer with the same song to be major in one version and minor in the other."

Riley had another thought.

"As far as that goes," he said, "on the recording that Gondos did of his tune, he didn't include the third variation at all. I don't understand why I see a major variation in the sheet music which he never played for me and didn't put on his record. Doesn't make sense."

"What did you say to Mr. Gondos after he played for you?" Sexton asked.

"I told him I didn't think he had a case."

"Did you say why?"

"With both melodies, Hagood's and Gondos's," Riley answered, "the whole idea is so generic that they're not original compositions."

Riley's declaration made three out of three defence experts unanimous on the point.

"I said to Gondos, comparing his tune to Hagood's," Riley went on, "neither one's an original tune. The melody's been done before."

"Do you believe Mr. Gondos wrote variation three of his composition?" Sexton asked, switching Riley back to the credibility issue.

"I can't say who wrote it," Riley said. "But from studying

Gondos's work, I can say he's a composer who probably *didn't* write it."

"What about the first variation?"

"I don't believe Gondos wrote that one either."

"From your examination," Sexton asked, "have you any reason to believe Mr. Hardy or Rudy Toth copied from Mr. Gondos?"

"I don't understand why they would," Riley said, his hands resting on the piano keyboard. "As a matter of fact, Gondos had more chance to copy from Hardy and Toth than Hardy and Toth had to copy from Gondos."

When Brian Wheatley cross-examined the defence's three expert witnesses, he went at them with questions that came from a variety of slants. He tried to get them to concede that, even if Gondos's work struck them as unorthodox, unsophisticated if they liked, the unorthodoxies could be chalked up to a composer's artistic licence. None of the experts would bite on that premise. Wheatley, loading up with clever and informed hypotheses, made an attempt to have the three witnesses agree that if Hardy had happened to hear "Variations", just maybe he might have been influenced in his writing of "The Homecoming". No, the experts answered, Hardy wouldn't need such a source. Wheatley tried Ciamaga, Dale, and Riley on several suppositions and scenarios and possibilities. But the three refused to budge — except on one point that Wheatley regarded as seminal.

"Is there any doubt in your mind," he asked Jimmy Dale, "that the third variation of the Gondos piece is exactly identical to 'The Homecoming' except for one note?"

"Yes," Dale answered. "They're the same in that way."

"The melody's the same?"

"Yes."

"And 'Moment of Love' is almost the same in melody as

Gondos's first variation?"

"Except for some notes," Dale admitted, "the two melodies are the same."

Wheatley smiled at the answers.

"It was basic," he said many years later. "When somebody goes to copyright a song, what is it they copyright? It's only one thing — the melody. The chords aren't subject to copyright. If they were, Vivaldi would roll over in his grave because his progression of chords is the same in dozens of his works, but the melodies aren't. So, if I had the defence's experts say that the melodies were the same in their songs and in ours, in the Hardy and the Toth and in the Gondos, well, then I was halfway home to winning the case."

By Friday morning, April 30, the defence had called all of its witnesses except one. Mr. Justice Carruthers put over the trial until the following Wednesday, when the final witness would be heard from. He was Hagood Hardy.

If the trial had gone according to Ed Sexton's plan, he would have called Hardy as his first or as a very early witness. But Hardy's health scuppered the plan, and he ended up in last place on the witness list.

Hardy began the trial sitting at a table in the courtroom with Sexton, Chris Morgan, and Linda Nascher. There were things about those first few days that ticked him off. The very fact that there was a trial at all made Hardy angry, but smaller events ate at him too.

For example, John Arena's behaviour.

"Hagood, good morning," Arena said, all heartiness and bonhomie when he ran into Hardy outside the courtroom before Arena's testimony. "How nice to see you."

"I couldn't believe the man," Hardy says today. "He gives

me a big hello and then goes in front of the judge and testifies against me."

Other events gave Hardy mild reason for cheer.

For example, Doug Carruthers' ear for music.

On the second day of the trial, Sexton asked a witness to listen to a recording of "The Homecoming" that Hardy put on the B side of the single he issued on his own Isis label, the single that came out before Attic Records took over and made the song into a hit. The version on the B side had a jazz feel with bossa nova rhythm and a flugelhorn solo played by a well-known jazz musician named Guido Basso. The record was on a 45-rpm disc, but in the courtroom the record-player was set at 33 rpm, and for a few seconds, thick soupy music poured out of the machine.

"If somebody doesn't fix that thing," Carruthers said, "the flugelhorn on there is going to sound like a tuba."

"I was amazed," Hardy says. "To have a judge who knew the difference between a flugelhorn and a tuba, who even knew what a flugelhorn was, it gave me hope that we'd get a just decision."

But more than hope or anger, it was plain and simple pain that Hardy felt in the early days, the ache in his head that made him look for relief at noon by lying on Ed Sexton's office floor. By Wednesday, the third day into the trial, the agony was unbearable, and by Thursday, Martha Hardy took her husband to St. Michael's Hospital.

The cause of the horrific pain, the doctors said, was a blood clot. It was on the right side of Hardy's head, towards the front, a clot of blood caught in the layer of muscle between the skull and the brain. The bump against the golf cart months earlier in Florida had been responsible for the clot, and now it had to be removed.

There was a choice of treatments. Drill two holes into the side of Hardy's head and suck the clot out. Or feed him steroids and hope they'd shrink the clot. The first took longer and was more certain. The second was quicker but might not work. Hardy chose steroids.

"If the doctors drilled the hole," Hardy says, "I wouldn't have been able to testify at the trial for maybe six months. I'd been waiting almost two years for my day in court. I couldn't stand another delay."

While Hardy lay in his hospital bed soaking up steroids, Ed Sexton worried in the courtroom.

"I knew Hagood would make a terrific witness," Sexton says. "He exudes integrity, and I needed him on the stand so that Carruthers could see for himself the kind of man Hagood really is, that he isn't the sort of person who'd steal anything."

Sexton got bulletins from Hardy's doctors twice a day, and at first he wasn't encouraged.

"I considered asking the judge to adjourn the case to Hagood's hospital room," Sexton says. "Carruthers was used to that sort of thing by then. He'd already had one person die in the case."

But the steroids did the trick. They shrank the blood clot, and Hardy left St. Michael's twelve days after he went in, not exactly perky but free of the headaches and set to testify.

If Hardy had any say in the matter, he knew the story he wanted to tell on the witness stand. He'd been thinking about Ivan Gondos's claim for a couple of years, and he'd figured out the things in Gondos's head, the ticks, that led to the absurd lawsuit.

"You start with the fact that Gondos was a cocktail pianist all his life," Hardy explained one afternoon years after the trial. "By nature, a cocktail painist's job is to pick up snippets of melody from all over the place and play them repeatedly night after night. Well, Gondos did that, and he got 'The Homecoming' or maybe the Salada Tea commercial and he got 'Moment of Love' and he pushed them into something he called a suite. Remember that Gondos's only recorded version of 'Variations' came after 'The Homecoming' and 'Moment of Love' were written and available. So the timing works out right for him to have stolen Rudy's music and mine. Never mind that 1962 sheet music of Gondos's which was fraudulent and not from 1962 at all. Anyway, Gondos kept playing this so-called suite and eventually he made himself believe that he actually wrote everything in it. His mind got just warped enough to imagine he composed it all."

What about the witnesses, including John Arena, who said they heard Gondos play "Variations on a Theme in A Minor" in the 1960s?

"People's ears fool them," Hardy said.

He was sitting in the living-room of his North Toronto home and moved to the piano.

"Listen to this," he said.

He played one melody, then a second, and a third. The three seemed almost alike. Hardy identified them. The first was "Someone to Watch over Me", the 1926 George Gershwin song, and the other two were much later tunes, "Crying in the Chapel" and "PS I Love You".

"There are areas of song that are similar, and people confuse them," Hardy said. "That's what I think happened here. Maybe Gondos started with some sort of romantic melody, but it wasn't 'The Homecoming' and it wasn't 'Moment of Love'. Those two he incorporated into his alleged suite and passed them off as his own. It got so he *thought* he wrote the whole thing and he went to court to prove something that wasn't true."

This is the story that Hardy would have told in court if he had had any say in the matter, but he didn't have much say. Ed Sexton wanted Hardy to show Mr. Justice Carruthers the kind of person he was. That was the prime reason for putting Hardy on the witness stand. And besides, the rules of evidence don't permit a witness in Hardy's position — a party to the action, not an expert — to testify about ideas and theories. The rules of evidence allow for facts, and Hardy had to keep his speculations, thoughtful and informed as they may have been, to himself.

On the morning of Wednesday, May 5, Ed Sexton summoned Hardy as the defence's final witness. Guided by Sexton's questions, Hardy talked for almost four hours about his training, his career, his music, the circumstances of his composition of "The Homecoming". As to specifics, Hardy denied that he was at Stop 33 on the night of September 25, 1970, that he'd ever met Ivan Gondos, that he'd heard "Variations on a Theme in A Minor" in any form on any occasion, that anything had influenced him in writing "The Homecoming".

"The thrill of being in music," Hardy said on the stand, "is to compose original music, not to copy someone else's."

Sexton monitored Carruthers' reaction to the testimony. He thought it was positive. Hardy was everything that Sexton wanted in his client — candid, straight-ahead, more than a little upset.

"I think I came across as a person who was indignant," Hardy says. "I *was* indignant."

And for one brief moment Hardy managed to squeeze in a line or two from his own theory. It happened when Brian Wheatley was cross-examining him and asked a question about the nature of Gondos's composition.

"Well, Mr. Wheatley," Hardy said, more than a trace of irony in his voice, "I think Mr. Gondos kept working on his song and adding to his song until he may have got it right."

Hardy gave his testimony just in time. Another couple of days later and he would have made a different, more loony impression on Carruthers. It was the steroids' fault. Hardy had a wild and crazy reaction to them.

"I went a little nuts," he says.

"Nuts?" Martha Hardy says. "He went through such a personality change he was impossible."

The steroids put Hardy on a three-week high. He slept only two hours a night. He talked in non-stop monologues. He embarked on a spending spree — a complete new wardrobe, a car, ghetto-blasters. He organized an all-star jazz band and booked it into the Imperial Room of the Royal York Hotel, a venture that was a financial disaster. And he wrote dozens of letters to politicians offering solutions to the problems of the day.

"My big disappointment," Hardy says, "is that not one of those politicians wrote me back."

Eventually the steroids ran through Hardy's system, and he thumped down to earth. But while he was on the high, he was ferocious.

"If I'd testified when I was in my manic phase," he says, "I would have told Brian Wheatley what I thought of him and his client, which is not really speakable or printable."

When Hardy finished his testimony on the afternoon of May 5, Wheatley flabbergasted the defence lawyers by calling two witnesses in reply to their case.

"The guy just wouldn't quit," Ken Cancellara says. "Sometimes at a trial, when a lawyer sees the case going against him, he'll plug the record with as much information as possible in the hope it'll help if he appeals the decision. But that wasn't what Brian was doing. The case we were on was mostly about credibility. Was Gondos a person to be believed? The way I read the trial, the answer was no. And I didn't think all the patching in the world was going to change that situation. But Brian was determined to fight the credibility thing even though his client was dead. It was ridiculous."

Wheatley's two reply witnesses were directed to one issue

— the Roy Robson copy of Gondos's 1962 sheet music. According to the testimony of Gondos and Robson, the copy was a Xerox that Gondos gave to Robson in 1965 or '66, a fact that helped to establish the early origins of "Variations on a Theme in A Minor". The defence witnesses whom Chris Morgan rounded up, Peter Schopfer and Ernie Sniedgzins, said that from their knowledge of the world of Xerox, the Robson copy couldn't have been made before 1974, and their expertise seemed to have carried the day. Now Wheatley was striking back with two experts of his own.

The first witness, a young man named Sanderson who worked in the copy business, took the stand, and Wheatley showed him a Xerox of the Gondos sheet music. It was over-sized and had music on both sides of the paper. It looked just like the Robson copy.

"What is this I'm showing you?" Wheatley asked Sanderson.

"It's a copy I made yesterday," Sanderson said. "I did it on an old Xerox machine over at Bell Canada."

Sitting at the defence table, Chris Morgan almost lost his cool and his lunch.

"I felt like death," he remembers.

"How did you make this copy?" Wheatley asked Sanderson.

"I fed it through the old machine on one side," Sanderson answered. "And then I fed it back on the reverse side. That's how it came out double-sided."

"Thank you," Wheatley said.

He called a second witness, a man named Robert Mobbs who worked at the Xerox Corporation.

"Would you identify the machine that made this copy?" Wheatley asked, showing Mobbs the copy that Sanderson had introduced into evidence.

"That came from one of our Xerox machines that were available throughout the 1960s," Mobbs answered.

"I was dying," Chris Morgan remembers. "The paper was

my baby. Ed brought me in to handle the engineering stuff, and it looked like I was blowing it. Maybe the Robson copy *did* date from 1965."

It was Sexton's turn to cross-examine Robert Mobbs. He stopped at the defence table, standing over Morgan. Sexton had both copies in front of him, the Robson copy and the document that Sanderson had put through the Xerox machine at Bell Canada.

"What do I ask?" he said to Morgan.

Morgan thought as fast as he could.

He said to Sexton, "Ask him why anyone would go to all the trouble of running paper through a machine on one side and doing it again on the other side."

Morgan was stalling for time.

While Sexton questioned Mobbs, Morgan sat at the table studying the two copies, the Robson and the Sanderson. He was fighting a battle with the panic he felt inside. He fought — and he won.

"Oh, my god," he thought. *"Track marks!"*

There were track marks on the copy that Sanderson had made the day before.

But there were no track marks on the Robson copy.

That meant, according to what Morgan remembered Ernie Sniedgzins telling him in the offices at Xerox, that the Sanderson copy really was made on a 1960s machine, a machine that operated in the days when the seals let ink dust leak on to the rollers and left rows of black dots along the bottom of the copy paper.

Morgan remembered all of Sniedgzins's lecture. Track marks. Right. And they were on the copy in front of him, the Sanderson copy with its rows of little black dots.

But the Robson copy had *no* rows of little black dots. *No* track marks. And as Sniedgzins had said, absence of track marks meant that the Robson copy came from the 3103 Xerox machine that didn't arrive in Canada until 1974.

It was so *simple*.

Wheatley's witnesses, Sanderson and Mobbs, were perfectly correct in their testimony. But the testimony didn't change the status of the Robson copy. It was still a 1974 document.

Sexton returned to the defence table.

"Now what?" he asked Chris Morgan.

Morgan hurried into an explanation of track marks and the significance of their absence from the Robson copy.

Sexton turned back to Robert Mobbs and showed him the Robson document.

"Could this copy have been made in 1965 or '66?" he asked.

Mobbs answered without a pause.

"No," he said.

"Why not?" Sexton asked.

And Mobbs talked for the next few minutes about track marks and their cause, the differences between Xerox machines of the sixties and those of the seventies, the look of the Robson copy that dated it some time in the mid-1970s.

"Dodged the bullet." Chris Morgan says today.

The trial ended that afternoon, Wednesday, May 5, and Mr. Justice Carruthers retreated to his chambers to begin thinking about his judgment. Over the following weeks, he had other cases to hear, some in the Toronto Courthouse, some in county towns around Ontario. He worked on *Gondos v. Hardy and Toth* in the evenings and on weekends. The judicial year shut down on June 30, and he had more time for the judgment, but the case seemed to have even more tricks and complexities to it than he remembered. He studied the case law on musical plagiarism, digesting the wisdom and flinty remarks of United States Justice Learned Hand, and he read through the thick notebooks he'd filled with his own accounts of witnesses' testimony and lawyers' arguments.

He started to write his judgment in longhand in early July. The writing went swiftly, and when he was done, he delivered the longhand pages to his secretary. She typed it out to forty-five pages of finished copy, and on Friday, July 16, the judgment was released to Sexton, Cancellara, and Wheatley.

Carruthers began in the usual manner of judges writing judgments by stating the facts. Except that in this case, there were two distinct sets of facts, the plaintiff's and the defendants', and they matched in very few particulars. Carruthers put both versions on paper and proceeded to assess their degrees of truth and falsehood.

When it came to credibility, Carruthers made it immediately clear that the issue was no contest. If there was a clash between the plaintiff's side and the defendants' side over memory of key events, and some not-so-key, Carruthers accepted the defence story hands down.

For example, the Roy Robson Xerox: was it made in the mid-1960s, as Gondos and Robson insisted, or did it date from much later, as the copy experts contended?

Carruthers had no trouble resolving the question in one succinct sentence, a sentence that justified all of Chris Morgan's sleuthing and compensated for his sweaty moment in the courtroom.

"The evidence of a witness called on behalf of the plaintiff, Robert Mobbs," Carruthers wrote, "along with that of the two witnesses called on behalf of the defendants, Peter Schopfer and Ernie Sniedgzins, requires me to doubt that Roy Robson received a Xerox copy in 1966 as he claims."

What of Marcel Febbo's statement that he *saw* Gondos write out the 1962 sheet music?

Carruthers dismissed that testimony almost as brusquely.

"I cannot accept the evidence of the witness Febbo that he saw the [1962 sheet music] being produced by the plaintiff," Carruthers wrote. "The event described, if it occurred, was twenty years ago; and Febbo gives no explanation as to how

117

he is able to relate what he was shown at trial, the 1962 sheet music, with what he saw copied, apart from the date shown on the manuscript, '10/11/62'."

How about Sharon Pagliuso's testimony that she, too, received a Xerox of the 1962 sheet music?

Maybe she did, Carruthers wrote, but "I am not prepared to find that [her copy] was what is shown on the 1962 sheet music as she claimed at trial."

Well, then, were Robson, Febbo, and Pagliuso lying on the witness stand to help their old friend and teacher, Ivan Gondos?

Not quite.

Carruthers wrote, "I think it is appropriate for me to say here that in concluding as I have about the evidence of Robson, Febbo, and Pagliuso, I do not suggest that any of them have consciously departed from the truth as they look upon it. Nor do I reject all of their testimony. I think they have been caught up with the cause of the plaintiff to such an extent that they are not able to be objective in their approach to the recollection of events, some of which occurred many years ago."

What of John Arena and the other witnesses who swore they heard Gondos play "Variations on a Theme in A Minor" in the 1960s and early 1970s? Did Carruthers class them with the trio who allowed themselves to be "caught up" in the Gondos crusade? Or was there something solid in what they, as well as Robson, Febbo, and Pagliuso, said they heard Gondos play on various pianos and in different homes and clubs around Toronto?

"I am prepared to accept," Carruthers wrote, "that all of these witnesses, with one going as far back as 1962, heard the plaintiff play, on a variety of occasions and times, a melody similar to that heard on the playing of the record, *Ivan Plays Favorites*."

The finding represented at least a partial victory for the Gondos side. The recording, it was true, contained only part of what Gondos put forward as the complete and final version of "Variations on a Theme in A Minor". More significantly, the recording lacked the third variation. It was mainly the third that Gondos accused Hardy of copying for "The Homecoming", and it was the third that the plaintiff's expert, Dr. Paul McIntyre, found to have twenty-five notes out of twenty-six in common with "The Homecoming". Those facts tended to weaken Carruthers' finding. Still, he was saying that Arena and the other witnesses had heard a piece of Gondos's music which had a main theme that resembled "The Homecoming" and a variation that sounded like "Moment of Love". Chalk up one for the plaintiff.

In all other matters of credibility, Gondos didn't get the tiniest nod from Carruthers. His lordship believed very little of Gondos's testimony, certainly not the parts that clashed with evidence from Hardy, the Toths, and their witnesses.

Did Hardy meet Gondos and listen to Gondos's music at Stop 33 on the night of September 25, 1970?

Carruthers reviewed Gondos's story and compared it to the evidence that Ed Sexton called about the alleged incident, and didn't hesitate in making up his mind.

"The plaintiff's evidence on this point is highly improbable," Carruthers wrote, "and I specifically reject it."

Carruthers went even further.

"I accept the evidence of the defendant Hardy in any event," he wrote, "wherever it conflicts with that of the plaintiff."

By the time Carruthers finished with Gondos's stories, they were in tatters. He rejected Gondos's explanations for his failure to register "Variations" with BMI. And he didn't believe Gondos's testimony that he first heard the Salada Tea commercial in August 1974; clearly, Carruthers wrote, after the evidence of Peter Lighthall of the Leo Burnett ad agency that the "Church" commercial stopped running in July 1974, and after the evidence of Alan Lowry, a plaintiff's witness, that Gondos talked about the commercial in 1973,

Gondos must have been aware of Hardy's Salada Tea music much earlier than 1974.

Carruthers found that Gondos had also been less than truthful about his education and about his use of "Variations" as a "theme song". And as for the Gondos tale about his midnight trip to Rudy Toth's cottage with Chris Toth and the record album *Ivan Plays Favorites*, Carruthers said it was rubbish.

"I accept all of the evidence of the defendants Toth," Carruthers wrote, "and in particular wherever it conflicts with any of that given by or on behalf of the plaintiff."

Then Carruthers summed up his overall impression of Gondos's credibility and tried to account for the reasons that it registered so low on his lordship's scale.

"To my mind," Carruthers wrote, "the overall effect of the plaintiff's evidence at trial is that it leaves a great deal to be desired. I find that the plaintiff was inclined to say things which he thought would promote his best interest without regard to actuality, factuality or, on some occasions, the truth. There were many involved in giving evidence on his behalf, and some I have indicated who were caught up in the promotion of the plaintiff's case to such an extent that they lost much of any objectivity they might otherwise have about the matters at issue. The plaintiff himself was in my opinion the worst offender. In making my findings of credibility with respect to the plaintiff, I am conscious of his condition, both mental and physical, at the time of giving his evidence. His condition may have had some adverse effect on his ability to recall accurately at times, but did not, in my opinion, cause him to go to the length he did in an effort to promote his position."

With the matter of credibility disposed of, almost entirely in favour of the defendants, Carruthers went on to make a crucial finding that worked mightily to Ivan Gondos's benefit. The finding had to do with the infamous third variation as it appeared in the 1962 sheet music of "Variations on a Theme in A Minor".

The evidence that Ed Sexton adduced had thrown variation three into plenty of uncertainty. When did Gondos write it? Indeed, *had* Gondos written it? Gondos said he began work on the whole composition including variation three as early as 1956. But Sexton's cross-examination of Gondos and testimony from Sexton's witnesses suggested strongly that Gondos might have tacked variation three on to his piece of music *after* he heard "The Homecoming". In short, the possibility was that someone else, namely Hagood Hardy, wrote the third variation and Gondos stole it. What made this possibility especially important was that Gondos indicated to Sexton on cross-examination that the third variation contained the sixteen bars that Hardy had copied for "The Homecoming".

"I'm showing you the 1962 sheet music for 'Variations'," Sexton said to Gondos in the room at the Westin Hotel in June 1981. "And I also have here a green pen, a pen with green ink."

And with Sexton, Carruthers, and all the others in the room watching, Gondos marked in green lines on the sheet music the bars that he said Hardy copied for the Salada Tea commercial and for "The Homecoming". The bars he marked were the last sixteen of "Variations", all of variation number three.

But Carruthers held that none of the fuss over the third variation mattered a whit, not Gondos's testimony in the hotel room, not his specific marking with the green ink of the sixteen bars on the sheet music.

Carruthers wrote, "While I am prepared to accept the position of the defendants that I should doubt that variation three was written at the same time as the balance of what is shown in the sheet music dated 1962, I do not find it necessary, for the purpose of determining the issues raised in this

121

action, to express any opinion as to whether someone other than the plaintiff was its composer."

Why did Carruthers say that?

"I say this," he went on, "mindful of the fact that insofar as the Hardy music is concerned, the plaintiff ultimately isolated his complaint to the sixteen bars of variation three. I am not at all certain that he intended this restriction to be placed on his case by making the statement in cross-examination."

Gondos didn't *mean* to mark off the third variation with green ink in answer to Sexton's question? How could that be? Was there some quirk in Gondos's demeanour which Carruthers read as indicating that Gondos didn't intend to say Hardy copied only and exclusively from those last sixteen bars of "Variations"?

"From my point of view," Carruthers wrote, "it is not difficult to look upon [Gondos's] statement as another example of the plaintiff saying something for the express purpose of advancing his case without realizing what it is that he, in fact, has said having regard to the totality of the evidence."

Ah, it was poor Gondos's own eagerness that betrayed him. He'd misspoken. He'd shot himself in the foot. He'd inadvertently painted himself into a corner. And now Carruthers was going to rescue him.

"Notwithstanding [Gondos's] statement," Carruthers wrote, "I think it is only fair to look upon the plaintiff's case as being a complaint that the melody of 'The Homecoming' and that of 'Moment of Love' were copied from his work 'Variations', whether it be stated in the 1962 sheet music or otherwise."

Carruthers was giving Gondos a giant break. In deciding the case, Carruthers was saying, he would look to the melody of the principal theme of "Variations" and not to variation three, which, though it was identical to "The Homecoming" with the exception of one note out of twenty-six, was of extremely doubtful provenance.

"For the purpose of this judgment," Carruthers wrote, "I am even prepared to say that the principal melody of 'Variations' and that of 'The Homecoming' are strikingly similar to my ear."

And what of "Moment of Love" and the first variation of "Variations"?

Well, Carruthers wrote, "the similarity between variation one and 'Moment of Love', again to my ear, is less." Still, he went on, the two pieces were close enough to get ahead with the business of deciding the merit of the plaintiff's claim against the Toths.

Thus, in Carruthers' opinion, Gondos may possibly have been a liar and a thief and an all-round cad, but he *had* written a work of music — one which, according to Carruthers' earlier finding, John Arena and other witnesses heard in the 1960s — that sounded strikingly like "The Homecoming" in one part and quite a bit like "Moment of Love" in another.

In what way had such a bizarre situation come to be possible?

To answer the question, Carruthers waded into the territory of the expert witnesses. He treated their testimony rather like a smorgasbord. He went down the line of goodies they offered, and took a taste of this, a bite of that, a sampling here, a *soupçon* there. And he rejected some dishes altogether.

First, Dr. Gustav Ciamaga, Dean of the University of Toronto's Faculty of Music and the defence's chief expert.

Carruthers was taken with Ciamaga's seminar on the state and evolution of the pop song.

He particularly liked Ciamaga's statistics.

"In the light of the fact that the first fifty years of the twentieth century have produced approximately half a million popular songs with copyright," Carruthers wrote, "Dr. Ciamaga finds it hard to believe, as a composer, that all of them were original."

123

And Carruthers latched on to more of the seminar.

"In Dr. Ciamaga's opinion," he wrote, "the popular song tradition is an aspect of tonal tradition which, very early, set out its own rules and delimited the amount of material available to a composer and the number of harmonic progressions."

All of which, as Carruthers interpreted Ciamaga, led inevitably to "the use of clichés and commonplaces in modern western music". And not just in any old anonymous western music but, right on point, in "Variations" and in "The Homecoming". "Dr. Ciamaga," Carruthers wrote, "found clichés and commonplaces to exist in the works under consideration."

Moving briskly on to Ciamaga's next proposition, Carruthers wrote, "That there are similarities in modern music does not, in Dr. Ciamaga's opinion, suggest influence of one work on others."

Finally, Carruthers said, put them all together — Dr. Ciamaga's lessons on cliché, on musical similarities, on the non-applicability of influence — and what is the conclusion? "Dr. Ciamaga," Carruthers wrote, "believes that two people could have written 'Variations' and 'The Homecoming' without one influencing the other."

When Carruthers considered the testimony of the other two defence experts, Jimmy Dale and Doug Riley, he passed up their learned demonstrations of Ivan Gondos's musical perfidy. Or it could have been that, without mentioning Dale and Riley, Carruthers took their critiques into account in assessing Gondos's credibility. In any event, the only use that Carruthers made of the Dale-Riley appearances in court occurred in one sentence in his judgment when he enlisted the two men to back up one of the Ciamaga points that Carruthers regarded as central to the case.

"I was impressed by Dr. Ciamaga's testimony regarding musical clichés and commonplaces," Carruthers wrote once again, "and by the support of his position given by two obviously talented and knowledgeable musicians, Dale and Riley."

Even when Carruthers focussed on the plaintiff's expert witness, Dr. Paul McIntyre of the University of Windsor's Music School, he co-opted McIntyre, unfortunate chap, to uphold the Ciamaga propositions. Carruthers doffed his hat to McIntrye's exquisite note-by-note comparisons of "The Homecoming" and "Moment of Love" with different sections of "Variations on a Theme in A Minor". And he agreed that McIntyre established breath-taking similarities among the melodies of the three pieces of music. But he drew far short of reaching the end point that McIntyre and Brian Wheatley were looking for.

To them, similarity equalled copying. The fact that Hardy and Rudy Toth wrote later melodies exactly like Gondos's earlier melodies meant, *ipso facto*, no question, that they copied from Gondos.

Carruthers turned away from that road.

"I accept that similarity does exist between the works," he wrote, "but I do not agree that this means the one has to have influenced the others."

Carruthers was sticking to the Ciamaga line that none of the composers — Gondos, Hardy, Rudy Toth — need have had an impact on their fellow song-writers. In fact, Carruthers further interpreted McIntyre's performance on cross-examination by Ed Sexton and Ken Cancellara as additional support for Ciamaga's view. No doubt to McIntyre's chagrin, Carruthers decided that the good doctor's reaction to the songs from the Dale-Riley tape confirmed the principle that lots of songs, which were written independently of one another by composers who lived in different places at different times, may sound almost identical.

Carruthers checked off the songs on the tape and McIntyre's responses. McIntyre, Carruthers wrote, found the 1969 Belgian song "Je ne songeais pas à Rose" "strikingly similar to the melodies of the plaintiff and Hardy". The same went

125

for the 1967 American pop tune "What Was Good Enough for Me". Carruthers continued down the tape, and when he reached the excerpt from Vivaldi's *Four Seasons*, he did something rather surprising — he substituted his ears for McIntyre's.

Dr. McIntyre had said the Vivaldi was "not even similar" to the Hardy and Gondos pieces. The most he granted was that if someone heard the Vivaldi, he might go on to write a composition like "Variations on a Theme in A Minor".

Carruthers disagreed with McIntyre.

"To my ear," Carruthers wrote, "the passage from Vivaldi alone would be sufficient to support the opinions of the witnesses Ciamaga, Dale and Riley. I found it to be very similar to the melodies of the works of the plaintiff and Hardy."

Carruthers covered most of the songs on the Dale-Riley tape, finding the first six to be similar, often "strikingly similar", to the main theme of "Variations" and to "The Homecoming", and the last five to be not quite so similar to variation one of "Variations" and to "Moment of Love".

Then he put his finger on what he thought to be the great significance of the tape and its sound-alike songs.

"The playing of those passages that are similar," he wrote, "is relevant to support the issue of coincidence."

With all the hints that Carruthers was dropping — his championing of the Ciamaga line, his slotting of McIntyre's testimony, his overruling of McIntyre on the Vivaldi piece — it seemed perfectly clear where he was headed: he was going to find that Hardy and Rudy Toth had arrived at their melodies and Gondos at his two melodies by separate, independent, and coincidental routes. But first Carruthers had to take care of the law on musical plagiarism.

He devoted several pages of his judgment to a review of some of the English and American cases and to the principles of plagiarism that they laid out. He touched on the issues of musical similarity and of causal connection, the need for the song-writer who is the alleged copycat to have access to the song composed by the complaining song-writer. He quoted from the judgments of a few leading cases — the George Harrison case, for one — and he reviewed the neat and telling distinction from the American cases between conscious and unconscious copying.

That done, Carruthers was ready to apply the law as he saw it to the case in front of him, *Gondos v. Hardy and Toth*.

First, similarity.

In order for Gondos to succeed, he had to show that the songs he was complaining about were "strikingly similar" or "substantially similar" to his song. That part was easy. To Carruthers' ear, to everyone's ear, the necessary degree of similarity was flat-out obvious. So much for the first hurdle.

Next, access.

With respect to the Toths, Brian Wheatley alleged that there had been conscious copying. It arose out of Gondos's story of Chris Toth's purchase of *Ivan Plays Favorites* and his delivery of the record to his father on the occasion of Gondos's midnight visit to the Toth cottage. That, according to the argument, was how and when Rudy Toth had access to "Variations on a Theme in A Minor". But, since "Moment of Love" was composed five years before those summer events and since Carruthers held that, anyway, the events never took place, he got rid of the allegation of conscious copying in a hurry. There had been, Carruthers held, no conscious copying by the Toths.

With respect to both Hardy and the Toths, Wheatley argued that there had been unconscious copying. He pitched his argument on two levels. One, the Hardy and Toth songs were so incredibly similar to passages from "Variations on a Theme in A Minor", almost note for note, that Carruthers had no alternative but to infer that unconscious copying had taken place. And, according to Wheatley's second argument, Carruthers should make the same inferential leap from the constant presence of all three song-writers, Gondos, Hardy, and Rudy Toth, on the Toronto scene at the same time. As Wheatley put it, Hardy and Rudy Toth *must* have come across Gondos's song and unconsciously squirrelled away its melodies until they emerged as "The Homecoming" and "Moment of Love".

Carruthers needed only a single paragraph of his judgment to dispose of Brian Wheatley's unconscious-copying arguments.

On the point that the very similarity of the songs begged for the conclusion that copying had occurred, Carruthers said simply that, the way he read it, that wasn't the law. There was nothing he could find in the English and American cases, Carruthers said, establishing such a far-out principle.

And on the second point, that just because Hardy and Rudy Toth worked around Toronto during the same period as Gondos, it should be inferred they heard and borrowed Gondos's music, Carruthers was equally quick to brush off Wheatley.

"This," he wrote, referring to Wheatley's request to make the inference of unconscious copying, "I will not do in this case."

Well, what *would* Carruthers do?

What he did was double back to the conclusion he arrived at as a result of his analysis of the expert witnesses' testimony. He picked up on the Ciamaga line of reasoning and adopted it as his own. He came down on the side of the simplest, funniest, most ironic explanation of all.

Coincidence.

"Having rejected that the defendant Hardy and the defendant Rudy Toth copied any part of the work of the plaintiff," Carruthers wrote in conclusion, "the similarity which I have found to exist among the songs must, of necessity, be the result of coincidence."

All three compositions, Carruthers wrote, "had the

required degree of originality necessary to give rise to a claim for copyright."

The three songs — here was Carruthers' point — were *equally* original. Gondos wrote "Variations on a Theme in A Minor". Hardy wrote "The Homecoming". Rudy Toth wrote "Moment of Love". And if the second two sounded like parts of the first, it wasn't the result of copying and plagiarism. It happened because song-writers in the same city fooled around with the same musical clichés and ended up with melodies that were accidentally, strangely, almost magically identical.

The whole mess, Carruthers held, was the result of . . . coincidence.

Carruthers' finding meant that Gondos lost the case. Gondos claimed that Hardy and the Toths copied from his music. Carruthers said there was no copying. Hence, Gondos was the loser.

Carruthers dismissed both of the Gondos actions, the first against Hardy and the second against the Toths, with costs. That meant the Gondos estate was obliged to pay most of the legal expenses incurred by Hardy and the Toths in defending against the lawsuit.

The Toths had brought a counter-claim against Gondos on the grounds that he copied from "Moment of Love" in writing the first variation of "Variations on a Theme in A Minor". But Ken Cancellara hadn't pressed the counter-claim. He used it more as a tactical ploy to keep pressure on Gondos, and Carruthers held there was no evidence that Gondos had access to Rudy Toth's music. He dismissed the counter-claim without costs. That meant the Toths were not obliged to pay any of the Gondos legal expenses in defending against the counter-claim.

Gondos v. Hardy and Toth had reached a finish.

Perhaps not so surprisingly, the side that was supposed to have come out on the short end of the trial — the Gondos side — found itself more content with the result than Hardy and the Toths, the people who were, on paper, the victors.

"Carole Anne Gondos didn't feel displeased by the judgment," Brian Wheatley says. "It said her husband wrote an original piece of music, which is what she and Ivan had been telling everyone all along."

But Wheatley had his own reservations.

"I thought I gave Mr. Justice Carruthers two plus two and I expected to get back a four," he says. "Instead, I got a 3.75. I showed him that the Toth and Hardy songs were substantially similar to 'Variations'. He accepted that. But he wouldn't go for my contention that the three musicians worked all around the same Toronto clubs in the same years, which gave Hardy and Toth access to Ivan's music, which, in turn, led to unconscious copying. I thought there was enough for Carruthers to make the jump. He wouldn't. But I can't say I was unhappy with the result."

Hagood Hardy and the Toth brothers were very unhappy. Part of the reason was financial. Carruthers ordered the plaintiff to pay the defendants' costs. But the estate that Ivan Gondos left at his death consisted of the grand piano he played in the lounge at Deerhurst Inn and not much else. When Hardy and the Toths pressed the Gondos estate for recompense, they came away with about four thousand dollars for Hardy and the same for the Toths. Those amounts made only a small dent in their total bills. Ed Sexton charged Hardy seventy-five thousand dollars for excellent services rendered, and Cancellara's account to the Toths was in the neighbourhood of fifty thousand. The defendants dug deep in their savings to pay the legal bills, and in the case of Rudy Toth, who assumed responsibility for most of the Toth family payment, he had to take out a mortgage on his house.

But Hardy's bitterness at the trial and its outcome went beyond money. He raged against the whole misguided process that put him through such a wrenching experience.

"Who received the least of amount of justice in the trial?" he asked. "I'd say it was me and the Toths, and we *won*!"

Hardy is saddened by one particular that, he feels, arises by implication out of Doug Carruthers' judgment. The way Hardy interprets part of the decision, it says that he may somehow have soaked up the melody for "The Homecoming" from an earlier musical source.

"To tell the truth, I've never been able to read the judgment all the way through," Hardy says. "I'm grateful to Judge Carruthers for finding in our favour, but I keep getting the feeling that the judgment says I borrowed from some place else. That really bothers me. It cheapens the original thought I had in composing 'The Homecoming'. As a matter of fact, I sometimes wish I never had the idea for the damned song."

Ed Sexton doesn't think his client should look back on the case with quite such doubt and sadness.

"Not many people in their lifetime have the opportunity to be adjudged in a public forum to be an honest person," Sexton says. "But that's what happened to Hagood. He was accused of stealing someone else's song, Ivan Gondos's song, and Doug Carruthers held that, no, he didn't steal anything and, yes, he's an honest man."

Hardy got back in gear.

"As long as the trial was hanging over me, I had trouble writing music," he says. "Even afterwards, after the trial, it took four months before I could write in a comfortable way."

It didn't help that many of the Canadian clients he composed music for — film-makers and television people — gave him a wide berth as if he were tainted goods.

"Nobody in Canada would touch me," Hardy says. "But down in California they heard about the lawsuit and they said, hey, no problem, come and write for us."

Hardy composed the music for a Movie-of-the-Week on

the CBS-TV network. Then he did a score for an NBC movie. The assignments flooded in. A total of ten network Movies-of-the-Week. The music for the Gerald Durrell nature series. And when the CBC got around to phoning, Hardy hit it big in both artistic and commercial terms when he wrote the music for one of the most acclaimed and popular programs in Canadian television history — *Anne of Green Gables*.

On the performing side, Hardy again took to the road.

"Over a period of four or five years, I've played in more than two hundred cities and towns in Canada," he says. "There are all these smaller centres with absolutely gorgeous seven-hundred-seat halls. Prince Rupert. Lethbridge. Corner Brook. I played them all and loved them all."

Most often Hardy performed with a trio, himself on piano, a drummer, and a bass player named Rick Homme who doubled on a synthesizer that filled the halls with enormous waves of sound. Sometimes Hardy took along strings and a few horns. And sometimes he appeared in Canada and the United States as a guest soloist playing the music from *Anne of Green Gables* with a full symphony orchestra.

"Music for me has never been so exciting and so busy," Hardy says. "And I can't see it doing anything except getting better."

In the years after the Gondos case, five more people made it known to Hardy that he'd stolen "The Homecoming" from them. Some had their lawyers contact Hardy. Others made noises about taking him to court. A musician in Belgium was among the claimants, and so were a couple of people who seemed to have impressive Hollywood music credentials. All eventually went away without beginning legal action.

"Some song-writers down in Nashville told me something that really got to me," Hardy says. "These were veterans in the business, and they said you don't really count as a song-

writer until at least seven people claim they wrote one of
your songs. I don't know why they said seven. But that's the
number. Seven."

Just before Christmastime of 1987, a Greek musician living in Austria hired a lawyer in Toronto who arranged for
Hardy to give a deposition in answer to a lawsuit brought in
the Austrian courts by the Greek gentleman. He said he
wrote and recorded a song in Greece in 1972 that Hagood
Hardy copied when he composed "The Homecoming".

The Greek was the seventh claimant.

LUKE'S CASE

Luke Elwood has never set foot, a small foot in his case, in a courtroom. If he did, he'd no doubt feel baffled, maybe terrified, though sometimes there's no telling about Luke's reactions to the world. He's just a kid, born at the Halifax Grace Maternity Hospital on October 29, 1977, which made him eight years old when all the legal excitement over his education started. But, apart from his very young age, something else might make Luke draw away in a courtroom. There are qualities about him that separate Luke from most other children. The differences are described in various ways depending on who's doing the describing. A man named Gary Hodson, a psychologist whose field is behaviour therapy for children, says Luke has "a language disorder with development delay". Lorne Verabioff, another man who figured prominently in Luke's life, the chairman of the Halifax County–Bedford District School Board, once told a meeting of his board that Luke was "a boy who can't interact with his environment". The current jargon of child psychology describes Luke as a "special" or an "exceptional" child. The old-fashioned language, much less enlightened, might call Luke "retarded". Either way, *any* way that Luke is categorized, he's different, and it's the difference that made him the centre of a struggle in the Nova Scotia courts that, in the end, may have done more for children like Luke than any other single act in recent Canadian social history.

The Elwood family wouldn't look out of place in a photograph on the front page of any newspaper's lifestyle section. Here's Rick the dad, medium-sized and muscular, his strong face set off by a moustache that's just modish enough. Maureen, the mom, suggests the beauty of a movie star from 1940s black-and-white, perhaps the young Greer Garson, delicate and brave and clear-eyed. Melissa is the older kid, lively and athletic, beginning to crowd toward adolescence and showing signs of growing into her mother's loveliness. Luke is straight and sturdy, nothing in the set of his face that hints at "language disorder" or "development delay", his dark hair cut close with a saucy little rat-tail poking down the back. The dog's name is Byron, a white Scottie who walks with an amiable slouch. Behind the family in the photograph, the house in Upper Lawrencetown, a bedroom suburb twelve miles down the road from Dartmouth, where Rick works as a fireman, is a compact bungalow on a big lot that backs on a hill of tall trees. On the deck that reaches around the side of the house, there's a set of chimes that the wind nudges into gentle rustles. The tranquil sound of the chimes might stand as a metaphor for the sort of family that the Elwoods are. In photographs and in life, they come across, Rick and Maureen, Melissa and Luke, as remarkably serene people.

And the way life has worked out for the Elwood family — fate, hard luck, the roll of the dice — they've had to show themselves to be something else besides serene.

They've had to be remarkably tough people.

The need for toughness set in when Luke was six months old. That's when a scary abscess grew on his shoulder. The family doctor told Rick and Maureen not to worry. But the doctor was mistaken. The abscess happened to be the first signal that all was not right with Luke. When he was ten months old, his eyes went funny. He didn't walk and talk at the age when other babies walked and talked. In fact, Luke didn't walk at all, and the noises that came from his mouth were guttural and incomprehensible and irritating. Hardly anything worked for Luke, not from the time the abscess showed up on his shoulder.

Life for Luke, for the whole Elwood family, revolved around trips to doctors. All kinds of doctors and medical experts. Pediatricians. Eye specialists. A neurologist, who was the first to diagnose Luke as "developmentally delayed". Luke was eighteen months then. Physiotherapists. Occupational therapists. A pediatric urologist. Speech therapists. And psychologists.

Gary Hodson was one of the psychologists. He met the Elwoods when Luke was almost three. Hodson developed a system for working with parents who had children like Luke. The system made use of videotape and other up-to-the-minute gizmos, but mostly it had to do with patience and repetition and understanding. It called for the Elwoods to work long and relentlessly to teach Luke the things that come naturally to other kids. Walking, for example. A week and a half after the Elwoods began applying the Hodson system, Luke took eight steps all by himself.

Under Hodson's guidance, Rick and Maureen helped Luke lick other problems. Wetting himself during the day was one. That called for the use of a bladder-control alarm, a little instrument that Luke wore in his underwear. It made a noise when Luke began to wet himself. The noise told Luke he'd better hustle to the bathroom. Luke caught on in a few days, and the wetting problem went away. Hodson recognized that Luke could understand events and concepts much better than he could express them. Hodson found that both puzzling and troubling.

Still, he and the Elwoods went hard at Luke's problems. There was the daily crisis of the bathtub, something that

137

invariably drew one of Luke's temper tantrums. Luke loved water. When Rick or Maureen gave him his nightly bath, he lolled in the tub, blissful, content, in seventh heaven. But when the bath ended and Rick or Maureen lifted him out of the tub and into a towel, he shook and screamed. How were the Elwoods supposed to handle Luke's bathroom grief? Hodson had an idea. Let the water out of the tub while Luke was still in it. The idea worked. Luke watched the water run out of his tub, and when it was gone, he stepped quietly into the towel his parents wrapped around him.

Simple?

Maybe, but not for Rick and Maureen. Not for Luke.

Before Luke was five, he had surgery on his eyes four times. He had his adenoids removed; the operation ended his recurring ear infections. He took speech therapy twice a week. He went into play-group classes. He participated in a program called Move and Grow, where a team of therapists taught him how to learn and practise movements that other kids would do as a routine part of growing up. Nothing was routine for Luke. Through all the treatments and operations and training, his favourite word was still "no", and he still liked to bang his head against a wall, and the temper tantrums still overwhelmed him. But he was pushing ahead, learning words, walking with confidence, getting attached to favourite toys, watching cartoons on television, playing with Melissa and his parents. And no matter what, under the "no's" and the temper tantrums he was a very sweet kid.

The work with Luke took a toll on Rick and Maureen's time. All the facilities — the doctors' offices, the clinics for speech therapy and other treatments, the Move and Grow program, Gary Hodson's office at the Izaak Walton Killam Hospital for Children — were in Halifax. The trips into the city and back meant drives that could eat up a couple of hours, especially on days when traffic stacked up on the bridge over the Narrows between Dartmouth and Halifax. Rick's schedule at the fire station added a complication. He worked shifts of forty-eight straight hours on duty, eating and sleeping at the station, followed by three or four days off. Maureen held a job at a federal government office in Halifax when she could fit it in. And, not to forget Melissa, she needed a natural share of space and attention from her parents. At the Elwood house, the alarm went off at 5 a.m. It took an early start to meet everyone's needs. Especially Luke's.

"I suppose there's never been anything ordinary or normal about the way we've lived since Luke was born," Maureen says. "On the other hand, to all of us, our life with Luke *is* ordinary and normal."

After Luke's fifth birthday, the age when kids start to public school, Elwood family life got even more mixed up. There were classes available for children with Luke's conditions. That wasn't a problem. Luke went to a school called Hillside Park for kindergarten and to Astral Drive Elementary School for Grades 1 and 2. But the classes that Luke was in weren't real kindergarten or real Grades 1 and 2. And, for Maureen and Rick, Maureen particularly, that *was* a problem.

For many years, ever since Luke's trouble became apparent, Maureen had been digging into the kinds of treatment and possibilities and education that were going to be available to her son. Maureen Elwood, beneath the placid front she shows the world, has true grit and plenty of ambition, a woman who likes to keep plans on the boil. Rick Elwood marvels at that side of his wife. "I'm the easy-going one," he says. "But Maureen, now, she has to be always on to something that'll make things better." With Luke, what she was on to from the start was his future.

When Luke was a baby, Maureen involved herself with the Nova Scotia branch of the Canadian Association for the Mentally Retarded (the organization changed its name in 1987 to the Canadian Association for Community Living). She met

Debby Smith, the Association's executive director for Nova Scotia. She met Bill Powroz, a paralegal and all-round trouble-shooter. And she met a remarkable woman named Margie Brown, a psychologist who lectured at Acadia University in Wolfville, Nova Scotia, on methods for teaching kids like Luke. Margie Brown's experience with exceptional children wasn't exclusively academic. She had five kids of her own, and two of them, both teenagers, one a foster son, had labels attached to them that Maureen understood all too well. Douglas Brown was called "moderately mentally retarded" and "autistic", while Derek Brown, who had Down's syndrome, was also tagged "moderately mentally retarded". Maureen talked to Margie Brown and the others, and she began to soak up ideas.

Almost from the beginning, Maureen recognized that Hillside Park School and Astral Drive Elementary seemed to be working against Luke's progress. The schools were "regular" schools for "normal" students, but Luke and other kids like him were for the most part grouped in classes by themselves. They had teachers with training in special education, and there were other experts on hand, speech pathologists and psychologists. But none of them, splendidly intentioned as they were, worked any wonders with Luke. Just the opposite. Luke was *regressing*.

"Luke has picked up some negative behaviours from the other children in the class," one of Luke's teachers at Hillside wrote on a report card. "He does not seem to be able to distinguish between appropriate and inappropriate behaviour."

It was the segregation that Maureen blamed. Luke took gym and music classes with normal kids, but, effectively, he was shut away in a ghetto of disabled children. And as far as Maureen could make out, he might pass the rest of his life in different corners of the same ghetto. He'd never escape. He'd never grow. If Luke was disabled, then the system seemed constructed to keep him disabled.

"Everybody means for the best at Astral," she said to Margie Brown one day in August 1986. "But what's happened is that Luke's being alienated from everybody around him."

"From the rest of the community," Margie said.

"It starts first thing in the morning," Maureen said. "Luke doesn't go to the school a couple of miles down the road from us, the school where all the other kids in the neighbourhood go. Oh no, he gets collected in a taxi and goes miles off in the other direction to Astral."

"The experience with my boys," Margie said, "is they needed the chance to interact with children their own age in natural ways."

"Just take Luke's speech," Maureen said. "The only way he's going to get into better speech habits is if he's around children who talk normally."

"Which isn't happening at Astral."

"Astral's just reinforcing bad habits in speech and behaviour and everything else," Maureen said. "He's got to be with kids that he can model himself on. Every day, I mean. Normal kids from around our neighbourhood."

"You know the answer as well as I do."

"Integration," Maureen said.

Integration — mixing handicapped kids in the same classes as their normal peers — had been taken up by several school boards across Canada. Over in Margie Brown's part of Nova Scotia, Coldbrook in Kings County, she'd lobbied to integrate her two sons in junior high, and they'd shown, she said, terrific academic and social gains. There were no Canadian laws that compelled integration, no court decisions, but lots of school districts were voluntarily going for it. Maureen Elwood's district — Halifax County–Bedford — wasn't one of them.

Margie Brown said to Maureen, "The argument you're going to hear is that, oh well, integration may be very nice, but Luke can't possibly keep up with the other children in reading and arithmetic and the other subjects."

141

"That isn't the point."

"You don't have to tell me."

"Luke'll progress at his own rate," Maureen said. "And that *is* the point. He'll *progress*."

"If you want to put Luke in your local school," Margie Brown said, "the Association'll be behind you all the way."

"Luke's the kind of disabled boy who's bound to get the best out of integration," Maureen said. "I know it."

"You may have a fight on your hands."

Margie Brown didn't realize that the Elwoods' fight would take them to the Nova Scotia Supreme Court.

Later that month, August 1986, something happened that shook Rick Elwood.

A group of children showed up with teachers and counsellors for a tour of Rick's fire station in Dartmouth. The kids were disabled. Rick recognized some of them, boys and girls who were Luke's age and older, from Hillside Park and Astral Drive. But these kids were wild. They were disoriented. Out of control. To Rick, they seemed hopeless.

He phoned Maureen at home.

"You won't believe what went on down here," he said.

He described for Maureen the appalling scene at the station.

"The thing I kept thinking," Rick said, "was that this could be Luke. He's going to end up like those kids if he stays in segregated classes."

"He doesn't have to stay in them," Maureen said.

Rick Elwood, who hadn't until then been as alive as Maureen to the dangers his son faced, said, "Let's make sure."

A week later, on the morning of Tuesday, September 2, the day after Labour Day and two days before school opened for the year, the Elwoods drove to Atlantic View Elementary

142

School for a meeting with Inez Collier. Atlantic View was the local public school, two and a half miles down the highway from the Elwood house, and Inez Collier was its principal. She was a strong-minded, efficient woman in her fifties, a salt-of-the-earth Maritimer, gruff when she had to be, and she was no stranger to the Elwoods. They knew and admired Collier from their daughter Melissa's years at Atlantic, and they realized she carried a heavy load, teaching class for half her day, and, for the other half, tending to the administration of a school that numbered 170 students from Grades 1 through 4.

Collier listened to Rick and Maureen as they talked about Luke's character and problems and education, and she seemed to take the information that they intended to enrol Luke at Atlantic in her stride.

"I think Luke'll fit in," Collier said. "Of course, he'll be learning at his own level."

"All we want," Maureen said, "is for him to be in his own age-equivalent class."

"Age-equivalent, yes," Collier said, pausing over Maureen's handy use of the lingo. "Well, it won't be necessary for Luke to pass Grade 3 academically."

"You see any problems?" Maureen asked.

"The only problem I see at the moment," Collier said, "is that the other children in the class might try to do too much to help Luke. I wouldn't want that."

Collier reached into her drawer and pulled out school-registration forms for Luke.

"Now, really, *that* was an interview that surprised me," Rick said on the drive home.

"Looks like there isn't going to be any trouble," Maureen said.

"Can't believe it."

But almost instantly, behind the scenes at the Halifax

County–Bedford School District, the bureaucracy began to grind. The district is the largest school region east of Montreal. It reaches down the eastern shore from Halifax and is responsible for almost thirty thousand students. Several dozen administrative employees are needed to run the district, and when the Elwoods left Inez Collier's office, she played it according to the book and telephoned the news of Luke's enrolment to one of the senior officers. He was Don Trider, the supervisor for the area that included Atlantic View School.

"If this young boy — Luke, you say? — has been at Astral," Don Trider said to Collier, "he must be TMH."

"TMH?"

"Trainable mentally handicapped."

"The terms keep changing, don't they?"

"Whatever we're dealing with in this youngster," Trider said, "I don't feel we should allow him to transfer to Atlantic until we've done some studies."

"The Elwoods have the application forms."

"I'm going to get Judy Harrity in the picture," Trider said.

Judy Harrity was the district's supervisor of resources, the officer who organized the services of teaching assistants, speech therapists, and other experts for students who needed them.

"What do you want from us at the school?" Collier asked.

Trider said, "We've got to hold off the Elwoods."

The next day, September 3, the phone at the Elwood house rang off the kitchen wall.

Inez Collier phoned at seven-thirty in the morning.

Keep Luke at home, she said to Maureen, until you've had a meeting with Judy Harrity.

Harrity called at eleven-thirty.

Leave Luke at Astral, she told Maureen, until I've reviewed his file and made my recommendation.

Between calls, Maureen talked to Debby Smith at the Mentally Retarded Association.

Don't back away, Debby said.

Were the lines already being drawn? Even this early, it seemed to be shaping up as a struggle over Luke between the parents, backed by the Association, on one side, and the school district's administration on the other.

Maureen dug in.

"As far as we're concerned," she told Judy Harrity in another long conversation, "Luke's a student at Atlantic."

At two-thirty that afternoon, Maureen took a break from telephone duty and drove with Luke to Atlantic View for a meeting with the woman who would play perhaps the pivotal role in the contest over Luke Elwood's education. She was Annette Garner, Atlantic View's Grade 3 teacher.

Garner was a petite, bubbly woman in her late forties. As Maureen was to learn in the following months, Garner brought enormous energy to her job, and all her students came to respect her. Garner grew up in England, where she took her education — an honours history degree, a teaching certificate — before she married, had kids of her own, and moved to Ottawa. Her teaching experience touched many bases — a Montessori school, a small public school in Newfoundland, a bilingual school in her own Montreal home. When she met Luke, she was in her third year at Atlantic View.

"Luke'll need special attention," Maureen said. "I guess you realize that."

Garner didn't seem fazed by the prospect of taking Luke into her class. At least that was the way Maureen read her reaction. Garner talked to Luke, looked at the report cards that Maureen had brought from Hillside and Astral Drive, and promised to read the literature about special education that Maureen also supplied.

"What about the bus to school?" Garner asked. "Is there someone to help Luke with it?"

145

"His sister won't be at Atlantic this year," Maureen said. "Melissa's going to Ross Road for Grade 5."

"I'll speak to Jenny Bezanson," Garner said. "She's in Grade 4 and very responsible."

"Jenny lives right near us."

"That's settled," Garner said.

Maureen went home and told Rick that after the blizzard of worrying phone calls in the morning, things were looking up again.

At seven-fifteen the following morning, a Thursday, Jenny Bezanson knocked on the Elwoods' side door.

Hi, she greeted Luke, and the two kids set off for the bus.

The two-lane highway where the school bus stopped was a couple of blocks down a hill from the street where the Elwood family lived. About twenty-five kids in the Upper Lawrencetown subdivision rode the bus to Atlantic View. Five years earlier, when Melissa started at the school, there'd been no crossing guard at the highway. Maureen Elwood led the agitation for a guard — and won.

Maureen stood at the top of the hill and watched Jenny and Luke join the other kids at the bus stop. She wasn't sure how she felt. Apprehensive? Excited? She knew only one thing for sure — that morning was one of the rare times when her son was doing something that all the rest of the kids in the neighbourhood took for granted. He was going to the local school.

The bus pulled up at the stop.

Luke climbed the steps.

"Good morning," he said to the driver.

"Hey, you kids," the driver called to the other children on the bus. "You hear that? Here's the only boy who's said good morning to me. There's a lesson for the bunch of you."

Early on Thursday afternoon, while Luke was in Annette Garner's class and Maureen was doing volunteer duty in the library at Atlantic View, Don Trider, the area's supervisor of schools, convened a meeting.

He gathered together eight people: Judy Harrity; John Caldwell, the district's supervisor of special services; and one man and five women from Astral Drive School: the principal, two teachers, two speech pathologists, and the school psychologist. This formidable array of personpower zeroed in on one subject: eight-year-old Luke Elwood.

The meeting, called a case conference in education circles, allowed all present to toss in their two bits' worth. Some speakers, no more than half, drew on personal experiences with Luke at Astral, and fairly quickly the mood of the conference — sober, responsible, grave — was expressed in a consensus. Barbara Simmons, the school psychologist, drew the assignment of putting the consensus on paper along with a collection of the conference's observations and comments. Simmons's report, two single-spaced, typewritten pages, pulled no punches:

"Luke is not self-initiated and is very dependent on teacher guidance. He requires constant supervision and direction."

And,

"Socially, Luke needs help to hang up his coat. He can put on his sneakers with effort but has not yet mastered left-right."

And,

"Luke likes to go places with the other children but doesn't do anything when he gets there."

Sometimes the report bogged down in educationese:

"Luke appears to be at a pre-readiness level academically and is cognitively functioning at a very low level."

But, altogether, the conference looked on Luke as a nearly hopeless case:

"Luke requires verbal and physical prompting to do anything."

And the conclusion was unanimous:

"It is felt by the group that the program instituted and available at Astral Drive School best serves Luke's needs at this time."

Rick and Maureen Elwood were not to see the report for several months, not until the litigation over Luke was almost done, but Maureen learned of the report's conclusion immediately after the case conference broke up.

"It's Don Trider," Maureen heard when she answered the phone at home on Thursday afternoon.

Maureen felt an automatic tightening in her stomach.

"We've had a meeting with teachers and speech people at Astral who know Luke best," Trider went on. "They feel very strongly about Luke staying with them."

Maureen said, "Luke's father and I feel strongly about him staying at Atlantic."

"There's something else, Mrs. Elwood," Trider said, trying another card. "I've talked to Mrs. Garner and she's exhausted after just one day with Luke in the class."

"I'm sure that's not so," Maureen said.

Trider had a fall-back position.

"May I just ask this?" he said. "Would you and Mr. Elwood come to a meeting with myself, Judy Harrity, and some others tomorrow afternoon? Let's talk things out."

Meetings. Phone calls. Case conferences. Talking things out. Maureen couldn't believe the red tape.

She said to Trider, "A meeting's fine if it'll get Luke's schooling settled."

"Good," Trider said. "This will be with Lloyd Gillis."

At the administrative end of the Halifax County–Bedford School District, Lloyd Gillis was the main man. His title was chief executive officer, and he looked the part, a Leslie Nielsen type, tall, handsome, a shock of white hair. He'd earned a reputation as a solid administrator, decisive, but a man who played his cards close to the vest, and at the meeting on Friday afternoon, September 5, he assumed immediate charge.

"I know the situation," he said. "And my decision is that Luke not go to Atlantic View."

Don Trider and Judy Harrity were grouped with Gillis at the meeting, and across the table sat Rick and Maureen and Debby Smith, whom the Elwoods brought in for reinforcement.

Gillis had a question for Maureen.

"What are your reasons for transferring your son to Atlantic View?" he asked.

Maureen glanced at Debby, took a breath, and turned back to Gillis.

"We've put a lot of thought into this," she said. "We want Luke in a class with his peers."

Maureen was getting polished at her spiel, and she laid it out once again for Gillis.

He didn't seem impressed.

"Luke should attend Astral Drive," he said when Maureen finished. "That's my decision. But if you disagree, you're entitled to appeal it."

"Appeal?" Maureen said. "Who to?"

"To the whole School Board," Gillis said, "The next meeting is September 17 if you want me to put you on the agenda."

"Sure," Maureen said. "But in the meantime, Luke stays at Atlantic View."

"That's your prerogative," Gillis said. "But my suggestion is you return Luke to Astral Drive. That way, you see, the Board will perceive you as co-operative parents."

"No way," Maureen said.

Annette Garner had her hands full with Luke. Later, many months later, she admitted that she probably didn't have a

149

handle on the best ways to approach the boy. "I was really stumped at the beginning," she said. "I felt so inadequate and insecure." But that observation came in hindsight. In the reality of the early days with Luke, Garner was frustrated and discouraged, and her feelings were expressed — perhaps *unleashed* was more accurate — in a report she wrote on September 15.

"Luke's attention span is very short," Garner said in the report. "He cannot continue a task by himself, e.g. using blocks to build an object. When left to himself, he will throw the blocks or bang them together. . . . Most of all language used in the classroom is beyond his comprehension. He is cooperative in that he will join a group for reading a story; however he does not understand what is going on. . . . He is frightened by the big space in the gym and the boisterous behavior of other students, so he tends to stand at the side and watch. . . . Luke's interest, his prior knowledge, and appreciation of concepts are unlike those of grade three students."

Maureen got together with Debby Smith and Margie Brown to thrash out programs for the classroom that would simultaneously involve Luke in the class's work and give him projects that he could carry out at his own speed. Maureen took the programs to Atlantic View, and Don Trider, ever conscientious, sat in on a meeting while Maureen went over her ideas with Annette Garner.

"From our point of view at home, Mrs. Garner," Maureen said, "we already see tremendous improvement in Luke. We think you're doing a great job."

"Well, that's good to hear," Garner said doubtfully.

"He's expressing himself more, playing with the other kids on the block, all kinds of little things that are real big for him," Maureen said. "And, I hope anyway, these programs should help you and Luke."

Maureen pressed the programs on Garner and appealed to

Trider for a part-time classroom assistant to work with Luke in class. After all, she pointed out, there was provision for such part-time assistants in the school system and its budget.

Trider said he'd look into it, and Garner promised to give things her best shot.

Maureen kept ringing the offices of the Halifax County–Bedford District School Board. Lloyd Gillis had said the Elwoods could appeal to the Board his decision to bar Luke from Atlantic View. But what was the drill for this appeal? Maureen didn't get the answer until Monday, September 15, when she reached Ruby Heffler, the Board's secretary.

"You have to submit a written notice to us," Heffler said on the phone. "You know, something that identifies the problem."

"That's easy."

"This is the meeting on Wednesday night we're talking about, the seventeenth," Heffler went on. "You'll have fifteen minutes to make your appeal."

"Fifteen minutes?" Maureen said. "That's hardly any time at all."

"Well, it's the rule," Heffler said. "And two spokespersons."

"Just two?"

This was getting worse by the second. Maureen planned to bring in parents who had special children integrated in other schools. They'd explain to the Board how the system worked for them. And maybe an educator from an integrated school would provide the same kind of enlightenment.

"After you're finished," Heffler said, "the Board members might ask a few questions, but there won't be anything like a back-and-forth debate."

"What about Mr. Gillis and the other staff people?"

"Oh, yes, they'll likely speak after you," Heffler said. "They'll explain the reasons for their decision."

From the sound of things, Maureen thought the appeal procedure might be loaded against Luke.

Terri Hill lived on the same street as the Elwoods. Her son Nicholas was in Grade 2 at Atlantic View, and sometimes he chummed around with Luke. Terri lined herself on the Elwood side of the fight to keep Luke at Atlantic View, and so did her organization. Terri Hill was president of the Atlantic View Home and School Association.

At a meeting of the Association on the night of September 16, the members passed this resolution:

"We the parents in Atlantic View Elementary School believe in total integration for all our children in the Atlantic View School District and will take steps to ensure all our children have the option and opportunity to attend our school."

"Maybe you'll come with me to the Board meeting?" Maureen asked Terri Hill. "The other half of the delegation?"

"Well, sure."

Fifteen members sit on the Halifax County–Bedford District School Board. Parents in the district elect five of them, the province appoints another five, and the remaining five get their appointments from the district's municipal councils. The members choose their own chairman from among the group of fifteen. For their meetings, the members gather in the boardroom of the Halifax County Municipal Building, a room designed by an architect who may have had little sympathy for the poor supplicants appearing before the Board. The members occupy desks in an elevated ring, while down below, "in the pits" as Maureen Elwood puts it, those presenting appeals and petitions take their places in a posture that invites a crimp in the neck and a poke in the confidence.

On the night of September 17, Maureen and Terri Hill handed up a few pages of written material to the members. They included a research study on the benefits of integration, and other printed stuff pointing out that the Nova Scotia Department of Education seemed to favour integrated schools.

Then Maureen stood, and, her voice trembling slightly, more Debra Winger than Greer Garson, she spoke from notes she had written earlier in the day.

She got started in formal style.

"Ladies and gentlemen," she said, "we are here this evening to make appeal to the Board regarding denial of placement for our son, Luke Elwood, in Grade 3 at Atlantic View School in Upper Lawrencetown, Halifax County."

But as Maureen talked of Luke and the improvement that she and Rick saw in him after only ten days of school, the formality broke down and the mother's enthusiasm shone through.

"In the past," she said, "other children said to us, 'Why doesn't Luke go to our school?' and 'Why *can't* Luke go to our school?' And now we hear, 'Luke belongs here,' and 'The kids are *glad* he's here.'"

Maureen talked about Luke's new independence in travelling with kids his own age on the school bus, the improvement in his play skills, his gains in reading and artwork, the fresh awareness he had for the community around him.

She praised Annette Garner and Inez Collier. "They've accomplished so much without the resources that can be made available in the school system." And she touched on some of those resources. "There already is a resource teacher and a speech pathologist in the system and in particular at Atlantic View, and approval has been given for a full-time program assistant for Luke's class."

153

The benefits, Maureen said, were for Luke, but the other twenty-eight kids in the class stood to be winners, too, just by having a boy like Luke among them.

"Their horizons are expanding," Maureen said, winding up with a few sentences that shouldn't have left a dry eye in the house. "And they're getting a broader knowledge of the real world. They're gaining skills at helping, and they gain one more thing — one more little friend who can share his own sense of humour, his wit and charm and loyalties and friendship."

Maureen sat down, and Terri Hill rose to emphasize the support for the principle of integration from the Atlantic View parents.

Maureen looked at her watch.

"Fourteen minutes," she whispered to Terri.

"Mrs. Elwood," the chairman, Lorne Verabioff, said, "do you want your son integrated into Atlantic View for purely social reasons?"

Maureen thought she detected hostility in the question.

"We want him to receive his academics at his own level," she answered. "And it doesn't seem a difficult job to teach him his academics along with the rest of the class."

"Well then," another member asked, "how do you think Luke's going to get through the school system?"

More hostility.

"He'll move with children his own age from grade to grade," Maureen said. "He won't have the same academics, but as long as he's progressing, he'll keep moving."

A third member spoke up.

"Why do you think Luke should pass on to the next grade," he asked, "and someone else be held back?"

"I had a sister who was handicapped," a woman member put in indignantly, "and she never even *got* to school."

Maureen was beginning to reel.

"Oh my goodness," she said to Terri Hill. "They don't get

what special education is all about."

"I guess it takes longer than fifteen minutes to explain," Terri said.

The questions ended, and Maureen waited for the staff people to make their presentation. Lloyd Gillis had been sitting beside Lorne Verabioff, the chairman, throughout the meeting. Surely he was going to speak to the Luke Elwood issue. But things didn't go in the direction Maureen expected. Instead, a member moved that the matter be put over until the following week, Wednesday the twenty-fourth, to hear representations from the staff. The motion carried, and Maureen left the boardroom wondering if she'd been set up.

The Elwood crusade drew the attention of Halifax's media, and on the morning of September 18, a radio report of the previous night's events at the School Board caught Blaise MacDonald in mid-shave. A disabled boy? Parents taking a stab at integration? That hit home to MacDonald. His own younger brother, Sean, back in Glace Bay, carried the retarded label. And his wife's sister had a boy, Matthew, who was a Down's syndrome child. The sister-in-law, Winnie, lived in Fredericton, New Brunswick, and she'd used her moxie and determination to get young Matthew integrated into a Fredericton public school. Blaise MacDonald knew what these Elwood people were up against, and after he finished his shave, he got Maureen on the phone.

"If you need help," he said to Maureen, "I'm your man."

MacDonald told Maureen about Winnie and Matthew and the events in Fredericton.

"Just put my phone number on a piece of paper," MacDonald said on the telephone. "It sounds like you might be needing legal advice and I'm a lawyer."

Blaise MacDonald arrived at law by a circuitous route. He

grew up the second-last of thirteen children — Sean came after him — in a devout Catholic family. The father of this great brood ran a bakery and was for twenty-one years the mayor of Glace Bay. Blaise trained as a boilermaker, and his work took him around the country in the late sixties and early seventies. It also took him into upper management for a couple of years. But he remained at heart a labour man, and when it dawned on him that the law was a fine tool for social change, he entered Dalhousie Law School.

"Law's the last place in the world you'll find revolution," MacDonald says. "But slow change, gradual change, that's a different proposition. That's how you use the law."

MacDonald's a fighter. He doesn't look or sound it, not with his soft, rounded face, his gentle Cape Breton accent. But wind him up and point him in the direction of a perceived injustice and he turns tiger. His law firm, Goldberg MacDonald, works out of the fourteenth floor of a steel-and-glass tower on Halifax's spiffy waterfront, and its specialty is labour cases. When a Nova Scotia union gets in a tight spot, the call often goes out for Blaise MacDonald.

After the phone conversation of September 18, Maureen Elwood had his number jotted on the calendar on her kitchen wall.

At the School Board meeing on the night of September 24, Maureen saw which way the wind was blowing.

In her presentation to the Board, she'd been allowed fifteen minutes.

The school administration took one hour and forty minutes to make its pitch.

Maureen's side was permitted two speakers.

The administration wheeled out three big guns: Lloyd Gillis, Don Trider, and John Caldwell, the school district's supervisor of special services.

Maureen had filed a few thin documents with the Board.

The administration brought in an avalanche of paper, eight thick studies that charted Luke's career and outlined administration policy on mentally handicapped children.

"Is this fair?" Maureen said to Rick as they sat listening to the presentation, unable to question the presenters or to read the thick studies.

Many of the Board members, entirely well intentioned and reaching desperately for the right answers, were relieved by the documentation that the administration people were throwing at them. They knew about special children in a general sense, but until Luke Elwood came along, they hadn't confronted a particular case. They were looking for guidance, something with authority to it, and Lloyd Gillis and company were delivering the goods.

"The placement of a moderately or severely disabled student in a mainstream setting," Gillis said, "is a complex process demanding careful planning and necessary support structures if it is to succeed at all."

Just so, the Board members nodded.

Don Trider explained that there were four levels on which handicapped children might be placed.

Level one was for children who can integrate into a regular classroom setting with minimal special help.

Level two: children who are full-time in a regular classroom with the help of extra support personnel.

Three: children who are in segregated special classes for part of the time and in integrated classes for the rest.

Four: children who take their full education in segregated special classes.

Where did Luke Elwood fit?

"The staff assesses Luke as between levels three and four."

Ah, said the Board members.

"Luke was making progress at Astral Drive in both social and academic skills," John Caldwell said. "Astral is where he belongs."

We see, said the Board members.

157

"It will be expensive to accommodate Luke Elwood at Atlantic View," Lloyd Gillis said.

How much?

"We project thirty thousand dollars."

Oh-oh, said the Board members, and they adjourned until October 1, when they would vote on the administration decision to keep Luke out of Atlantic View.

The people from the Canadian Association for the Mentally Retarded — Debby Smith, Margie Brown, Bill Powroz the paralegal — let the Elwoods know they were behind them for the long haul. Maybe legal counsel was needed at this stage? The Association would put up the money for a lawyer. Maureen mentioned the phone call from Blaise MacDonald. Bill Powroz knew MacDonald from their days together at the Dalhousie Legal Aid Clinic. First-class lawyer, Powroz said, and he lined up an interview for the Elwoods with MacDonald on September 30.

At the meeting in MacDonald's office, he mapped out swift strategy for the next night's Board session. He'd present the members with a letter. That might slow them up.

"I was careful not to overstate our legal position," MacDonald says of the letter. "I just made it clear there could be difficult times ahead for both sides."

The letter sent up two warning signals. For one thing, MacDonald wrote, the Board was in possible danger of running afoul of the Charter of Rights if it refused Luke admission to Atlantic View. And, secondly, MacDonald called the Board's attention to a line in a booklet published by the Nova Scotia Department of Education. "No child," the line read, "may be placed in a special class without the consent of the parents."

The next night, October 1, voting night, the motion to refuse Luke Elwood's admission to Atlantic View was made and seconded. Maureen and Rick, MacDonald, and a few

Elwood supporters sat in the audience waiting for the show of hands that would determine Luke's immediate future. Despite the rough ride that Maureen thought she'd taken on the night of her presentation, she felt optimistic. Cautious but optimistic. Anyway, she said to Rick, at least it's going to be settled one way or the other.

"Mr. Chairman. Mr. *Chairman!*"

Lois Wiseman, one of the Board members, wanted Lorne Verabioff's attention, and she looked worried.

"Wouldn't it be wise," she said when she had the floor, "to defer the vote? I mean, we have this letter before us from the Elwoods' lawyer. Shouldn't we have advice on the matters it raises from our own lawyer?"

Verabioff made up his mind in a hurry.

"We'll discuss it," he said. "In private."

The Elwoods and company waited in the corridor for what seemed to Maureen to be a ridiculously long time before Lois Wiseman appeared out of the boardroom.

"We've been phoning all over town," she told Maureen. "Our lawyer's away somewhere."

"What's that do to the vote?" Maureen asked.

"It's postponed," Lois Wiseman answered. "Don't you worry, I'll see you get notice when it's coming up."

"This is sure an anticlimax," Maureen said to Blaise Mac-Donald.

"Letter's got them thinking," MacDonald said.

The fighter thought he'd taken a round.

When Wayne MacKay speaks, there seems to be a laugh in his voice.

MacKay is a legal scholar who's written dozens of learned articles on the Charter of Rights, a distinguished lawyer who served a year as law clerk to the late Chief Justice Bora Laskin of the Supreme Court of Canada, a full professor of law at Dalhousie University, a fit, bearded man in his late thirties,

159

husband and father of four, but the characteristic that sets him immediately apart is the sound of laughter in his voice. It appears to be a permanent fixture, something he surely brought with him from his boyhood in Nova Scotia's Pictou County and has never surrendered.

MacKay grew up in a tiny spot on the map called Mount Thom, where his father served as the unpaid champion of all causes. "He was nominally a farmer," MacKay says. "But he pretty much neglected the farm because he was too busy looking after this constant stream of neighbours who came through our house to get my father to fill out their income-tax forms, to get him to go after the government for better services in the area, to find them jobs. He had a great concern, my father, for disadvantaged people."

Wayne MacKay graduated from university and taught high school in Dartmouth. So did his wife Laurie. Her field was special education. The MacKays adopted two children, both girls, both black, and Laurie gave birth to two more, another girl, then a son. After three years of teaching, MacKay enrolled at Dalhousie Law School. He was a wizard student, his class's gold medallist, and he won the clerkship with Bora Laskin. "The most amazing part of the job," MacKay says, "is that the Chief Justice used to ask my opinion about the cases the court was hearing."

From Laskin, MacKay returned to Dalhousie Law as a teacher. He concentrated on constitutional law and administrative law, ran a seminar in criminology, and developed a specialty in education law. And, on the side, he acted as counsel in a series of cases that centred on court challenges under the Canadian Human Rights Act.

It was that background — the know-how in education law, the human-rights concerns — that led Bill Powroz to suggest that MacKay be brought into Luke Elwood's fight. If this thing ever gets to court, Powroz said, Blaise MacDonald and Wayne MacKay would make a dynamite duo, MacDonald on the nuts and bolts, MacKay on the Charter angles, both of them on other legal points. Everyone — including MacKay — went along with Powroz's brainstorm.

"The reason I chose teaching law in the first place, apart from liking it," MacKay says, "is I thought, with a young family, it'd be a better lifestyle. More time with the kids and so on. But these special cases seem to make me busier than if I was a normal practitioner."

MacKay speaks the mild complaint with the laugh in his voice.

On the morning of October 15, Maureen Elwood telephoned a Board member named Betty Rix on a subject that had nothing to do with Luke.

"By the way, Betty," Maureen said as the conversation was winding down, "we're getting anxious about the vote on Luke. He's coming along so great at Atlantic we don't want to see him leave."

"I can't promise how it'll go," Betty Rix said. "But you'll know after tonight."

Maureen exploded into the phone.

"*Tonight*?!"

"Didn't you hear? Tonight's the meeting."

"When you vote?"

"Luke's on the agenda," Betty Rix said. "Our lawyer apparently says its okay to go ahead with the vote."

"But Lois Wiseman said she'd let me know."

"Poor Lois," Betty Rix said. "She's been laid up in hospital."

Maureen signalled battle stations. She rounded up Blaise MacDonald. Wayne MacKay couldn't make it; he had a commitment to deliver a speech on, of all appropriate subjects, "Education and the Charter of Rights". But Maureen corralled a dozen neighbours to drive to the meeting. The Elwoods were making a show of force.

So were the media.

161

When the Elwood gang arrived at the Municipal Building, they stepped into a crush of reporters with pens, pads, tape-recorders, cameras, and TV lights.

"When Rick and I made the decision there'd be no more special classes for Luke," Maureen told a reporter, "we never dreamed it'd turn into a public monster. We're just trying to get a kid into school."

As the meeting started, the Elwoods handicapped the Board members and votes. They knew Eric Hill was on Luke's side. He represented the area that took in Upper Lawrencetown, and the previous week he had dropped into Annette Garner's class and had come away impressed. Another member, Sharon Stewart, had spoken in favour of integration, and Betty Rix was at least a possible vote for Luke.

And then there was Percy Baker.

"I remembered Percy as soon as I walked into the first meeting," Blaise MacDonald says. "Back in 1965, when I hadn't a clue what to do with myself, I enrolled in the Maritime School of Social Work. Pretty soon I decided it was a useless institution and I only stayed a few months. But at one point another fella and I got sent as interns to the County Home over in Cole Harbour. It was for mentally disturbed children, and it was a regular horror show. Children locked up. Children sitting in the halls grunting and groaning something fierce. The other fella and I decided we were gonna blow the whistle on the place. Tell the newspapers what was happening in this snake pit. Well, the administrator of the Home had us into his office and he opened up the books. 'So you're going to the papers,' he said. 'While you're at it, you might tell them I get $2.33 a head to feed and clothe and care for these poor children. If you boys want to do something useful, why don't you get me some money?' We never went to the newspapers because we realized that man, the adminis-trator, was hard-headed but he had a great heart. The man was Percy Baker, and I knew he'd be with Luke Elwood on the vote."

Lorne Verabioff called the meeting to order and recognized Lloyd Gillis, who swung once again into his recommendation that Luke be removed from Atlantic View.

"Luke Elwood is mentally handicapped and needs specialized education," Gillis told the Board. "His needs cannot be met at Atlantic View without additional support, and the cost of that is unwarranted."

Gillis had more stats. He pointed out that there were sixteen other disabled students in the district served by Atlantic View, and if all of them followed Luke's example and enrolled at the school, the cost could hit a half-million dollars.

"If he can make all these arguments," Maureen whispered to Blaise MacDonald, "how come we can't give the Board more of our side?"

"Seems to be their rules," MacDonald said.

Betty Rix asked Gillis about the amount of time that regular students at Atlantic received from resource people and speech therapists. Gillis thought that, well, yes, those specialists would possibly have time left over from regular students to help with Luke.

The debate pinged back and forth from member to member. It produced no storm or fire. No member shouted or grew angry. Some members seemed to be looking for a resolution of what was bound to be a mess. Some remained disturbed or hesitant or both, and a few had apparently shut down their minds on Luke.

Percy Baker wasn't one of them.

"We may not think it's right to put this boy in Atlantic View," he said. "But the parents want it, and it's been my experience over the years that the parents are most often right in deciding what's best for their children."

Lorne Verabioff shifted in his chairman's seat, looking over

163

the documentation in front of him, listening to the buzz of discussion, and he grew itchy. To him, the issue was sliced as cleanly as it could be. The Elwoods, sincere people, thought their son was making progress at Atlantic View. The administrative staff didn't see it that way, and the staff, the men and women in the firing-lines, close to the action every day, studying Luke, *they* should know.

Verabioff was a stocky, good-looking man in his late forties, the head of the department at Dalhousie University that trained physical-education teachers. And he was not one for shilly-shallying.

"I have something to say," Verabioff told the other Board members.

He slid out of the chairman's seat.

"Mrs. Rix," he said to Betty Rix, "would you chair the rest of this part of our meeting?"

"What's that all about?" Maureen asked MacDonald.

"Person in the chair doesn't vote unless there's a tie," MacDonald answered. "Rix just lost a vote. Verabioff's got one."

"I looked up integration, the dictionary meaning," Verabioff began, speaking from prepared notes. "It's defined as 'free and equal association'. I stress *equal*. The educational system is based on individual progress. If a person can't interact with his or her environment, no learning takes place. Now the point is we are *not* all equal. The world is based on merit. So that integration is not absolute and society is not all integrated. Society, I believe, is based on merit."

"Oh my goodness," Maureen sighed.

"He's gonna back Lloyd Gillis all the way," MacDonald said. "Bloody jock mentality."

"When I review Luke's case," Verabioff continued, "I have difficulty. On the one hand, there is an element of real progress. But there are problems. Luke needs cuing to initiate tasks. He's a passive watcher, not a mixer. He has trouble

164

communicating. The teachers at Atlantic View say he has difficulty interacting with his environment without one-to-one support. As far as simple socialization goes, I believe that if the goal of integration is socialization, then Astral Drive is providing socialization for Luke Elwood."

"Can't *anybody* get this straight?"Maureen said to Mac-Donald. "It's way *more* than socialization."

"I urge the Board," Verabioff finished, "to support the recommendation."

Percy Baker broke in.

He said, "I thought the chairman of the Board was supposed to be impartial."

"May I speak on a point of order," Verabioff said before Betty Rix in the chair could sort out Baker's objection. "Mr. Baker is not addressing the motion on the floor. We're debating the Luke Elwood matter. We're not talking about the chairman's role. Perhaps that's for another time. Right now, we have a motion to settle."

The Board prepared to vote.

The secretary read the motion: moved and seconded that the staff's recommendation that Luke Elwood be placed in the special-education class at Astral Drive School be approved.

Lois Wiseman was in the hospital and Betty Rix was in the chair.

That left thirteen votes.

The hands went up.

In favour of the motion: Lorne Verabioff's and seven others.

Opposed: Percy Baker's and four others.

Motion carried, eight votes to five.

Luke was out of Atlantic View.

Blaise MacDonald said, "Our next step is we get an *ex parte* injunction."

"What's that?" Maureen asked.

"Temporary order from a judge keeping the Board from kicking Luke out of Atlantic."

MacDonald, the Elwoods, and a few others were gathered in MacDonald's office later on the night of the vote. MacDonald had a phone to his ear. He was trying to track down a Nova Scotia Supreme Court Justice who might hear his application for the injunction that night. But he was coming up empty.

"These fellas go to bed too early," he said.

"What do we do about Luke tomorrow?" Maureen asked.

"Send him to Mrs. Garner's class," MacDonald said. "Nobody's won this fight yet."

At midnight, everyone left for home.

Don Trider chose an awkward moment to knock on the Elwoods' side door. It was one-thirty in the afternoon on the day after the vote, and inside the Elwood house, Maureen, Rick, Debby Smith, Bill Powroz, and Margie Brown were talking strategy.

"Like to come in for coffee, Don?" Maureen asked at the door.

"Thanks, no," Trider said, holding out an envelope. "It's just this letter."

Lloyd Gillis had signed the letter, and in the crisp Gillis style it requested the Elwoods' immediate compliance with the School Board vote to return Luke to Astral Drive.

Maureen's heart took a tumble.

"Call Blaise," Debby Smith said.

"I suppose what they did," MacDonald said on the telephone, "was nip over to the school, and when they saw Luke sitting in class, they had a pow-wow with their lawyer and whipped off the bloody letter."

"From what it says," Maureen said, "we won't be sending him back to Atlantic tomorrow. Or maybe ever."

"Bugger the letter, Maureen," MacDonald said. "Wayne and I'll be in front of a judge in a couple of hours."

At four o'clock, MacDonald and MacKay walked the three blocks south from MacDonald's office to the Halifax Courthouse. It's a glum, contemporary stone building that does little with its magnificent view over the harbour except block it. MacDonald and MacKay, without a prearranged appointment, found only one Supreme Court Justice in his chambers. He was Alex MacIntosh, an erect, snowy-haired man from MacKay's neck of the woods in Pictou County. MacIntosh agreed to see the two lawyers.

"Do I really need to read those documents you've got for me?" he said in his chambers. "I've been following this business on TV and in the papers."

MacDonald and MacKay hadn't brought along much in the way of documentation, just enough recital of facts to convince MacIntosh — they hoped — that they deserved an interim injunction.

An interim injunction is a useful but risky sort of legal remedy. For one thing, a judge grants it for only a very short term, usually a matter of days. For another, the judge hands it out in anticipation that two further court proceedings will follow. One is a much more formal and complete hearing on the injunction; at this later hearing the judge decides whether the injunction should be dissolved or left in place until a trial is held. The second proceeding is the trial itself. It's a trial that leads to a final decision on the issue that was the subject, way back at the beginning, of the interim injunction.

In the Elwood matter, the trial would decide whether the School Board had the right to bar Luke from Atlantic View. MacDonald and MacKay knew they'd have to get the paperwork started that would lead to such a trial. But until it took place — and that was bound to be a long way down the road — they wanted to try to keep Luke at Atlantic. And the interim injunction was the first step in the process.

167

Another wrinkle in the application for this kind of injunction is that it can be conducted *ex parte*. In English, that means the hearing takes place with the lawyers for only one party to the proceeding before the judge. "You have no obligation to advise the other side," Blaise MacDonald says of *ex parte* applications. "Maybe it's courteous to let them know. But in the Elwood case I didn't bother." Thus, at that stage, on the afternoon of October 16, the lawyers for the School Board had no idea what MacDonald and MacKay were up to.

Mr. Justice MacIntosh's first question in his chambers came as an echo of a line of thought the Elwood lawyers had grown accustomed to.

"What about the special classes at Astral Drive School?" MacIntosh asked. "Wouldn't this young lad be better off in them?"

MacKay fielded the question.

"Luke's in regular classes at this minute, your lordship, and we feel he's doing just fine," MacKay began. He talked of Luke's days at Atlantic, the Elwoods' feeling about his progress, and went on to tell MacIntosh about arguments that might be raised under the Charter of Rights to prevent the School Board's action. Then he emphasized that the application that afternoon was, after all, merely for a temporary injunction to keep the Board from sending Luke back to Astral.

"We'll be arguing a permanent injunction very shortly," MacKay said.

His talk — too chatty to be called a speech — lasted no more than ten minutes.

MacIntosh, not a judge to beat around the bush, said, "I'll grant your injunction."

"Is your lordship going to make it returnable on a stated date?" MacDonald asked, a touch of anxiety in his voice. If MacIntosh set a short limit on the injunction — a couple of days or so — the Elwood team wouldn't have long to prepare for the tough legal fight against the Board to keep the injunction in place until the trial was held.

"I'll do it this way," MacIntosh said. "I'll make the injunction last until the day you go to trial or to the day the court makes some other order. But I'll provide that either side can give the other forty-eight hours' notice that they're applying to have my injunction set aside. That suit you?"

"Perfect," MacDonald said.

He knew that the wording of MacIntosh's injunction was extended enough to hold off the Board's lawyers for a week or two.

Peter McLellan was the principal lawyer for the Halifax County–Bedford District School Board, and, not for the first time, he was miffed at Blaise MacDonald.

McLellan has deep roots in Nova Scotia's legal community and in its gentry. His father ended his career at the bar as a County Court judge, and Peter is a partner with McInnes, Cooper & Robertson, one of Halifax's oldest, largest, and most proper law firms. In his early forties, McLellan is a man who keeps his appearance pleasant and well-groomed, tidy moustache, dark-brown hair, suits that suggest he was born to them. As a lawyer, he is a letter-of-the-law craftsman. He speaks smoothly, observes the niceties, and is generally the very antithesis of Blaise MacDonald. Since McLellan's firm represents large corporate clients, he's bumped up against MacDonald and his union clients in a handful of litigious rows. In style and politics, in background, probably in their views of something as lofty as the quality of life, the two lawyers face each other across a vast gulf. McLellan projects a steady front, and that drives MacDonald crazy.

"Lawyers like Peter view emotion as being the enemy of the law," MacDonald says. "I say bullshit. You shouldn't fear shedding the odd tear. We see dramatic stories about real

169

people in our courts, and there's no use biting your lip for three stitches when you come up against them."

For McLellan's part, in the Elwood matter, he would have liked advance notice that MacDonald and MacKay were applying for the temporary injunction. *Typical* MacDonald tactic. Nevertheless, entirely professional, McLellan proceeded quickly to counter the Elwood lawyers by giving them notice that he was lining up a court hearing which would decide whether Mr. Justice MacIntosh's injunction should be continued or set aside.

The hearing was set down for October 29.

While the adults batted around Luke Elwood's future, the boy who was the subject of the debates and the voting, of the injunction proceedings, Luke himself, eight years old, went to school. Each morning at seven-fifteen he walked down the hill and rode the bus with the other kids. He filed into Mrs. Garner's class, and as the school days went by, a small and wonderful thing seemed to be happening. Slowly, Luke was getting caught up in the class and in the other kids.

Rick and Maureen recorded the signs.

"When he went to school over at Astral," Maureen says, "the other kids on our street, the neighbourhood children, didn't pay much attention to him. He spent most of his time alone, and even when there were other children around, Luke avoided them. But after he'd been at Atlantic for a while, it was like night and day. Luke was one of *them*. He went over to see other kids, and they came over to call on him."

Luke's vocabulary started to expand. He recognized words on the page. "Dog" and "Byron". He registered numbers. "1 + 2 = 3". He began to talk in five-phrase and ten-phrase descriptions. He learned to hang up his coat at school. And he arrived home one afternoon with the announcement that he wanted to see a hockey game.

"What was so satisfying about that," Maureen says, "is

that before, at Astral, he wasn't around children who talked about things like hockey. But now that he was, he developed a hockey vocabulary."

Maureen took him to a kids' hockey practice on October 26 where another event amazed her. Luke spotted a boy who had been in his class at Astral. Luke spoke to the boy.

"By *name*," Maureen says. "Luke hadn't seen this boy in four months, but he actually remembered his name."

Luke's mind and world were expanding.

One day after school he told the family there was something new in his life.

"What?" Melissa asked.

"Girlfriend," Luke answered.

"Well, now," Rick said.

A memory that sticks in Wayne MacKay's mind from the two weeks of hectic research and talk and planning that led up to the injunction hearing on October 29 is this:

"Rick Elwood emerged as a strong force. It was Maureen who had always been front and centre, and she still was. She had this incredible determination, and she was the advocate. But over time, in his quiet way, Rick asserted himself and he became a real anchor."

Here is what Blaise MacDonald remembers:

"I got Susan Coen to draft an affidavit by a fella named George Flynn. This was a very important affidavit because Flynn was a school administrator from up in Ontario who knew everything in the world about integration. Susan was the articling student in our firm, and when she brought in the affidavit she'd drawn, I more or less told her it was a piece of crap. So she snatched it off my desk, wheeled around, and banged out of my office. What she came back with next day was a work of art. It was the best affidavit I read in my life. Susan had spunk, and that's when I decided I wanted her to join the firm as a lawyer. Which she did."

Maureen Elwood remembers this:

"The long meetings at Blaise's office. We'd be there, all of us, until midnight, till two in the morning. I never saw such mountains of paper as those lawyers piled up."

What the late-night sessions and the affidavits and Susan Coen's spunk and everything else produced was a brief of 296 pages that the Elwood side would present to the court on the October 29 injunction hearing. The brief was intended to persuade the judge at the hearing to continue Mr. Justice MacIntosh's injunction against the School Board, thus allowing Luke to remain in Atlantic View until the whole issue of the Board's action in attempting to return Luke to Astral Drive School could be thrashed out in a full-scale trial.

One section of the fat brief was made up of a Memorandum of Law. In it, MacDonald and MacKay argued that the Board, in casting its vote against Luke, had erred in law. The errors, so the argument went, invalidated the Board's vote, and they were errors that essentially fell under two headings.

First, the Board had denied Luke procedural fairness at its meetings on September 17 and September 24. The unfairness arose out of several bits of business in the boardroom at the Municipal Building. The short time that Maureen was allowed to make her argument to the Board was one, a mere fifteen minutes as against an hour and forty minutes for Lloyd Gillis and the other staff people. Another was Maureen's lack of opportunity to ask the staff questions at the September 17 meeting. And then there was the staff's failure to share its many reports on Luke with Maureen.

Second, the Board's action deprived Luke of a bunch of rights that he was guaranteed under the Charter of Rights. The Charter spoke of the right of freedom of association, the right of equality, the right to be free of discrimination on the basis of mental disability. And by its October 15 vote, the Board had cheated Luke out of all of those rights.

In the Memorandum of Law, MacDonald and MacKay also dealt with the dodgy legalities governing injunctions. In order to keep the judge at the hearing from setting aside the interim injunction that Mr. Justice MacIntosh granted, the two lawyers had to pass a three-part test. Under the law of injunctions, they were required to show that they had a good case to take to trial on Luke's behalf against the School Board; that Luke would suffer "irreparable harm" if the injunction were lifted and he was returned to Astral Drive; and that the "balance of convenience" for all parties concerned in the matter — the Board, Atlantic View, Luke, the other kids in his class — was weighted in favour of Luke.

To meet those tough requirements, MacDonald and MacKay crammed their brief with a batch of affidavits from experts, educators, psychologists, and those who knew Luke best. The affidavits included these:

An Affidavit by Gary Hodson.

Hodson was the child psychologist who worked with Luke from his earliest years. His affidavit emphasized the improvement he saw in Luke in the few weeks the boy had been at Atlantic, and it urged that "the best way for Luke to learn is to be among peers who use language properly, and a regular classroom setting could meet that need."

An Affidavit by George Flynn.

Flynn was the director of education at the Waterloo Separate School Board in Ontario and a long-time champion of integration for special children. His affidavit, the handiwork of Susan Coen, said that, from the experience in his schools, there were two compelling reasons for going the integration route. One was that it produces a better education for special children, and the other was that it saves money. On the money point, Flynn said, at the Toronto Separate School Board where he was superintendent for special services from 1979 to 1985, it used to cost eighteen million dollars a year to bus special kids to their special schools. With integration, that outlay was eliminated. And Flynn's affidavit made one other point: integration does no harm to normal kids in the class. If a special child misbehaves, Flynn said, "the self-

173

correcting nature of peer influence is more powerful than anything a teacher can do for a disabled student."

Affidavits from the parents of twenty-seven of Luke's classmates.

All the parents said they and their kids welcomed Luke to Atlantic View, and they offered a rainbow of reasons for the welcome.

Monica Hiltz, mother: "Erica came home one day and told me how much better Luke was doing in school. She said that when the teacher asked what is two plus two, before anyone could answer, Luke said, 'Four.'"

Judy Nelson, mother: "Daniel is a little chubby, and Luke is the one child in the class who does not call him names."

Dorcus McNaughton, mother: "I believe it is beneficial for Jake to have Luke at school with him. I do not want to teach Jake that we should separate children who are different. It is beneficial to Jake to learn how to cope with disabled children and to grow up together and work with them as adults."

An affidavit by Maureen Elwood.

In eighty-two pages, it told everything that a judge would need to know about Luke and about the weeks from September 2 to October 15 when the Elwoods set out to send Luke to school with the kids on their block. The last sentences of the long affidavit carried Maureen's small cry:

"I have seen the difficulties Luke's isolation has caused him. His life was so separate and different from the lives of the children on the street who were born at the same time as him. Since he started at Atlantic View, he laughs more. He's learning to relate to other children in the neighbourhood. They've learned to relate to him. They have day-to-day experiences in common. Luke looks at you. You can see the happiness in his eyes. He's included now."

When MacDonald and MacKay learned who they'd drawn for the injunction hearings — the Chief Justice for the trial division of the Nova Scotia Supreme Court — they did handsprings.

The Chief Justice was Constance Glube. She had been named to the court in 1977 and bumped up to the Chief Justice's office five years later over several more senior and male judges. No one, least of all the judges she vaulted past, resented the appointment.

"Glube," Wayne McKay says, "is known for giving you a good hearing and keeping an open mind."

That wasn't the only reason MacKay and MacDonald were delighted — even delirious — to have her on the injunction hearing. They also knew that Glube had served in the 1970s as Halifax's City Administrator, the top bureaucratic job in civic government. With that background, she'd appreciate the gaffes that the School Board had committed during the Elwood debate and vote. And Glube was a mother, a circumstance of nature that, MacDonald and MacKay thought, might make her warmer to Maureen and her maternal drives.

At 9:46 on the morning of Wednesday, October 29, the Chief Justice — dark, attractive, fiftyish, businesslike — called the hearing to order in a courtroom on the fourth floor of the Halifax Courthouse. Glube had already read the 296-page brief submitted by MacDonald and MacKay. Peter McLellan had also filed material, a much shorter brief which included affidavits from Lloyd Gillis, Inez Collier, and Annette Garner. Both sides, McLellan for the Board, MacDonald and MacKay for Luke, told Glube that they wished her to hear further evidence in the form of testimony. MacDonald led off by calling to the witness stand George Flynn, the integration expert from Ontario.

"Hell of a powerful witness," MacDonald said later of George Flynn. In appearance, Flynn was a heavy-set man with short hair. By temperament, he was thoughtful. By

175

conviction, he was deeply religious. "In other words," Mac-Donald says, "he wasn't a half-cocked guy."

MacDonald's main purpose in putting Flynn on the stand was to give Glube another perspective on two points that Lloyd Gillis was gung-ho on in his affidavit. Gillis said that, one, Luke was bound to find himself isolated from normal students at Atlantic View, and, two, a formidable list of specialists costing a fortune would be necessary to help Mrs. Garner cope with Luke in her classroom.

"In my experience," Flynn started off, addressing the first point, "when a youngster like Luke is placed in a regular classroom and done so appropriately with the proper intent, that kind of isolation does not — *should* not — occur."

Before he got any further, Flynn executed a sharp detour and brought up a problem he called "labelling".

"We're talking here about classification," Flynn went on in a long, uninterrupted speech. "I often see reference to a 'mentally handicapped child'. Well, once you've assigned that label and made that identification, there's a mind-set established from which some very destructive kinds of thing can follow."

Such as?

"That there are tremendous costs to integrate a child with that label. In my opinion, this is simply not the case."

Flynn thought all the head-shaking over the cost of educating Luke illustrated the pernicious results that come from labelling.

"I've met Luke and I can appreciate that his teacher will require some assistance," Flynn said. "But that assistance can be of a paraprofessional nature that is relatively inexpensive. In fact, that resource is already in the [Halifax County-Bedford] system. It's just a matter of redeployment. It seems to me this youngster can be accommodated quite easily, effectively, and efficiently."

MacDonald, happy as a clam to have a witness who just

took off and flew on his own, asked a few more questions, and for MacDonald, Flynn's testimony did nothing except get better.

"Some resources are needed, no question," Flynn said. "But I think the need diminishes very quickly as soon as the school community begins to feel comfortable with this young person in their school, and that's a matter of a few weeks."

Chief Justice Glube had a question.

"Perhaps, Mr. Flynn," she said, "you could tell me what your view is on the preparation system necessary for bringing a child into an integrated school."

It was like asking Winston Churchill to say a word or two about the Second World War. Would Flynn talk about integration? Are you kidding? This was Flynn's subject. His *obsession*.

For several minutes, with Glube breaking in with an occasional question, Flynn spoke of the role of the principal and the teacher in preparing for integration, the duty of the administrative staff, the atmosphere that should be engendered in the school. "It's critical that when the child first arrives at the school there is a welcoming, inviting kind of attitude." And towards the end of his little forum on integration, speaking specifically of Luke's situation at Atlantic View, Flynn dropped a surprising statistic. Even without advance preparation for Luke, the plain fact that he'd already spent a few weeks in Mrs. Garner's class meant that, in Flynn's experience, "seventy-five to eighty per cent of the task is accomplished."

Peter McLellan had to challenge Flynn on that one.

"Do you mean," he asked, "that if the teacher physically accepts the child in the classroom, seventy-five per cent is *done*?"

"I mean," Flynn said, "that it's true if the teacher is philosophically, pedagogically comfortable and is committed to

177

this child experiencing success."

With the answer, Flynn had, in McLellan's view, dug himself into a hole.

McLellan said to Flynn, "Let me refer you to a statement that Annette Garner made on October 14."

"It is becoming obvious," Mrs. Garner wrote in the statement, "that another teacher, rather than a program assistant, is required for Luke."

McLellan asked Flynn, "Is that statement consistent with your opinion that seventy-five per cent of what Luke could hope to accomplish is now being accomplished?"

"I don't see anything in her statement that says the teacher is not accepting," Flynn said, not at all rattled by the question of Garner's declaration. "The teacher appears to be raising issues related to program, and if I may — a personal opinion — it appears to me that the teacher is making avail to cry for help. I don't in any way think she's saying I don't want him and I can't cope. She's saying I'd like some help."

Flynn stepped down from the stand.

Maureen Elwood was next to testify.

In answer to Blaise MacDonald's questions, she did her usual heart-tugging job of describing the Elwood struggle to give Luke a chance in life and the ways in which Luke's time at Atlantic View had already begun to open up his mind.

"You mentioned," MacDonald said to Maureen, "that Luke's memory ability has improved since he started at Atlantic."

"Yes."

"Could you give some example of a story, a poem, whatever, that Luke has recently memorized?"

"Well," Maureen said, "I can think of one poem in particular that's he's memorized. It's called 'Garbage Delight'."

Glube broke in.

"I don't know the poem," she said to Maureen, interested.

"No?" Maureen said, turning on the stand to face Glube. "I'll show it to you some time. It's really very nice."

"Did he learn it at school?" Glube asked, getting more interested. "It must be something new they're teaching."

MacDonald leaned close to Wayne MacKay and murmured, "Are the channels of communication opening up between those two or *what?*"

Maureen was saying to Glube, "Luke's ability to remember things that are happening in his day is improved very, very much."

MacDonald explored more of Luke's gains with Maureen, and he took care in the questioning to make it clear that Maureen wasn't an utter fanatic about her son's education.

"If you were to feel," MacDonald asked, "that Luke's best interests were not served at any time in the future anywhere he was, what action would you take?"

Maureen answered, "If I ever saw a situation that was causing Luke harm or he wasn't progressing or was having great difficulty, I'd take steps to remedy it."

In Peter McLellan's cross-examination, he threw a few encomiums at Maureen — "tremendous admiration for your dedication" — and sat down. Very wise. No sense monkeying around with a witness who talks like the heroine from a Frank Capra movie.

The two women on the tightrope at the hearing were Inez Collier and Annette Garner, respectively the principal and the Grade 3 teacher at Atlantic View. Peter McLellan had filed affidavits from them in which they sounded less than optimistic about Luke's chances in the school. The Elwood crew, forever partisan, suspected that the School Board had put pressure on the two women to lean on the negative side in the affidavits. Whatever the truth of the suspicion, Collier and Garner did come across as much more sympathetic to Luke in their testimony before Glube. The major difference was that they offered explanations for the problems they might have in dealing with Luke.

Collier, somewhere between laconic and cryptic in many of her answers to questions, left no doubt that, in Luke's case, she was operating on a shoestring. She had access at Atlantic to a resource teacher — a teacher who assists the regular teacher in any classroom in setting up individual learning programs for students who need them — and a speech pathologist, but those two were too busy with other, non-handicapped students to give Luke a hand. And besides, Don Trider told Collier early on not to assign resource help or speech therapy to Luke Elwood.

Why?

"Because," Collier testified, "at the time they felt Luke would only be with us a very short time."

MacDonald jumped all over this lack of planning to help Luke at Atlantic.

"Was it your position," he asked Collier, "that you found it more difficult because no program was in place for Luke?"

"It put me in a difficult position as a principal."

"Where would that program normally come from if it was going to come from anywhere?"

Collier answered, "I would expect it would come through the special services department."

When Annette Garner testified, MacDonald went after the same point about the apparent administrative indifference to Luke and the absence of help for him in the classroom. But, first, he checked out with Garner her views of Luke's status and his progress, if any, at school.

"How do the other children behave towards Luke?" he asked.

"They treat him very much like a younger brother without the sibling rivalry," Garner answered. "They're very willing to help him and make attempts to draw him into every activity in the classroom."

"So in terms of Luke's socialization," MacDonald said, "you're making progress?"

"I don't see his interaction with other children a problem."

MacDonald said, "It's the actual teaching that's causing the problem?"

"I divide it into social and academic," Garner said. "And, yes, it's the academic side that's causing me problems."

MacDonald said, "Did you ever report to your superiors that without assistance and a program you were having difficulty coping with your job?"

"Coping is the wrong word."

"Okay, sorry."

"As a teacher," Garner said, "I like to do the best for every pupil, and I don't feel I'm doing my best for Luke at this given time."

"Assuming," MacDonald said, stepping ever so carefully, "that everything you needed could be supplied to you — a program, resource people — would you have any problem with Luke being in your classroom?"

"No," Garner answered.

Glube had a pre-trial conference on another case scheduled in her chambers at twelve-thirty, and five minutes before that appointment, she adjourned the injunction hearing for an hour.

"What's your feeling?" MacDonald asked Wayne MacKay.

"I think Glube started out leaning to the Board's side," MacKay said. "Now I think she's getting her mind changed."

"It was Maureen."

"Maureen's the star," MacKay said. "But I think Glube liked it when George Flynn talked about expense."

"It's the old City Administrator in her," MacDonald said.

"She loves it when witnesses tell her good things aren't gonna cost much."

At 1:34 p.m., the hearing resumed, and Peter McLellan called Lloyd Gillis to the stand. Gillis's testimony was mainly of the motherhood–apple pie variety. The school administration, he assured Glube, "has been most responsive to the disadvantaged children within the system." Gillis saluted a few other flags, and he made the specific point that, in the administration's opinion, children with special needs could only be taught by teachers with special training and not, by implication, by the Mrs. Garners of the school system.

Yes, McLellan agreed, but what about this testimony of George Flynn's that a concerned teacher without special training could meet seventy-five to eighty per cent of the needs of a child like Luke Elwood?

"I would have to submit," Gillis answered, "that that is very difficult to believe."

MacDonald had no questions for Gillis. And neither did Glube, but she wanted to hear more from an earlier witness.

"Perhaps I could have Mr. Flynn back on the stand," she said.

Glube needed Flynn to clear up a couple of puzzles. The first was the recurring chatter about the seventy-five or eighty per cent. What did it really mean?

Flynn obliged.

"The major hurdle is having the child there in the classroom, present and accepted." he said. "And it seems to me we've accomplished that here in Luke's case. It's a small step now to bring the resources together that are required to provide the youngster with the appropriate program."

"All right," Glube said to Flynn, "you testified earlier that Luke would need a speech pathologist and a paraprofessional. What kind of time are we talking about for a paraprofessional? And what *is* a paraprofessional?"

"Usually a lady," Flynn said. "Someone who's prepared to come to the school. A mom whose children are all in school. Often these people are nurses or former teachers, or sometimes they have no professional training whatsoever but are just willing to come and offer another pair of hands as directed by the principal or the teacher to assist in any way."

Flynn made it sound so easy.

"In our school system in Waterloo," he said, "paraprofessionals are paid by the hour, and it works out to about eight thousand dollars a year, as high as eleven thousand, if they work with lots of different children in class."

Eight thousand bucks? That was a damn sight better than the thirty grand Lloyd Gillis projected.

And what about the amount of time a paraprofessional would need to spend with Luke?

"People on the scene would have to make the judgment," Flynn said. "It might be seventy-five per cent of his time in the beginning, and that would gradually decrease."

Glube looked grateful for the information.

MacDonald whispered to MacKay, "Never paddle downstream."

The two lawyers had cooked up an elaborate plan to bring Luke to court. Rick and Maureen were dead set against the idea. Throughout the whole blasted controversy over Luke's schooling, they'd kept him away from the media and from public scrutiny of other sorts. But MacDonald and MacKay thought it might be essential to let Glube have an in-person look at the boy whose future she was going to affect. They conferred with Gary Hodson, the psychologist, about the best way of presenting Luke to the court, the way that would be least stressful to Luke, and they laid out a scheme full of back alleys and service elevators for smuggling him in and out of the courtroom without reporters getting a peek at him.

183

But, the way things were going with the hearing, Mac-Donald and MacKay were rethinking the plot. Maureen's testimony had impressed Glube. And the combination of testimonies from Flynn, Garber, and Collier laid out the message that, given help from a paraprofessional in the classroom, Garber ought to be able to get through to Luke on his academics. And the cost to the school system would be, relatively speaking, peanuts. With so much breaking in favour of the Elwood case — or so it seemed — MacDonald and MacKay asked themselves whether it was really necessary to bring Luke to court. Hey, why take the risk?

"Never paddle downstream," MacDonald said to MacKay, and they cancelled the elaborate plan.

By twenty minutes after two, the witnesses had been heard from, and it was time for the lawyers to talk law to Glube.

MacDonald and MacKay split the responsibilities for their argument in a ratio of one-third MacDonald, two-thirds MacKay. It was up to them to make the case for continuing the injunction, which would prevent the School Board from returning Luke to the special classes at Astral Drive School. And to accomplish that task, they were required to pass the three-part test.

They had to show that Luke would suffer "irreparable harm" if he were forced to leave Atlantic View.

They had to show that "the balance of convenience" for all parties involved in the matter was weighed in Luke's favour.

And they had to show that they had a good case, "a triable issue" in the language of the courts, to take to trial on Luke's behalf.

This was the test that the law of injunctions prescribed, and to hurdle it, MacDonald and MacKay decided that Mac-Donald would argue the first two parts — "irreparable harm" and "balance of convenience" — and MacKay would speak to Glube about the "triable issue". MacKay's share was more demanding in time and complexity because it would get him into the thickets of the Charter of Rights. Hence, two-thirds for him.

MacDonald went first.

In his inimitable style, just a touch on the pugnacious side, he sketched the events of the previous six weeks that had worked against Luke. The September 4 case conference convened by Don Trider. The one-sided School Board meetings. And everything else that effectively excluded the Elwoods from decisions about their son. But, MacDonald said, through all of this administrative disorder, Luke has hung on at Atlantic. What's more impressive, MacDonald continued, according to testimony in court, especially from Maureen Elwood, Luke is beginning to thrive. What is even more impressive, according to testimony from others, from Flynn and Garber, the odds are awfully favourable that, with a little help from friendly hands, he'll discover even brighter days ahead.

So, irreparable harm?

If Luke is removed from Atlantic View at this stage, MacDonald argued, "he's denied the opportunity to grow, and he would fall farther and farther behind his peers."

And, balance of convenience?

Who, MacDonald asked, is being inconvenienced?

Not the other kids in Luke's class. Their parents swear in affidavits that the kids are profiting from having Luke in their midst.

Not Mrs. Garner. She testified that, given a resource person and a little programming, she could teach Luke his academics.

And, for sure, not the Board. The cost to it in accommodating Luke at Atlantic is no formidable barrier, and, anyway, if the case comes to trial and the Board wins, the Elwood side will be obliged to compensate the Board for everything it's out of pocket in taking Luke into Atlantic.

That leaves the balance of convenience in Luke's favour.

Part didactic lecturer, part honeyed counsel — that was how Wayne MacKay put across his argument. And there was inevitably the faint sound of laughter in his voice.

MacKay also played the honest diplomat by reassuring Glube on two scores.

One was that the Elwood team didn't presume to hold a monopoly on virtue. "We've never really questioned the bona fides or good intentions of the School Board," MacKay said. "Both sides clearly have Luke's best interests at heart. It's a question of means, not motives or objectives. I think we have the same objective. We're debating the means."

And the other was that the Elwood intention wasn't to condemn the entire system of special-education classes for disabled children. "We've never taken the position that nothing good happens in special education," MacKay told Glube. "Lots of good things happen in special education. And there are many good special-education teachers, one of them being my wife." Special education wasn't wrong *per se*. It just wasn't the answer in this one instance for this one boy, Luke Elwood.

By making the two points, MacKay thought he'd created a comfort zone for Glube. Nothing screamingly radical is going on here, he was saying, nothing that's going to bring the school system tumbling down. Let's just keep our sights on Luke, and let's see if, down the line, there is a "triable issue", a case to be made in a courtroom on behalf of Luke to upset the School Board's ruling on October 15 that ordered him back to Astral Drive.

In arguing the triable-issue factor, MacKay wasn't required to show that, at the future trial, Luke would have a sure winner of a case. The burden wasn't that high. MacKay needed only to demonstrate that there was a case with a little meat on it to take to court, that there was a genuine issue for a judge to make a decision on. If MacKay could satisfy Glube that such a case existed, she could continue the injunction and leave Luke at Atlantic until the trial was held.

MacKay had two areas of argument to back up his contentions in favour of the triable issue.

The first was rooted in good old-fashioned basic administrative law, the stuff of the second-year course at law school, and the theme that MacKay pounded was unfairness. In arriving at its decision on Luke, he said, the School Board had violated several maxims of proper and decent conduct that the law requires of administrative tribunals.

"I am well aware," MacKay told Glube, "that the kind of procedure appropriate for a School Board is not a full-blown court procedure with lawyers and judges. But I am saying that even in relation to the standard rules of fairness, those rules have been breached."

MacKay had a little list of breaches. There was the huge disproportion between the time allowed to Maureen before the Board and the time given to the staff people. There was the failure to let Maureen question Gillis, Trider, and John Caldwell. And there was the "unusual activity" of the chairman, Lorne Verabioff, leaving his chair to make submissions and cast a vote.

"Pretty unreasonable," MacKay said, "pretty restrictive." Indeed, he went on, the conduct at the meetings was so unfair that it would be open to a judge at trial to upset the Board's October 15 vote.

MacKay's second area of argument got him into the thick of the Charter of Rights, and he went at it with a half-apology on his lips.

"The Charter is often seen as an obstacle to sensible common-sense solutions," he said to Glube. "I certainly don't see it that way. I suggest the Charter should be seen as a vehicle to preserve the best interests of Luke."

MacKay had a reason for his caution. He was aware of a recent study that showed the Nova Scotia Supreme Court tied with one other province's court as having judges who were, among the Canadian judiciary, most resistant to Charter arguments. MacKay didn't think Glube was remotely anti-Charter, but he elected to stick in his tiny note of restraint.

Then he let fly.

First, section seven of the Charter. It's the section that guarantees life, liberty, and security, and the right not to be deprived of them except in accordance with the principles of fundamental justice.

"I would say this," MacKay said. "Life, certainly liberty and security, encompasses the right to be educated and the right to be educated with equality."

Second, section fifteen, the one that guarantees, among other rights, freedom of association.

That, MacKay said, "gets us into the question of freedom of mandatory association with other disabled students as opposed to freedom to associate with either disabled or non-disabled students."

Where did Luke fit into all these guarantees in the Charter?

MacKay made a series of skilful links for Glube. He went back over the testimony and the affidavits — mainly George Flynn's, some of Maureen's — which indicated that once a kid gets hit with the disabled label, as Luke had, things happen to him and his education that are out of his control. He is segregated into something called a special class. And this segregation, MacKay argued, constitutes a violation of the equality guarantee in the Charter. He doesn't go to school with the other kids in his own neighbourhood. And this separation, MacKay argued again, represents a violation of the Charter's guarantee of freedom of association.

Luke, MacKay went on, is being discriminated against. Nobody *means* to discriminate against him, not the School Board or anyone else. But intention doesn't matter. It's a *fact* that, through segregation and separation, Luke isn't being treated with equality. He's being discriminated against

188

because he happens to be mentally disabled. And — it's right there in the Charter of Rights — discrimination based on mental disability is forbidden.

If there isn't a triable issue in all of this, a good case for arguing on Charter grounds that the School Board's decision should be upset, then, MacKay said, though not in so many words, I'll eat my hat.

For the School Board, Peter McLellan raised what lawyers call the "slippery slope" argument.

It's the argument that asks the question, how far are we going to go? Are we going to skid down the slope? Who will make the final decisions about the education of children? A school board that's elected and appointed to make such decisions? Or the parents? And if the parents get into the act, where will it all end? Will parents be able to say they don't want their kids to take mathematics or English literature? And make it stick? Where *will* it all end? Isn't this a terribly slippery slope?

McLellan had an impeccable courtroom manner. He gave his arguments a seamless flow, and nobody had the least difficulty following his presentation to Glube.

"Does a parent of a child handicapped or requiring special needs," McLellan said, "have the right to decide not only what school but what class the child should attend? That's ultimately the issue the court is being called upon to decide. Do the parents have a right to set the school curriculum? Establish the format? That, to me, is something unheard of."

McLellan saw chaos ahead, and he argued it was ridiculous even to imagine that a court should have to consider such an issue as which school Luke was to attend. McLellan asked whether in Luke's case "the court is positioned to make an assessment of this child." His answer was a resounding no. In fact, McLellan said, there's only one group, out of all the bunch who've had their say at the hearing, that is qualified to decide how and where Luke should be educated.

The School Board.

"Nobody," McLellan said, "has done an assessment of this child except the School Board."

He expanded on the theme.

"There are a number of people from the School Board who have worked with Luke Elwood," he said. "There's his teacher, his principal, his psychologist [all from Astral Drive School], a multitude of others in the system who have worked with Luke. Should their assessment that he remain at Astral Drive be disregarded in favour of the wishes of the parents?"

To McLellan, it was a match-up of "assessment" versus "wishes", and in that contest, assessment should come out on top.

McLellan hopscotched over a few other points. Administrative unfairness on the part of the School Board? Nothing of the sort. In the Board's meetings, McLellan said, "we have seen democracy in action." Violation of Luke's rights? "The Board," McLellan said, "was bending over backwards to ensure that controversy was avoided and to attempt to have a solution worked out by consent."

But the bedrock argument for McLellan was that there was no reason in law or common sense for Glube to continue the injunction, for a trial to be held, or for anyone to contemplate interference with the Board's handling of Luke Elwood. The Board, thanks to its assessment, knew best.

"To grant an injunction," he said to Glube, "is to disregard an assessment program without proof of malice, without proof of procedural deficiencies, without proof of any new assessments which show the Board's assessment was wrong."

In a short reply to McLellan's argument, Wayne MacKay thought he could put to rest the horrors of the slippery slope.

"In this case," he told Glube, "both litigants have tried to focus on the best interests of Luke and not on a dispute between parents and School Board. So, whatever solution is decided in the future trial to be in Luke's best interests is not going to open the floodgates to unrealistic demands on the part of parents. It would do Luke an injustice to pitch this affair as strictly a parents-versus-school-board debate."

At six minutes after four, Glube said to the lawyers, "Perhaps I'll take a few minutes and see if I feel I can present my views adequately at this time or if I need more time to develop them."

"The lady's full of surprises," MacDonald said to MacKay when Glube left the courtroom.

"This is unexpected," MacKay said. "I thought sure she'd reserve judgment."

"Sounds like she might be right back with an answer."

In the courtroom seats, the natives were restless. The trio of Smith, Brown, and Powroz sat in on the hearing with Rick and Maureen. So did a handful of Elwood neighbours and plenty of media, and across the back of the room a couple of rows were filled with young people. They were students from MacKay's education-law seminar at Dalhousie. The seminar was scheduled to meet that afternoon, but, since the professor couldn't go to the class, the class came to the professor. And everyone was getting jittery at the prospect of Glube's decision.

She returned to the courtroom exactly twenty minutes after she left, and she had a gripe.

"In the court's view," she said, "in spite of the fact that there is clearly no evidence before me of any other motive than to try to do what is best for Luke, I find it unfortunate

191

that matters were not dealt with in advance of any move of the child."

In other words, Glube was complaining, why didn't you people get yourselves organized on programming and para-professionals and the rest of the plan for helping this boy before you shuffled him from one school to another?

"I'm not placing any blame," Glube said. "I'm just saying it's unfortunate."

That rap on the knuckles administered, Glube dropped her decision on the waiting courtroom.

"I am not lifting the injunction," she said suddenly.

Luke had won.

He'd stay at Atlantic until the trial.

Glube, speaking from no notes, off the cuff, didn't offer elaborate reasons for her decision. She kept things short and snappy.

"I accept the evidence that there could be irreparable harm to Luke," she said. "And in my opinion, the balance of convenience goes in Luke's favour."

She said that MacDonald and MacKay had satisfied her that there was a triable case, something to take to trial, but she issued a warning.

"This injunction application doesn't decide the issues involved," she said. "If the parties work things out, that's fine. But if the matter goes to trial, the parents must recognize the possible detrimental effects which could result if the court dismisses the action. That would mean Luke would go to another school setting."

Glube urged everybody — the lawyers, the School Board, the Elwoods — to get two jobs done in a hurry. Set a date for the trial and arrange a program of assistance for Luke in Annette Garner's classroom.

"Okay?" Glube said. "Thank you."

She left the courtroom at twenty minutes to five.

The gang — Rick and Maureen, MacDonald and MacKay, Susan Coen, Smith, Brown, and Powroz, a few others — whooped it up in restrained style at a pub in Historic Properties, a small shopping complex next to the Courthouse. They drank draft beer and watched television reports of the victory in the Chief Justice's courtroom. But Rick and Maureen couldn't hang around long for the celebration. They had to drive home for another party.

That day, October 29, was Luke's ninth birthday.

The first open date on the Nova Scotia Supreme Court's calendar for the trial of *Luke Elwood v. The Halifax County–Bedford District School Board* wasn't until the week of Monday, June 1, 1987.

"No problem," Blaise MacDonald said. "That means Luke'll have a whole year of integration, and we can go to court and show the judge how great the boy's doing."

At Atlantic View, the ministrations of the resource people began about a month after Chief Justice Glube's decision. A speech therapist named Lynn Healy arrived first in Annette Garner's classroom. She worked a few hours each week with Luke — and with six other kids in the class who happened to need her services — on articulation and pronunciation and the rules of clear and proper speech. By mid-December, a paraprofessional named Bruce Nunn was coming to the class for parts of two or three days a week to lead Luke in little projects. He was replaced in March 1987 by another paraprofessional named Shannon LeBlanc, who had more experience working with disabled kids. Other experts of various sorts — a psychologist, a couple of assistants who were running liaison with Don Trider and Judy Harrity — popped in and out of the classroom at odd and unscheduled moments.

How did Annette Garner react to all of this help?

"It was quite a strain," she said.

The thing was that, with and without assistance, Garner and Luke found their own level of co-operation and progress and growth.

Small inspirations helped.

Garner decorated a tape-recorder in a way that enticed Luke into playing the tapes of music and poetry that were his favourites.

She set up a water tank where Luke could manipulate containers that floated or sank depending on the amount of sand he measured into them.

And she taught him to group different-coloured crayons — though Luke hadn't mastered the names of his colours — in separate boxes for reds and blues and greens and yellows.

Slowly, methodically, Luke made his way into the rhythms of the classroom. He began to respond to the stories that Garner read to the kids. He learned to cut and paste. And he played the drum in a class play about Indians.

And there were larger, more encouraging episodes.

"We had a theme going in class on dinosaurs and Indians," Garner said in the late spring of 1987. "They happened to be going side by side. Luke did a project on dinosaurs, and it was nicely done. His dad helped him, and Luke presented it in class. Still, I didn't know how much understanding there was in it for him. But one day, I said, 'Luke, we're going to do a film-strip,' and he said to me, 'Is it about dinosaurs and Indians?' Now, that showed me, since it was completely uncued, that he had some understanding of what we had been doing. The information had been absorbed."

Wayne MacKay says, "One way of putting it is that, in those months, April, May, leading up to the date for trial on June 1, we conducted a royal commission on education in the Halifax County–Bedford School District."

To prepare for the trial, MacDonald and MacKay were

exhaustive. They held examinations for discovery of nineteen witnesses. They examined child psychologists, experts in special education from across Canada and the United States, and almost every school principal, teacher, and official who ever came in contact with Luke, including Chairman of the Board Lorne Verabioff. MacDonald and MacKay were building a case that would persuade a judge to overturn the School Board's decision returning Luke to Astral Drive School, and they overlooked no persuasive possibility. They brought in Dulcie McCallum for advice. She was a lawyer with the national office of the Canadian Association for the Mentally Retarded, and, apart from knowing the ropes in litigation on behalf of disabled people, she was a tough cookie. "She looks like a mature Anne of Green Gables," MacDonald says. "But she eats fire." And, getting really creative, MacDonald and MacKay hired a CBC cameraman to shoot a forty-minute video of A Day in the Life of Luke Elwood.

"I'd describe it as a home movie," MacKay says. "Nothing fancy, but it would give the judge a good idea of who we were talking about."

It cost big money, the video and the discoveries and the importation of experts and the hundreds of hours of lawyers' time. MacDonald and MacKay practically donated their services, and the out-of-pocket expenses were paid by the CAMR. But money was a constant pain in the neck.

"When you crusade with the Charter," MacKay says, "the system works against you. The School Board didn't need to hire experts because they had them in-house. They could call on psychologists and professionals in special education who were already paid members of their staff. But we had to dole out money to bring experts to town and get their expertise."

For the School Board, Peter McLellan conducted no more than a handful of discoveries. He examined Luke's psychologist, Gary Hodson, and he examined an officer from the

CAMR. He questioned Rick Elwood for fifteen minutes. And he grilled Maureen for a day and a half.

"He asked me a lot of repetitive questions," Maureen says. "I think he was hoping I'd contradict myself."

She looks at Rick.

"You didn't," he says.

Of all the discoveries on both sides, on McLellan's and on the MacDonald-MacKay side, the set of answers that went the longest way in putting Luke and his education in perspective came, once again, from Annette Garner.

Wayne MacKay examined Garner on May 23, and, gently, sympathetically, he led her through the catalogue of Luke's achievements during the school year. The trick with the tape-recorder. The drummer's role in the class play. And the project with the dinosaurs and Indians. But what was most vivid about the discovery was the way in which MacKay, the empathetic questioner, got Garner to contrast her reaction to Luke in his first weeks in her class with her feelings about him in the spring of 1987.

"I was expecting more than he could give me," Garner said when MacKay asked about her early problems with Luke. "I was expecting some independence, and there wasn't any. I hadn't given him any strategies to use in independent play, and I didn't realize he didn't have any. My expectations were wrong."

"In your reports in September on Luke," MacKay said, "you were to some extent negative."

"I was really full of frustration," Garner said.

"This is not the picture you see today?"

"No, no," Garner answered. "It took Luke a while to orient himself to the school. That was what the big problem was. I didn't appreciate how difficult it was going to be for him. I wasn't used to children with his needs, and my expectations were really too high."

"Would it be fair to say you're more comfortable with him at this point than you were in September?" MacKay asked.

"And you're teaching Luke in a way that's meaningful to you and to him?"

"I think what I'm doing is right for him," Garner answered cautiously. "I'm just trying to encourage him to gain the most from the atmosphere he's in."

"Are you more positive about his academic progress?"

"There's more verbal communication, which means his vocabulary has increased somewhat," Garner said. "He's learned to ask for something specifically. Instead of 'Help me,' it's 'Help me with my sandwich.' He doesn't seem to ask 'What? What? What?' so often. And his tolerance level of discussion and sitting with the group is much longer now, either because he understands more or he enjoys it more. We still do a lot of heavy cuing. Like, when we ask him to read back the story, we've learned to take it from a much lower level."

MacKay got out a report that Gary Hodson had written in the fall of 1986 and quoted a line. Integration for Luke, Hodson wrote, would help him in "developing his potential for occasional employment and independent living."

MacKay asked Garner, "In relation to the admittedly negative comments that came out of those early school reports, would you be more positive now about Luke meeting his needs in the integrated Atlantic View?"

"Can I say his needs as a nine-year-old?" Garner asked back.

"Yes."

"Okay," Garner said. "I think we've met some of his needs as a nine-year-old in the integrated system at Atlantic View."

MacKay said, "I guess I'm curious why you say it that way."

"Well," Garner said, "I don't like this business about 'developing his potential for occasional employment and independent living'."

"Your crystal ball is not that accurate?"

"No," Garner said, solid and no-nonsense. "I believe we've

197

helped Luke this year, whether more or less than in any other situation, who can tell?"

MacKay thought Garner had told it as exactly as anyone.

On April 29, Rick and Maureen sat down to a meeting in Lloyd Gillis's office. Out of the blue, Gillis had invited the Elwoods to drop around. He wanted to talk, just the three of them.

"I've got some possibilities I'd like you to think about," Gillis said.

Rick said, "We'll always listen to anything that'll help Luke."

"This is just a suggestion," Gillis said. "What about, as an alternative to the present situation, we send Luke part-time to Atlantic and the rest of the time to Astral Drive? That way, you follow me, he'd have the benefit of the special-education teachers over at Astral and still be mixing with his peers at Atlantic."

"I'm not sure," Maureen said. "Luke's settled with Mrs. Garner and I'd hate to break up his day."

"Well, let's not rule out anything," Gillis said.

"You have other ideas?" Rick asked.

"Perhaps it would be to Luke's best advantage in the long run," Gillis said, "if he finished out at Atlantic."

"You mean to the end of Grade 4 next year?" Rick said.

"Exactly," Gillis said. "And then he could move to the special-education classes for older children at Ross Road."

"Oh my goodness," Maureen said. "We've done so much to get him *out* of special education, I couldn't agree to the idea of sending him back into it."

"Just suggestions," Gillis said. "Keep them in the back of your mind."

When Rick reported the conversation with Gillis to Blaise

MacDonald, MacDonald said, "By jeez, they're starting to think settlement."

So they were, and for the next four weeks, through May, MacDonald and MacKay made like jugglers.

"With the right hand, we were preparing full steam for trial," MacKay says. "With the left, we were negotiating toward a settlement before trial."

Lloyd Gillis was the key player on the other side. He understood more about the school system than anyone else elected, appointed, or hired at Halifax County–Bedford. He knew how the system worked, what it cost, and how it could make room for Luke Elwood. If Gillis wanted a settlement of the Elwood case, the School Board would undoubtedly agree. More than that, if Gillis recommended a specific settlement, the Board would approve. Gillis was the man who had to be sold, and the way MacDonald correctly assessed the situation, he was now in a buying mood.

Why?

"Probably a number of reasons," MacKay says. "I don't think he liked the *idea* of litigation. He didn't want to put his Board into a public fight with the expense and mess. But perhaps most of all, the word must have been filtering through that Luke was coming along so nicely, and after all, everyone's aim, ours and the Board's, was to do what was best for Luke."

The paper flew by messenger and mail between Mac-Donald's office and Peter McLellan's. Memos. Draft agreements. Letters of amplification. MacDonald and MacKay knew how much they wanted for Luke. They wanted the moon. They wanted a guarantee that Luke would proceed through the entire regular school system in Halifax County–Bedford. But would Lloyd Gillis and Peter McLellan go for the whole bundle?

The negotiations ticked down to Friday, May 29, one short weekend to the trial date.

"On that Friday," MacKay says, "I thought it was ninety-per-cent certain we'd settle. But it was awfully tight."

It was so tight that the Elwood team went ahead with two last examinations for discovery they'd arranged for the Friday. Everyone was scrambling. MacDonald was fresh back in the office from a trial in Cape Breton. Dulcie McCallum, the national CAMR lawyer, flew in for the last hard negotiating strokes. Rick Elwood was stuck at home with two young patients: Luke had an infection, and Melissa had been laid low in a baseball game when another kid accidentally smacked her with a bat. And Maureen was in MacDonald's office on a conference call with MacDonald and Dulcie McCallum joining her at one end and Peter McLellan and Lloyd Gillis on the other end.

Settlement was inching closer.

A draft agreement travelled late Friday morning from MacDonald's office to McLellan's. Then back to MacDonald's. Another trip to McLellan's. At each stop, the lawyers applied small amendments. The document made two more shuffles between offices for fine-tuning, and late in the afternoon, after another round trip, they had a settlement.

It consisted of two separate documents. One was two pages long, the other seven pages, and they contained preambles and definitions and qualifications and projections of future possibilities that ran to exquisite detail. But the essential paragraphs of the settlement said this: Luke would finish with his classmates to the end of Grade 4 at Atlantic View and he would move, just like the rest of the kids in his neighbourhood, to Ross Road School for Grades 5 through 9 — not special-education classes but regular, normal, ordinary classes — all the way to graduation from junior high school.

Luke had the moon.

There was a hitch.

The School Board, which approved the settlement on Friday night, refused to pay costs to the Elwood side. In theory, the Elwoods "won" the case. They were suing to keep Luke at Atlantic View in defiance of the Board order sending him back to Astral Drive, and they succeeded. They could make a good argument for demanding that the Board, the "losing" side, pay the hefty legal bill they'd run up. But the Board dug in its heels. It wouldn't pay the Elwood bill, and it insisted that the subject of costs not be mentioned in the settlement or in court.

Over the weekend, the Elwood crew aired out its anger. The settlement hadn't been signed, and it wouldn't be signed, sealed, and delivered until Monday, when all parties appeared before the Supreme Court Justice who was scheduled to hear the trial. Since the case had been docketed for trial and since one of the litigants was an infant, the judge was required to put a formal stamp of approval on the settlement. But the people on the Board side made a two-part stipulation about the settlement and the appearance before the judge: both sides would be responsible for their own costs, and neither side would whisper a word about this unwritten arrangement to the judge. And that double whammy had the Elwood gang up in arms.

"This refusal to pay costs, it's the same tactic the big corporations use when they go around breaking all the pollution laws," Blaise MacDonald said at a meeting in his office. "What happens, environmental groups bring an action against the bloody polluter, and the corporation resists right down to the last minute before trial's gonna start. Then it agrees to cut back on polluting and signs an agreement. But it says to the environmentalists, hang on, you fellas, we're not paying costs. Well, the environmental people have fought so long and they don't want to take a chance of losing in court. So what do they do? No choice, they swallow their costs. It's a really criminal situation."

MacKay had to agree that MacDonald's comparison struck close to the mark.

"The Board's saying to us," he said, "you can have your *cause célèbre*, but you have to pay for it."

"Thing about those people," MacDonald said, "they don't differentiate between General Motors and a disabled child. It's just whoever's on the other side."

"We have to be balanced about this," MacKay said. "Suppose we went to trial and won, the best result we could hope for is probably one more year of integration for Luke."

"But the settlement leaves him in the system till he's ready for senior high."

"Say we ask the judge to award us costs," MacKay said. "The whole agreement might come unravelled."

"If there's one chance in a million of disturbing the settlement," MacDonald said, "it's no use risking the one chance."

"I think the sensible course is to go along with the Board."

"But I'm itching to fight."

"I could hardly tell."

At nine-thirty on Monday morning, nine people trooped into Mr. Justice Mac Rogers's chambers in the Halifax Courthouse.

For the Elwoods: Rick and Maureen, MacKay and MacDonald, Susan Coen and Dulcie McCallum.

For the School Board: Peter McLellan, Lloyd Gillis, and another lawyer from McLellan's office.

"I'm delighted at the result of this settlement," Mr. Justice Rogers began. "Delighted for Luke Elwood. For myself, I'm a little disappointed. I was looking forward to a good Charter case in my court."

Mac Rogers was in his late fifties, down to earth, a man who put everyone, even the Elwoods, right at home in his chambers. He was outdoorsy, a fervent environmentalist, and after the Elwood case he was hopping a plane for the

Queen Charlotte Islands. Had to see what was happening to the forests out there.

"Mr. MacKay," Rogers said, "if you've got anything more on this subject, writings of yours on education and the Charter I mean, I'd appreciate if you'd drop them off for me. Just in the event, you know, another case like this comes along."

"I'd be glad to, my lord," MacKay said.

MacKay was feeling embarrassed. On Friday, the lawyers had agreed they'd wear their gowns to Rogers's chambers. But some time between Friday and Monday morning, Mac-Donald and McLellan decided to forget about the gowns, and MacDonald didn't relay the word to MacKay. He showed up in his gown, vest, and tabs. When he saw the other two lawyers in civvies, he took off the gown and tabs. He looked half dressed in his white shirt and vest.

"I must apologize for my appearance this morning, my lord," he said to Rogers.

Rogers waved him off.

"No need for a lot of ceremony in here, Mr. MacKay," he said.

All was sweetness and light as MacDonald, McLellan, and MacKay took Rogers through the settlement, clause by clause.

Rogers nodded.

"I congratulate the School Board," he said to McLellan and Lloyd Gillis. "Very enlightened."

Smiles all round.

It was close to ten o'clock, and the meeting seemed to be running smoothly toward a calm, natural, and satisfying resolution.

Which was when Blaise MacDonald chose to give the tranquillity a good smashing.

"You'll notice, my lord," he said, "there's nothing said in the settlement about costs."

That ended the unwritten agreement not to mention money to Rogers.

"It was a frozen moment," MacKay remembers.

MacDonald pushed on with the explanation that each side was expected to look after its own costs.

Peter McLellan stared daggers at MacDonald.

"I give Peter a great deal of credit," MacKay says. "He didn't say a word in chambers about not bringing up the subject in front of the judge. Later, though, he wrote a sharp letter to Blaise and me."

"We're not asking for costs, my lord," MacDonald plunged on. "We're just directing your attention to the subject."

"Do I have jurisdiction with respect to costs?" Rogers asked.

MacKay rallied behind MacDonald.

"Probably not under normal circumstances, my lord," he said. "But the case is perhaps exceptional in two aspects. One is that it concerns an infant, and the other is that it's a Charter case. Those two factors might provide grounds for you to take jurisdiction."

Rogers needed a few seconds to think over MacKay's point.

"I think I'm bound by the agreement you gentlemen have made," he said finally. "I might have my own reservations about what you've done on the costs question. But that's as far as it goes if all of you are agreed to the settlement in front of us."

"Oh, sure," MacDonald said quickly. "We're agreed, my lord."

"Agreed, my lord," McLellan said.

"Well, that's the end of it," Rogers said.

The lawyers whipped out copies of the settlement.

Lloyd Gillis signed for the School Board.

Rick and Maureen signed twice, once for themselves and once for Luke.

The deal was done.

Rick and Maureen took a room that night at the Château Halifax. Neighbours came over from Upper Lawrencetown to celebrate. Margie Brown was there and Debby Smith, the gang from Blaise MacDonald's law firm, and people from CAMR. Blaise brought his VCR machine from home, and everybody watched reruns of the earlier newscasts that a neighbour had taped, the newscasts that showed the press conference in the courthouse after everyone left Mac Rogers's chambers. There were a few drinks in the room at the Château Halifax, a lot of talk that lasted late into the night, a tear or so, many laughs, the sounds of joy and relief.

And somewhere in the evening, fairly early on, Wayne MacKay went on the CBC radio program *As It Happens* and tried to explain the significance of what had happened that day.

"I think you could compare the Elwood case, even though it didn't come to trial, to *Brown v. Board of Education* in the United States," he said. "That was the 1954 case that first called for desegregation of the American schools. Maybe the Elwood case is the *Brown v. Board of Education* for the disabled in Canada. The settlement we worked out, with a Nova Scotia Supreme Court Justice's approval to give it judicial force, says that any disabled child in Canada doesn't have to be taken out of his own neighbourhood to get his education in a segregated class for special children. It says that the child's parents can say to their school board, look, we want our child to go to the local school with his friends and peers. And they can get what they want."

On the night of Saturday, November 14, 1987, the Canadian Association for Community Living — formerly the Canadian Association for the Mentally Retarded — held its annual national banquet at the Sheraton Hotel in Halifax. A couple of hundred delegates and guests sat down to dinner in the hotel's main ballroom. They ate and drank and greeted friends from across the country. They listened, to speeches, and paid tribute to their hard-working leaders, and towards the end of the evening, they grew especially quiet when the CACL president, Gordon Porter, announced the inauguration of a new prize. It was called the President's Award, Porter said, and it would be presented by the CACL each year to those people or groups who had contributed most significantly to the rights of the disabled in Canada. In this year, 1987, the first year of the President's Award, it would have two recipients, and Porter asked them to come forward.

The first recipient was Gordon Fairweather, the distinguished Canadian who had for years fought for the disabled as head of the Canadian Human Rights Commission.

The second recipient was a family. The Elwood family. All four of them, Rick and Maureen, Melissa and Luke.

The Elwoods walked through a standing ovation to the head table. Gordon Porter handed them the award — a plaque framed in brass with black-and-gold scroll-work — and shook everyone's hand. Maureen spoke a few words of thanks into the microphone. The crowd in the ballroom applauded, and cameramen shot pictures of the family. It was the first time, from the very beginning of the fight fifteen months earlier, that Rick and Maureen had permitted the newspaper and TV people to photograph their son.

Luke looked great.

DOUG PALMER AND THE GREAT POLYNESIAN LOUNGE DRUG CONSPIRACY

Doug Palmer made the mistake of his life when he decided to trust Fred Ford. His excuse, though Doug Palmer wasn't the kind of guy who dealt in excuses, was that he'd known Ford for almost twenty years. He'd gone to Hastings Public School in the East End of Vancouver with Ford's older brother Billy. Palmer had been a bright student. His IQ was close to 150, and the kids he ran with in the East End, including Fred Ford, recognized he had plenty of street smarts. But he was too restless for school and dropped out after Grade 8 at Templeton Junior High. He got jobs on the tugboats in Vancouver harbour. He drove a cab, worked in a cannery, tended bar at the Waldorf Hotel on Hastings Street close to the line between downtown Vancouver and the East End. And he ran his own small trucking outfit from an office at 22nd Street and Renfrew, an intersection that was several blocks deeper into the East End from the Waldorf.

Beginning in the late 1960s and lasting until he stood trial in the winter of 1976, Doug Palmer put his brains and talents into another activity — the heroin business. Palmer masterminded the most lucrative heroin ring on the west coast, an enterprise that employed at least a dozen men and turned over annual profits in the millions of dollars. It wasn't until Palmer hired his old pal Fred Ford that the heroin business was fixed on a path that led to its collapse and Palmer's own downfall.

Ford dropped around to Doug Palmer's trucking offices at 22nd and Renfrew in June of 1971 and asked for a job. He didn't mean a job in the trucking company. He was talking about the heroin trade. Ford knew about Palmer's drug operation. Every rounder in the East End knew that Doug Palmer was *the* big shot in heroin. Palmer laughed at Ford. Maybe he laughed because he thought Ford was a loser. Ford had done time twice, first in the British Columbia Penitentiary in New Westminster for wounding with intent and again in the Saskatchewan Penitentiary at Prince Albert for theft. Out on the street, he turned a dollar by selling penny-ante amounts of drugs and by doing break-and-enters. Doug Palmer had no criminal record — no arrests, no convictions apart from a simple driving offence. For reasons he was never to explain to anyone, Palmer said he'd think over Ford's request and get back to him in a few weeks.

Palmer was as good as his word. One night in mid-July he summoned Ford to a meeting in the bar at the Waldorf Hotel. The two had a couple of drinks. Ford, a short, squat, sour-faced man, was twitchy and talkative. He needed the job. Palmer was his customary cool self. He wasn't a big man, about five-seven and 145 pounds, but he gave off a heavy charge of authority. It was in the eyes. Doug Palmer could lock his gaze on a man's face and hold it, unblinking, until he stripped the man of his nerves and defences. A lawyer who later acted for one of Palmer's co-accused at the 1976 trial said of Palmer, "He was the only drug trafficker I ever met who wasn't a cry-baby or a wimp." At the Waldorf Hotel, after the second drink, Palmer told Ford to come out to his car. He was going to give Ford a lesson in the major-league heroin trade.

Palmer drove about twenty blocks east of the Waldorf and another dozen blocks south to the edge of Rupert Park. He stopped the car, a yellow Charger, and instructed Ford to wait. Ford watched Palmer walk into the gloom of the park toward the pitch-and-putt golf course. Two men were waiting for Palmer. One held a briefcase. He handed it to Palmer, and Palmer returned to the car.

"This here's what it's all about," Palmer said to Ford.

He snapped open the briefcase. Inside were eight small glass coffee jars. Each jar held several condoms. Each condom was stuffed with gelatin capsules. The capsules were filled with white powder. The powder was heroin.

"Works out to five ounces of heroin in every one of them jars," Palmer said. "Forty ounces in the briefcase."

He started the Charger and drove further south on Rupert to an alley that ran behind a row of stores. Palmer led the way out of the car and into the darkened alley. He was carrying the briefcase. In the other hand he had a shovel that he'd taken from the back of the car. Several yards up the alley, he stopped beside a telephone pole and lifted one of the jars from the briefcase.

Palmer said to Ford, "The thing happening now, we're gonna bury the jar."

"What're you talking about?" Ford said.

"Start digging."

Ford shovelled a small hole beside the telephone pole. Palmer placed the jar at the bottom of the hole, and Ford covered the jar with dirt. He patted the ground until it was level and solid.

"This is what you're gonna be doing regular," Palmer said to Ford.

"Digging holes in the ground?"

"Your job," Palmer said, "it's called the back-end man."

"I don't get it."

Back in the car, Palmer enlightened Ford. The heroin, Palmer explained, arrived in Vancouver, usually from Montreal, in bulk form. It had to be capped up for retail sale on the street. Capping up was an intricate, time-consuming process. First, the heroin was reduced in strength by adding lactose; the strength reduction, or "cutting", meant more product for sale and more profits down the line. Next, the cut heroin was weighed in one-ounce portions, and the ounces were subdivided into empty gelatin capsules. The caps of heroin, which sold for fifteen dollars apiece on the street, were stuffed inside condoms in numbers of twenty-five or fifty per condom, and the condoms were packed into jars that held the heroin in even amounts, one ounce or two ounces up to a usual maximum of five ounces.

"We got different people all over take care of the capping up," Palmer said. "Maybe in a motel room, somebody's house, keep moving around like that."

"Yeah, that part I understand," Ford said. "What about the holes in the ground?"

"Reason for them," Palmer said, "is when you sell the stuff to a guy, to the addict, some other dealer, whoever, you don't actually hand over the heroin to the guy."

"Why not?"

"You crazy?" Palmer said. "Narc comes along, he nails you with the stuff in your pocket."

"So, look, the addict or dealer or somebody pays you," Ford said. "What's he get for his money?"

"A map."

"Of what?"

"Of where the jar of heroin's buried."

"I'm starting to get it."

Palmer told Ford that, as the back-end man, he would be kept in a regular supply of heroin that was capped up and stored in jars. Ford would hold on to the drugs until he received instructions to make a bury. He'd be told the amount to put in the ground, but the location was up to him. Wherever he chose to bury the drugs, he had to make a map or write out a careful description of the spot. He'd deliver the map or description to Palmer or one of his associates, who would arrange to pass it on to the paying customer.

210

"Other thing," Palmer said. "When you write the information down, the map or whatever, use cigarette paper."

"How come cigarette paper?"

"Suppose a cop's watching you," Palmer said. "It isn't gonna happen, but suppose a Mountie gets on your case. All you do's swallow the cigarette paper. Goes down real easy. The cop's got nothing and you're the only one knows where the stuff's in the ground."

There were more fine touches calculated to guarantee security.

"I phone you up to go out and put jars in the ground," Palmer said. "I'm not gonna say on the phone, like, 'Bury five ounces.'"

"In case somebody's listening," Ford said. "Line's tapped or something."

"I'll give you a licence-plate number."

"Like a code."

"If I say SJ7945," Palmer said, "that means you bury a five-ouncer."

"Last number's what I bury."

"Right," Palmer said. "Maybe I'll say SJ76422. That means you bury two two-ouncers. A twenty-two. Last two numbers are the same, it's a double."

Ford absorbed his lessons.

"Only question I got, Dougie," he said, "how much you figure on paying me for this back-end job?"

"Two hundred bucks every time you make a bury, maybe two-fifty," Palmer answered. "That's the usual I pay back-end."

"Beauty."

"You'll be out burying two, three times a night," Palmer said. "More even. Business is real good."

This was better than Ford had imagined.

"The other seven jars you got in the briefcase," he said to Palmer. "What about those?"

"Take them to your place," Palmer said. "I'll phone you tomorrow probably."

"I start burying."

"Back-end man," Palmer said.

The first small passing moment when the RCMP cottoned on to Doug Palmer as a possible player in the Vancouver narcotics trade may have come on a day in early February 1969. The place was the courthouse at 475 Main Street. The occasion was the preliminary hearing of six men on charges of conspiracy to traffic in heroin. During a recess in the proceedings, RCMP Sergeant Frank Kilner of the drug squad noticed a man talking to two of the accused, Conrad Gunn and John McKeoff, in the hall of the courthouse. The three appeared to be pretty tight in their conversation, and Kilner filed away the face and name of the third man for future reference. The third man was Doug Palmer.

Gunn, McKeoff, and another man, Dave Ponack, were eventually convicted on the charge of conspiring to traffic in drugs. The three had two biographical facts in common with one another and, as it turned out, with Doug Palmer: they earned their living in the drug business and they grew up in the East End. Vancouver's East End is relentlessly working-class. It stretches from the edge of the downtown, where smoky factories and flophouse architecture define the skyline, to the rolling hills of the middle-class municipality of Burnaby. For some of the East End's residents, its narrow streets and weathered single-storey houses are a stopping-off point. It is the neighbourhood where many immigrants to Canada find their first homes — poor English, Irish, Chinese, Sikh — and the ambitious among them move on to more upscale sections of Vancouver. For the people who stay behind, life can be a grind, and many of the kids of the East End grow up tough. Over much of two decades, the 1960s and

1970s, it was the East End's grown-up tough kids who controlled the heroin trade in Vancouver.

Doug Palmer came from hard-core East End stock. His father, Garnet, was a working man. His mother, Cecile, took in boarders and practised her Catholic faith. Neither parent ran up against the police. It was their first son, Ray, three years older than Doug, who introduced the family to trouble with the law.

Ray Palmer was a smooth operator, a man with wit and a neat line of patter. He used both to ease his way into the upper reaches of the drug business with Conrad Gunn, Dave Ponack, and their partners. But it wasn't drugs that sent Ray Palmer to prison. It was stolen bonds. When Ray was caught with them, he received a six-year sentence in the British Columbia Pen. A couple of years after he began the sentence, on January 19, 1970, he and another convict named Murray Boyd climbed a rope up an eight-foot wall and escaped. In the two months following Ray's break-out, four people with credentials in the underworld, two men and two women, turned up murdered. Police reasoned that Ray had the four taken out because they were trying to use his time in prison to muscle in on a larger share of the drug trade than they deserved.

Murray Boyd, the con who went over the wall with Ray, didn't last long in the outside world; the police caught up to Boyd 102 days after the escape and killed him. Ray survived longer. He made his way to Australia and got work as a plumber and roofing contractor. Australia was well known in the Palmer family. Doug lived there off and on for much of the late 1960s. It was in Australia that he met his second wife, Diane, the mother of his two sons, and it was in Australia, so the RCMP later theorized, that Doug stashed most of his earnings in the Vancouver drug business. The Mounties figured that while Ray Palmer was out of commission, either in prison or on the lam, Doug took over his brother's respon-

213

sibilities in keeping the heroin enterprises ticking over. Ray's period at liberty ended on February 24, 1973, when he was arrested in Australia and extradited to Canada to finish out his prison term. Doug Palmer, all the while, was raising the volume and profits of the drug business to levels that the former bosses, brother Ray, Conrad Gunn, Dave Ponack, and the others, had never dreamed of.

Some of the men Palmer employed in his ring were left-overs from the heroin trade of the Gunn-Ponack era. Some were newcomers to the business. Almost all were East End guys. Tommy Duncan, Johnny Smith, and Cliff Luhtala reached back to school days with Doug Palmer. Duncan was a big man, six-three and 240 pounds, who worked as a meter-reader for B.C. Hydro. He had no criminal record. Smith and Luhtala had medium-long records. Smith, lanky with a thin face marked by a fondness for booze, served prison terms for breaking and entering. Luhtala was hard and smart — he got his high school diploma while he was doing time — but he was convicted in March 1971 for his role in a pre-Doug Palmer drug ring. The conviction didn't deter Palmer from including Luhtala, before he went into prison and after he came out on an early-release program, in his own diverse and wildly profitable heroin dealings.

Along with other members of Doug Palmer's crew, there was his twin brother, Donald. Poor Donald, the Palmer brother whom life had short-changed. When he was a young-ster, an automobile accident had knocked Donald uncon-scious for six weeks. He needed another eighteen months to recover from amnesia, and forever after his thought processes seemed scrambled. He made mistakes that weren't worthy of a Palmer brother. In January 1961 he was sentenced to eight-een months in prison for, of all undignified offences, bigamy. Nevertheless Doug Palmer stuck by his twin. He hired Donald as a dispatcher in his trucking business and he made him a senior partner, though with limited authority, in his heroin business.

After Sergeant Frank Kilner registered Doug Palmer's presence in the Main Street courthouse in February 1969 and after the Mounties dug deeper into Palmer, they wised up to his commanding role in the Vancouver drug trade and organized themselves to bring down him and his gang. The RCMP's drug squad, working out of offices on Heather Street handy to the East End, numbered about forty men. All forty were thrown into the Palmer case at one time or another. They held little hope of catching any of the Palmer crew, especially Doug Palmer, in flat-out possession of a large quantity of heroin. The drug dealers were usually too cagey for such easy pickings. Instead, the RCMP approach, as it had been in many major drug cases in the 1960s, was to build toward a charge under the Canadian Criminal Code of conspiracy to traffic in narcotics.

Conspiracy is a crime of inference. The evidence in a conspiracy case is rarely of a direct variety; rather, it's evidence that invites the conclusion that a criminal act has taken place. What the police gather against the accused people, and what the crown attorney presents in court, is testimony about a series of suspicious events. By themselves, the individual events may seem harmless, but strung together they have a cumulative impact and raise a presumption of a concerted purpose on the part of the accused people which entitles a judge or jury to conclude that they have made an agreement to do something unlawful.

In conspiracy cases, it's the volume of evidence that counts, the huge number of incidents that demonstrate the accused people's criminal purpose, and in the Palmer case, the RCMP officers from the Vancouver drug squad set out in mid-1969 to record, within the limits of their manpower, each devious act and questionable meeting that Doug Palmer and his cohorts took part in. Some officers wore jeans, let their hair grow long, and drove unmarked cars. They tailed Palmer and his pals as they moved around the East End. They took up surveillance outside the gang members' houses. And they hung out at the Palmer crew's favourite drinking-spot, the bar at the Waldorf Hotel. For the rest of 1969, through 1970 and '71, the Mounties in mufti stuck to Palmer and company like glue and documented every episode, no matter how apparently trivial, that might indicate the men were conspiring to traffic in heroin.

Among other pieces of undercover work, officers tracked two Palmer people, Cliff Luhtala and another East Ender named Allan Cressie, on regular trips to downtown banks where they exchanged stacks of ten- and twenty-dollar bills for thousand-dollar bills. The Mounties knew it was an old drug-dealer custom to get rid of the tens and twenties of everyday dealing and hide away the profits in bills of larger denomination.

Officers trailed Luhtala on the night of February 2, 1970, when he slipped up an alley off the 2500 block of East 18th Avenue and appeared to do something shifty behind a garage. After Luhtala left the alley, the Mounties searched the area around the garage and dug a jar of capped-up heroin out of the ground.

In late 1969 and early 1970, officers tagged after Doug Palmer as he slid away to meetings with Conrad Gunn in a variety of places — in the bar at the Doric Howe Hotel, on gas-station lots, in cars parked on side streets. Since Gunn had been named in an earlier drug-conspiracy charge, on which he was convicted and jailed in the fall of 1970, the association between him and Doug Palmer suggested that Palmer might be transacting heroin business with Gunn.

On April 20, 1970, seven Mounties temporarily chucked the tactics of stealth in favour of something more bold. They rapped on the door of Donald Palmer's house at 6628 Vivian Street. It was one-fifteen in the morning. Donald answered the door, looking befuddled and carrying a shotgun. When the Mounties identified themselves, Donald put down the gun and invited them in. The Mounties searched the house and asked Donald to open the safe they found in the basement. Donald refused, and the Mounties woke up a mechanic from the Diebold Safe Company, who hurried over and drilled open the safe. Inside were bills of every denomination. The Mounties counted ten thousand dollars, returned the money to Donald, and left the house, taking with them the firm belief that Donald was keeping company with profits from the drug business.

Undercover officers hit on a bonanza of material in their observations of the Palmer gang's mixing and mingling at the Waldorf Hotel. The Waldorf, a dumpy yellow building, sits on Hastings Street in a down-at-the-heels commercial neighbourhood. Its bar, called the Polynesian Lounge, glories in a Hawaiian motif. Wicker tables and chairs, bamboo trim, palm trees with tiny white lights blinking in the fronds, walls hung with paintings of dusky bare-breasted beauties. The Waldorf filled the bill as informal office quarters for the Palmer guys. They dropped by the Polynesian Lounge at all hours of the afternoon and evening, knocked back drinks, had a few yuks, talked business. Many afternoons and nights, for almost three years, RCMP officers in work pants and windbreakers sat at the long, curving, pink-topped bar in the Polynesian nursing beers and noting the action. They saw plenty of table-hopping. Doug Palmer would sit at a table with Cliff Luhtala and Johnny Smith. Then he'd switch to the bar to join his brother Donnie and Bill Turner, another tough nut from the East End. Everyone was on the move around the room. Sometimes Doug or Luhtala or Smith or Turner or Tommy Duncan or another East Ender named Bobby Porter would duck out to their cars, transact commerce of some subtle import, and stroll back to the lounge.

The Mounties on undercover duty soon recognized the regulars: the Palmer twins, Bill Turner, Luhtala, Duncan, and the others, plus Allan Cressie and Johnny Smith's brother Andrew and another guy named Mike Watson. All of them flocked to the Waldorf, talked, drank, laughed, and went on their way. On one level, the conduct might shape up

217

as perfectly innocent, just a bunch of the guys who got together over drinks and discussed bowling scores. But to the Mounties charting the comings and goings in the Polynesian, the conferences of Palmer and friends had much more significance. The meetings demonstrated that the dozen or so men were in frequent and intimate contact, and thus, if it could be shown that a few of them, even two or three, were involved in a conspiracy to traffic in heroin, the law said the conspiracy could extend to all the guys who gathered in the suspicious conclaves at the Waldorf.

The Mounties got lucky in their surveillance of Tommy Duncan, the B.C. Hydro meter-reader. Tommy lived in a duplex at 2116 Eton Street in the East End, but he liked to pass the time at the homes of other Palmer associates. He and Bobby Porter struck up a particularly amiable relationship, even though, on the surface, two guys couldn't have been more unlike. Tommy, a phlegmatic sort, had no record of arrests or jail time, while wild Bobby's conviction sheet, reaching back to his teenage years, was a document of astonishing length and variety. Among his crimes, there was theft in Willow Branch, Saskatchewan, false pretences in Lethbridge, Alberta, forgery in Vancouver, break-and-enter in Prince George. The last caper got him three years in the B.C. Pen in July 1965, but after he came out, Bobby gave signs of calming down. He found a job at the Gulf service station in Ladner, a village in the Delta area south of Vancouver, and he settled into the community. The lads who drank at the Ladner Legion took to Bobby and elected him captain of the Ladner Legion A Team in the Fraser Valley Darts League. Bobby used to bring Tommy Duncan around to the Legion and the other Ladner hot spots. People warmed up to Tommy. What none of the locals knew was that, over at Bobby's apartment, he and Tommy were busy capping up Doug Palmer's heroin.

218

Late on the night of January 23, 1971, Bobby and Tommy made a run into Vancouver, met Doug Palmer at the Waldorf, and drove back to Ladner. A car of Mounties was on their tail. The Mounties couldn't be certain whether or not Bobby and Tommy picked up a fresh supply of heroin from Palmer. But they were suspicious enough to summon a back-up squad of a half-dozen officers who staked out Bobby's apartment, the Legion Hall, and the bar at the Ladner Hotel, another place where Bobby and Tommy liked to bend their elbows.

Tommy bent his elbow out of shape on the night of January 25. He was drinking boilermakers at the Ladner Hotel, and, since Bobby was on late duty at the Gulf station, Tommy whiled away the time playing shuffleboard with a new pal named Doug Manuel. Manuel was a ferry-master from Comox on Vancouver Island, a man who enjoyed his beer, good company, nice guy. Around midnight, when the boilermakers began to fuzz Tommy's head, he asked Doug Manuel to drive him to Bobby Porter's apartment. No problem, the accommodating Manuel said. The two men walked out to Manuel's pickup truck. It was of the crew-cab style, double-sized, with four doors and both front and back seats. Tommy and Manuel hoisted themselves into the cab, Tommy a trifle unsteadily, and as RCMP Corporal Terry Hart watched from his stake-out position in a second-storey room in the building across the street from the Ladner Hotel, the pickup drove down the street.

"Hey, man," Tommy said to Manuel after the truck had gone ten or twelve blocks. "Right here. This's where I wanna stop."

"Here?" Manuel said. "Nothing here. This is vacant lots."

"S'okay."

Manuel pulled on to the shoulder of the road. Tommy jumped from the cab and wobbled into the field. Manuel thought he was probably going to take a leak, but when Tommy returned, he was carrying a small bundle wrapped in a green garbage bag. He flipped the bundle into the back of the pickup, and as it hit the seat, the garbage bag burst open.

"Oh shit," Tommy said.

White powder sprayed the rear of Doug Manuel's cab.

"For chrissake, Tommy," Manuel said, no longer Mr. Nice Guy. "You're messing up my truck."

"Don't get pissed, man," Tommy said. He made clumsy passes at sweeping up the spilled powder.

"What's the stuff anyway?" Manuel asked, uneasy, his temper rising. "What the hell's going on with you?"

"Pot's all it is," Tommy answered, still brushing the powder into his hand and stuffing it in the pockets of his coat.

"Marijuana, that what you're talking about? *That's* marijuana?"

"Yeah," Tommy said. "Relax, okay. I'm cleaning things back here."

"Get that stuff the fuck out of my truck!" Manuel shouted. "You nuts or what? Get the stuff out and you get the fuck out too!"

The white powder wasn't marijuana. It was heroin. But the notion of marijuana was enough to scare Doug Manuel. As soon as Tommy swept up most of the loose powder and stepped down to the road, Manuel swung the truck in a U-turn and gunned back to the Ladner Hotel. He drove behind the building and stopped next to a row of extra-large garbage pails. Tommy Duncan's cleaning job had been perfunctory and Manuel stared at the shambles in the back seat. White powder, a ripped green garbage bag, two loose condoms. He gathered up the debris and stuffed it into a Ladner Hotel garbage pail. A film of powder still clung to the seat and floor in the back of the truck. Manuel decided he'd take care of that in a later scrub-down. His main concern at the moment was to put plenty of distance between himself and the crazy events in Ladner. He drove from behind the hotel and pointed his truck in the direction of the freeway to Vancouver.

Which is where Corporal Terry Hart picked up his trail. When Tommy Duncan left the Ladner Hotel in Doug

Manuel's pickup, Hart hadn't moved from his stake-out post across the street in time to follow the two men in his own car. He'd spent fifteen minutes driving in a criss-cross pattern through the streets looking for Manuel's truck. When he spotted it, Manuel was alone in the cab. Hart realized that much, but what he couldn't know, as he followed Manuel on the freeway north to Vancouver, was that Manuel was engaged in some serious rethinking of his situation.

At the Deas Island Tunnel, Manuel steered off the freeway to a telephone booth, got out, and dialled a number. Hart, watching Manuel as he talked on the phone for five, then ten, then fifteen minutes, chose to abandon his tail on the truck. Better pickings, he thought, back in Ladner. He noted the licence number and description of Manuel's truck and turned his car south on the freeway.

"Where you been, Terry?" a constable named Fred Hammond said when Hart reached the Ladner RCMP office a few minutes later. "I just had someone on the phone about your guy."

"Which guy?"

"Listen to this," Constable Hammond said. "According to the fella on the phone, name of Douglas Manuel, Tommy Duncan spilled white powder, marijuana he said, all over the back of this Manuel's truck."

"Pickup truck?" Hart asked. "One of those double jobs? Four doors?"

"Crew-cab model, yeah," Hammond answered. "Anyway, the guy on the phone, Manuel, said he dumped the stuff round back of the Ladner."

The Mounties scrambled over to the hotel. It was all there in the garbage pail — the loose heroin, the ripped green bag, the two condoms packed full of capped-up heroin. The RCMP were now on a roll. In the next couple of days they uncovered a hidden package of heroin at the Gulf station where Bobby Porter worked and they found a weigh-scale in Bobby's apartment, the sort of implement used in measuring heroin for capping up. The Mounties had a witness, Doug Manuel, and enough physical evidence to hit Tommy Duncan with a charge of possession of heroin for the purposes of trafficking. They also had plenty on Bobby Porter. But, even better, since Tommy and Bobby had been seen in regular association with Doug Palmer and company at the Waldorf, the RCMP now possessed evidence of a key link in tying everyone, including Palmer, into a conspiracy to traffic in narcotics.

In the Mounties' gathering of evidence, luck didn't always break their way. Sometimes, through misfortune or mismanagement, they blew golden opportunities to nail Doug Palmer and his pals with the goods. That was particularly the case in the Horrendous Bus Depot Fiasco, which began in meticulous planning and grand promise and ended in low comedy and furious embarrassment.

The episode took first shape when the Quebec Mounties, acting on instructions from their counterparts at the Vancouver drug squad, put a tail on Walter Guay in Montreal. Guay was a dapper, balding man in his mid-fifties. He wore a pencil-line moustache and had taste in clothes that ran to latter-day Al Capone. Boxy suits, light-brown cashmere topcoat, wide-brimmed fedora. Guay owned two sets of false teeth, one for everyday wear and a second set for party time. The second set boasted two diamonds up front. Guay paid for his flashing teeth and big fedoras with money he earned in the drug trade. He was a courier, the man who escorted bulk heroin from Montreal to Doug Palmer's distributing network in Vancouver.

The RCMP tail on Walter Guay picked him up on Friday, April 9, 1971, when he took delivery of a brown package from a sneaky character at the Green Garden Café in downtown Montreal. Guay stowed the package in a green Lucerne-brand suitcase and caught a cab for the CN train station. The

Mounties stuck with him. Guay and the suitcase checked into a roomette on the Supercontinental leaving for Vancouver. Three Mounties from the tail team climbed on, and the train pulled out of the station. When Guay ambled down to the parlour car for a drink and a display of his party teeth, the Mounties let themselves into his roomette and peeked inside the green Lucerne suitcase. It held the brown package that came from the man at the Green Garden Café, and the package held a couple of pounds of white powder. The Mounties, figuring the powder was heroin, snicked out a pinch for testing and resumed their tailing detail on Walter Guay.

Somewhere they lost him. It was probably during the stop at Capreol in Northern Ontario. Maybe Guay spotted the tail. More likely, as he later claimed, he got sick. Either way, he disappeared from the Supercontinental and boarded another train back to Montreal. The Mounties were chagrined that Guay had flown the coop but not devastated. What rescued the situation was that the three Montreal Mounties knew from the people at the Vancouver drug squad that the primary purpose of the exercise wasn't to bust Walter Guay, though he'd be swept up in due course. The real reason for the tailing job was to nab the people at the other end of the transaction, the guys in the Palmer gang who picked up Guay's package in Vancouver. On that score, the Montreal Mounties knew they were still on track because when Guay bailed out at Capreol, he left the green suitcase with contents intact in the roomette on the Supercontinental.

Corporal Emil Beaulieu met the train and the suitcase in Vancouver and put into effect stage two of the plan that the drug squad had painstakingly conceived. Beaulieu was a resourceful and tireless worker, and within five years he would be promoted to inspector and placed in charge of the RCMP's drug squad in Toronto. For the Guay plan, he was concerned to carry out three swift moves at the Vancouver train station.

First, Beaulieu rushed the green suitcase to RCMP headquarters on Heather Street and removed the white powder from its package inside the suitcase. On testing, the powder proved to be heroin, thirty-four ounces of the stuff. Beaulieu secured the heroin in a locker where evidence was stored for future use at trial, and in its place, in the package inside the green Lucerne suitcase, he substituted thirty-four ounces of plain white flour.

Next, he hurried the suitcase back to the train station in downtown Vancouver and placed it among the other bags in the CN luggage room. Beaulieu's expectation was that Guay would have been in touch with Doug Palmer to advise him that the suitcase had proceeded to Vancouver without him. Where would Palmer come calling for the suitcase? At the CN luggage room.

And, finally, Beaulieu posted teams of plainclothes men on lookout around the train station. One man sat behind a *Vancouver Sun* in the waiting-room. Another was hidden in an office adjacent to the luggage room. And a third, decked out in a CN smock, lounged inside the luggage room. All the men were on the alert for anyone who inquired after the green Lucerne suitcase that came in on the Supercontinental from Montreal.

While Beaulieu was orchestrating his manoeuvres in Vancouver, the Quebec RCMP once again picked up Walter Guay's trail in Montreal. On Monday, April 12, Guay rode to Dorval Airport and got on a plane to Vancouver. The Montreal Mounties flashed the news to the Vancouver Mounties, who fell in behind Guay when he arrived at Vancouver Airport. They followed him downtown and watched him check into the Hotel Vancouver. The Mounties stood by waiting for Guay's next step.

Over the following thirty hours, Guay pulled a few moves that seemed suspicious. But nothing excited his Mountie followers until eight o'clock on Thursday morning, the fifteenth. That was when Guay hopped in a cab at the Hotel Vancouver and directed it to the train station.

"Get set, everybody," Corporal Emil Beaulieu said into a walkie-talkie radio. "We have Guay in here."

Beaulieu was positioned in the office that adjoined the CN luggage room. He was broadcasting to Sergeant Frank Kilner, who was parked in an unmarked car with two other Mounties outside the train station. Kilner was in place to get on the trail of anyone who emerged from the station with the green suitcase and its cargo of flour. If Beaulieu was surprised that it was Guay who showed up at the luggage room, he had no trouble resolving the puzzle. Probably, Beaulieu reasoned, Guay had been reluctant to tell Doug Palmer that he'd let the shipment of heroin out of his sight. Instead, he'd claim the suitcase and proceed with the delivery as if nothing had gone wrong.

Guay stepped up smartly to the luggage room, identified the green suitcase, signed his name to a form for the baggage-master, and returned to the cab that was waiting for him on the street.

"There goes our man," Beaulieu said into his radio.

"Got him," Sergeant Kilner answered back.

Guay's cab drove south and east through the downtown morning rush-hour.

"Where the hell's he going?" one of the Mounties in the following car asked Sergeant Kilner.

"Bus depot's over this way," Kilner answered.

"Bus depot?" the other Mountie said. "We just left the train station."

Vancouver's bus depot is a low-slung, cramped building on the south side of Dunsmuir Street flanked by Cambie Street on its west side and Beatty Street on the east.

Guay's cab stopped at the front entrance to the depot and Guay got out. He was carrying the green suitcase.

"All right," Kilner said in the RCMP car. "Check it out."

The three Mounties, affecting a nonchalant look, fanned through the depot and watched as Guay walked up to a bank of lockers. He inserted a couple of quarters in the slot to locker 610, swung open the door, pushed the suitcase inside, shut the door, removed the locker key, and ambled back to his cab. Another RCMP car tracked Guay on his return trip to the Hotel Vancouver, and as Guay left the depot, Corporal Beaulieu joined Kilner and his men beside locker 610. With the help of the depot's manager, he opened the locker and examined the suitcase. Everything inside was as it should be, thirty-four ounces of flour in a brown package. He shut locker 610.

"Next thing we do," he said, "we stake out the depot."

Beaulieu felt satisfied. The exercise was progressing just the way the textbooks prescribed. Mounties on their toes. Flawless team-work. Solid job of shadowing Guay. The heroin was in hand, and now the stage was set to nab the dealers who would undoubtedly be calling around to collect the suitcase as soon as Walter Guay passed on the key to locker 610.

Beaulieu marshalled the men. Fifteen Mounties, almost half the drug squad, were summoned to the stake-out duty at the depot. They were split into co-ordinated teams that worked inside and outside the depot, on foot and in cars, all attention focussed on locker 610. Beaulieu ran the first shift from the morning of April 15 to early evening. No one arrived to pick up the green suitcase, and over at the Hotel Vancouver, while Walter Guay seemed to be putting in an active day, in and out of the coffee shop, stepping into phone booths, strolling the streets, none of the RCMP officers on his tail could detect whether or not he passed the locker key to anyone. The stake-out continued.

At eight o'clock on the evening of the fifteenth, Corporal Beaulieu ended his day at the depot, and a new shift of officers went on duty. Corporal John Paterson and Corporal Karl Richert settled themselves behind the depot's ticket counter. It faced the row of lockers that included locker number 610. About twenty feet separated the counter and the row of lockers, and Peterson and Richert had a view of number 610 that was unobstructed. The two men wore casual clothes, and Peterson was equipped with a walkie-talkie radio that put him in touch with five other officers who were in position outside the depot.

Sergeant Frank Welychka sat in the window of an empty service station on the north side of Dunsmuir Street facing the front entrance to the depot. Sergeant Welychka's unmarked police car was parked on the station lot.

Corporal Doug Chan was stationed in a car, also unmarked, on the north side of Dunsmuir a block and a half west of the depot. Corporal Chan had a distant view of the depot's front door.

Corporal Tom Brown and Corporal Norman Schafer were parked in their unmarked car on Mortimer Street half a block north of Dunsmuir. Since Mortimer was a north-south street one block west of the bus depot, Corporals Brown and Schafer couldn't see the depot from their post. Corporal Brown sat in the front passenger seat, and Corporal Schafer was behind the wheel of the car.

Sergeant Stan Domansky was in his unmarked car on Beatty, the street that ran along the east side of the depot. Sergeant Domansky's post was south of Dunsmuir. That meant he, too, had no direct sight-lines on the depot's front door.

The five outside men — Welychka, Chan, the team of Brown and Schafer, and Domansky — tuned in their radios and waited.

Inside the depot, Paterson and Richert kept watch on locker 610 from their spot behind the ticket counter.

Nothing happened until 9:45 p.m.

"Oh-oh," Paterson said to Richert at 9:45. "I think we got a guy at the locker."

Richert looked over the counter.

"Hold it," he said. "The guy's *close* to the locker."

The two corporals watched.

"Hell," Paterson said. "Now he's *in* the locker."

The man at locker 610 was about five-seven. He had on a tweed hat, sport jacket, open-neck shirt, and no tie. He wore long sideburns. He slid a key into the locker and pulled open the door.

Corporal Paterson ducked behind the counter and spoke into his walkie-talkie in a low voice.

"Everybody out there, alert," he said. "Male person taking possession of suitcase. Male wearing hat, sports coat. Long sideburns. Approximately five feet, seven inches. You read me?"

Sergeant Welychka, in the window of the gas station across the street, listened as his radio began to broadcast.

His radio said, *"Squawk, blip,* male, *squeak, buzz, buzz,* suitcase, *bzzzzzz."*

In their car, Corporals Brown and Schafer heard their radio say, *"Zip, zap,* sports, *cuhzip, cuhzap,* sideburns, *buhzup, buhzip, bihzap."*

Corporal Chan's radio said, *"Zzzzzzzzzzzzzzz."*

Sergeant Domansky's radio didn't say anything. At 9:15, Sergeant Domansky had started up his car and driven a few blocks west to the streets around the Hotel Vancouver. He thought he might spot Walter Guay. His drive took him out of range of Corporal Paterson's radio.

Sergeant Welychka stared at his radio.

"What the hell?" he said to himself.

"What the hell?" Corporal Brown said to Corporal Schafer.

Corporal Chan didn't say anything.

Sergeant Domansky hummed.

In the depot, the man with the long sideburns removed the green suitcase from locker 610. He walked through the depot toward the door on to Dunsmuir Street.

"Suspect's leaving the premises," Corporal Richert said to Corporal Paterson. "Dunsmuir door."

Paterson spoke into his radio.

"Alert, alert," he said. "Male suspect exiting bus depot at Dunsmuir."

Sergeant Welychka's radio went, "*Bleep*, male, *bleep*, Dunsmuir, *buzzizz*."

Corporals Brown and Schafer's radio went, "*Buhlip*, exiting, *buhlip*, Dunsmuir, *buhleep*."

Corporal Chan's radio went, "*Zzzzzzzz*."

Sergeant Domansky's radio was silent.

While Corporal Paterson was sending his second message, Corporal Richert ran from behind the counter. He crossed the floor and stopped at Locker 610. Empty, he signalled back to Corporal Paterson, his hands outstretched, palms up. Richert hurried toward the Dunsmuir door. He saw the man with the long sideburns, carrying the suitcase, pass through the door to the street.

Corporal Paterson finished his second broadcast and left his post at the counter. He trotted out the back door of the depot, turned left, and started around to the front by way of the Beatty Street side.

Sergeant Welychka pondered his radio.

"What in damnation's going on?" he said to himself.

"Something weird's up," Corporal Brown said to Corporal Schafer.

Corporal Chan said nothing.

Sergeant Domansky whistled.

Corporal Richert ran through the Dunsmuir door of the depot and spotted the man with the long sideburns. He and the green suitcase were disappearing into a yellow cab at the taxi ramp on the west side of the depot. The cab pulled on to Dunsmuir, turned right, drove several yards, and turned left at Beatty.

Corporal Paterson steamed around the corner of the depot.

"I think something's wrong with the damn radio," he said to Richert.

"The guy's gone with the suitcase," Richert said to Paterson.

"Hell," Paterson said.

He raised the walkie-talkie to his mouth and spoke into it. "Alert, alert," he said. "Losing our man. Repeat. Losing our man."

"*Buzink,*" Sergeant Welychka heard. "Losing, *budink,* repeat."

"*Zip, zap,*" Corporals Brown and Schafer heard. "Alert, *zip,* losing."

"*Zzzzzzzz,*" Corporal Chan heard.

Sergeant Domansky heard silence.

On Dunsmuir Street, Corporal Richert turned and raced back through the front door and into the depot. He went behind the ticket counter and dialled the RCMP offices on Heather Street. He asked for the radio dispatcher.

"Put this out," he said to the radio dispatcher. "We have a man in a yellow cab near the vicinity of Dunsmuir and Beatty. Long sideburns, sports jacket, no tie. Has a green suitcase in his possession. This man must be apprehended."

In the window of the gas station across Dunsmuir from the depot, Sergeant Welychka watched Richert and Paterson. He didn't notice a yellow taxi. He noticed only Richert and Paterson. He thought they looked frantic.

"Somebody must've picked up the suitcase," he said to himself.

Sergeant Welychka went out to his car and started it.

"Maybe we better go down there and see if the guy's come for the suitcase," Corporal Brown said to Corporal Schafer. "Start'er up."

Corporal Chan didn't start his car.

Sergeant Domansky circled his car around the Hotel Vancouver and pointed back to the bus depot.

Sergeant Welychka's car pulled off the gas-station lot and headed east.

Corporals Brown and Schafer's car rounded the corner of Mortimer and Dunsmuir and drove east along Dunsmuir.

Corporal Chan's car remained at the curb on Dunsmuir.

Sergeant Domansky's car covered the blocks from the Hotel Vancouver to the bus depot.

Corporal Richert finished his phone call to the Heather Street dispatcher and dashed back through the depot to the sidewalk on Dunsmuir, where Corporal Paterson was shaking his radio up and down.

"Don't know what's the matter with this thing," Paterson said to Richert.

Paterson and Richert turned their attention to the street.

They saw Sergeant Welychka drive past the bus depot in his unmarked car.

They saw Corporals Brown and Schafer drive by in their unmarked car.

"Hey," Sergeant Welychka said out loud inside his car, "there's that bloody Walter Guay."

Guay, wearing a dandy outfit of jacket, tie, slacks, and shiny shoes, was standing on the sidewalk at the northwest corner of Dunsmuir and Beatty. He was alone and seemed to have nothing much on his mind.

"Hey," Corporal Brown said to Corporal Schafer in the car behind Sergeant Welychka's car. "There's Guay."

"What's he doing?" Schafer asked.

"Not a damn thing," Brown answered.

Behind Guay, a car was parked on Beatty a few yards north of Dunsmuir. It was a 1963 green Chevrolet and there were three people inside it. The driver of the Chev drove away from the curb.

Sergeant Welychka turned his car hard left and fell in line a discreet distance behind the Chev.

So did Corporals Brown and Schafer in their car.

"Must be the people who came for the suitcase," Sergeant Welychka thought to himself.

"Gotta be the people we're supposed to be looking for," Corporal Brown said to Corporal Schafer.

The cars drove north on Beatty and turned east on Hastings. The order was, first, the green Chev, then Sergeant Welychka's car, then the car with Corporals Brown and Schafer. Corporal Brown asked on his car radio for more back-up cars to follow the green Chev. Soon five cars from the RCMP and the Vancouver city police were driving in surreptitious pursuit of the green Chev on Hastings Street East.

Sergeant Domansky's car was on Dunsmuir two blocks west of the bus depot.

"Yellow cab in vicinity of Dunsmuir and Beatty," he heard over his radio from the dispatcher at the Heather Street offices. "Please locate. Male suspect. Long sideburns. Green suitcase."

Sergeant Domansky drove past Corporal Chan's parked car, past the bus depot, past Corporals Paterson and Richert on the sidewalk. He turned north on Beatty and cruised back and forth on the streets near the bus depot. He didn't see a yellow cab carrying a man with long sideburns and the green suitcase.

At the corner of Hastings Street East and Nanaimo Street, about three miles from the bus depot, a Vancouver city police car pulled alongside the green Chev and ordered it to stop. The driver, who looked very frightened, parked his car on Hastings, and he and his two passengers got out. The passengers looked as frightened as the driver. They told the policemen from the car that stopped them that they didn't know anything about a green suitcase. The policemen believed them.

"Think we got a false alarm here," one of the policemen said into his car radio.

"Attention all officers on stake-out duty at the bus depot," the dispatcher at Heather Street broadcast. "Please report back to the office."

Sergeant Welychka peeled off Hastings Street East and drove to Heather Street. Corporals Brown and Schafer did likewise. Sergeant Domansky abandoned his search for a yellow cab. And Corporals Paterson and Richert caught a ride from the bus depot.

At Heather Street, Paterson and Richert looked through photographs of the members of Doug Palmer's crew.

"I'd say it was Johnny Smith walked out of the depot with the suitcase," Paterson said, ignoring Smith's height, which was several inches taller than the five-seven of the man who took the suitcase.

"Smith's the guy," Richert said, making the same omission.

"Well, he didn't get away in that green Chev," Sergeant Welychka said.

"Nothing but civilians in the Chev," Corporal Brown agreed.

"For sure," Corporal Schafer chimed in.

"Wait a minute," Corporal Paterson said. "Where's a green Chev come into this?"

"We didn't say anything about a green Chev," Corporal Richert said.

"Well, what about Walter Guay?" Corporal Brown said. "He was standing right there at the corner when the Chev started up."

"Coincidence is all that was," Sergeant Welychka said.

"Wonder where the damn cab got to," Sergeant Domansky said.

"Cab?" Sergeant Welychka said.

"What cab?" Corporals Brown and Schafer said.

"The yellow cab," Sergeant Domansky said.

"Yellow cab?" Sergeant Welychka said. "Then why'n hell were we chasing a green Chevy?"

No one answered him.

Corporal Chan arrived at the office and looked at the others. He said, "Slow night out there."

Corporal Emil Beaulieu was livid at the outcome of the bus-depot stake-out, but he soldiered on. Two days later, at eight o'clock on the evening of April 17, he and three other officers were camped near Ed Stenson's house at 1449 Gordon Avenue in West Vancouver. Stenson ran a business that supplied nightclubs with young women who sold flowers to the clubs' customers and offered to take their photographs. The Mounties suspected that Stenson was also a member of Doug Palmer's ring, with possible responsibilities as a cap-up man.

Beaulieu and his men watched Stenson's house through the late evening of the seventeenth and into the small hours of the eighteenth. At 4 a.m., as they trained their binoculars through Stenson's kitchen window, they saw him busy at a table with a variety of implements and a mound of white powder.

"That's it," Beaulieu said. "We've got the bastard cold."

The four Mounties burst through the door at 1449 Gordon, handcuffed Stenson, scooped up the white powder, and packed the prisoner and the evidence to Heather Street. It was an exhilarating early-morning's work.

An RCMP lab technician carried out tests on the white powder that came from the Stenson kitchen, and it was he who broke the bad news to Corporal Beaulieu.

The white powder wasn't heroin.

It was plain white flour.

It was undoubtedly the same plain white flour that Beaulieu had substituted for the heroin in Walter Guay's green Lucerne suitcase.

If Emil Beaulieu was upset at the news, one man was even angrier. Ed Stenson. He thought he'd taken delivery of thirty-four ounces of heroin.

Despite the occasional glitch in the investigative process, the Mounties had become so confident of the evidence they accumulated against the Palmer gang that on June 22, 1972, Emil Beaulieu, promoted to sergeant in early '72, swore an information declaring he had reasonable and probable grounds for believing that ten men had conspired to commit the indictable offence of trafficking in heroin.

The ten were Doug and Donald Palmer; Cliff Luhtala and Johnny Smith; Tommy Duncan, who had messed up so disastrously in Ladner; Duncan's sidekick, Bobby Turner; Walter Guay, the Montreal courier; Ed Stenson; and two other regulars around the Palmer tables at the Waldorf Hotel, Bill Turner and Mike Watson.

Sergeant Beaulieu's information alleged that the ten had conspired among themselves to commit the offence and had also conspired with seven other people. These seven, so the RCMP believed, were part of the trafficking conspiracy, but the Mounties decided they lacked evidence to charge the seven. The co-conspirators were Conrad Gunn and Johnny Smith's brother, Andrew; Allan Cressie, the man who changed tens and twenties into thousand-dollar bills; another Waldorf habitué named Leo Baker; and two women, Jackie Lampen and Liesilotte Weber, along with Weber's husband, Carl. The last three — the Webers and Lampen — never appeared in court in person or through their legal representatives. They were dead, three of the four people who were murdered, possibly on Ray Palmer's direction, in the two months after Ray broke out of the B.C. Pen on January 19, 1970.

Sergeant Beaulieu laid his information, and the ten men named in it as conspirators were arrested. They hired lawyers who arranged for their new clients to be released on bail. The next step would be a preliminary hearing at which a Provincial Court judge would decide whether there was sufficient evidence against the accused men to send them on for trial in a higher court on the conspiracy charge. The preliminary was set down for the autumn of 1972.

Until then, everybody had his work cut out for him.

The attorney for the crown was kept busy conferring with Sergeant Beaulieu and the other members of the drug squad and organizing the case for the prosecution. The crown attorney was an employee of the federal Department of Justice, which holds authority in drug cases in Canada.

The defence lawyers were occupied in contemplating the crown's case and picking at it for holes.

Doug Palmer and his East End pals were hustling to carry on business as usual in the heroin trade. The drugs continued to come in from Montreal and the customers were thick on the streets. Why let a little conspiracy charge get in the way of a crack at more profits?

And the Mounties were staying active in surveillance of the Palmer group. There was no telling what fresh evidence they might come up with before court time rolled around.

While Doug Palmer was contending with the conspiracy charge in the summer of 1972, things showed signs of going wrong at another end of his drug network. The source of the trouble was Fred Ford.

Throughout the year after Palmer hired him as a back-end man, Ford carried out his burying duties with efficiency and dispatch. There were no errors, no mishandled drugs, no runins with the police. Ford grew so reliable that Palmer included him in more areas of the operation. On many Thursday nights, Ford picked up two other members of the Palmer outfit, usually Tommy Duncan and Johnny Smith, and drove them to a motel where the two took a key of heroin, 2.2 pounds, and cut and capped it. Duncan and Smith needed two or three days to handle the work. When they were done, Ford collected them at the motel and kept the jars of heroin that the two had prepared. Ford was a trusted member of the Palmer enterprise.

And he was bringing home important money, about one hundred thousand dollars in the first year. That was what bothered Ford's older sister. Why, she asked, couldn't he spread the gravy? Specifically, the sister, whose married name was Mortimer, wanted Ford to let her son Jimmy in on the good times. Jimmy Mortimer was in his late twenties, only a couple of years younger than his Uncle Fred, and he was out of work. Ford's sister put on the heat and Ford caved in. All right, he said, he'd share his booty with Jimmy. He instructed Mortimer on the techniques of a back-end man and took him on several burying excursions. And he began to pay Mortimer small amounts from his own fees. But the one step that Ford left out was to advise Doug Palmer that Palmer had a new man on the payroll.

During the late summer and early fall of 1972, Ford continued as before, receiving deliveries of heroin, hiding jars in the ground, doing his job. The only difference was that, unknown to Palmer, Ford was employing Jimmy Mortimer as a paid assistant. Ford came to depend on his nephew. He permitted Mortimer to make burials on his own, and perhaps inevitably, in the early morning on October 9, 1972, Jimmy Mortimer got caught. Until that morning, the RCMP hadn't registered Ford as a member of the Palmer organization. Somehow, probably through plain dumb luck, Ford — and Mortimer — evaded the Mountie surveillance, but on October 9, officers nabbed Jimmy Mortimer close to a hole in the ground that had sixteen hundred caps of heroin in it.

A few hours after Mortimer's arrest, at eight-thirty in the morning, Fred Ford was waiting at the station where the Mounties were holding Mortimer. The station was in Burnaby, the suburb of Vancouver that adjoins the East End on its eastern border. Mortimer had been making his bury in a Burnaby back alley, and the Burnaby detachment had jurisdiction in the case. An RCMP sergeant named Harold Kryhul was in charge. It was on him that Fred Ford, sweating over his predicament, tried out a proposition.

"The truth of things here," he said to Kryhul, "is I can straighten out what's happening about Jimmy. His mother's a little sore at me. Matter of fact, a *lot* sore, and I got to make everything okay."

"That'll need plenty of making, Mr. Ford," Sergeant Kryhul said. "Our officers have a connection between Mortimer and more than fifteen hundred capsules of what we believe to be heroin."

"Sixteen hundred," Ford said. "Well, that's my point. See, those sixteen hundred, they were mine."

"Yours?"

"Jimmy was the messenger," Ford said. "I sent him out to handle a job."

"What are you doing, Mr. Ford?" Kryhul asked. "Confessing?"

"All I'm saying is this," Ford said. "I can give you some real good information, and the trade is, you let Jimmy off the beef you got him on."

Kryhul said, "We're not usually in the business of making trades, Mr. Ford."

"You will be this time," Ford said. "You ever heard of Dougie Palmer?"

"I might have."

"That's who I'm talking about," Ford said. "Where do we go from here?"

Kryhul had only recently been transferred to the Burnaby detachment from Ottawa. He wasn't familiar with all the drug traffickers in the Vancouver area, but Palmer was one name he'd heard. He knew about the Vancouver drug squad's long investigation of Palmer and about the preliminary hearing that would begin in a few weeks. Kryhul put in a swift phone call to Sergeant Jim Locker of the Vancouver drug squad, and within thirty minutes Locker arrived at the

Burnaby offices to interview Fred Ford.

"Just so's you know I'm not jerkin' you," Ford said to Locker, "I'll tell you right off, I'm a back-end man for Dougie Palmer. You understand what I'm talking about?"

"You're the guy who wants to cut a deal, Fred," Locker said. "Keep on talking."

"I handle the laying down for Dougie," Ford went on. "He gives me the stuff, and when he phones in an order, I go out and bury it somewheres and tell Dougie where I done it."

"What else do you know, Fred?"

"About Dougie Palmer," Ford said, "I know plenty."

"Tell me."

Ford was thinking as fast as he could. Looking for a route out of the jam. Considering his choices. He didn't want to hand Locker enough information to shut down Doug Palmer's entire drug empire. If he did, he, Fred Ford, would be dealing himself out of a hundred-thousand-dollar job. But he had to come up with something sufficiently juicy to per- suade Locker that it was worth while to go easy on Jimmy Mortimer. Ford had an idea.

"Well, all right," he said to Locker. "I happen to remember this guy in a white Chrysler, '61 or '62, beat-up old car. Couple of nights, more than a couple actually, I went with Dougie and he picked up packages of heroin from the white Chrysler."

"Who was he?" Locker asked. "The man in the Chrysler?"

"I don't know no names," Ford said. "But I know where the guy works that owns the white car. I was up there once, this welding shop on Marine Drive right in Burnaby."

"What about a name?"

"I told you I never heard the guy's name," Ford said. "He's a short guy, old guy, wears glasses."

"Your nephew's looking at a long sentence, Fred," Ser- geant Locker said. "We got him on possession for the pur- poses of trafficking. That won't go easy."

"Think about this," Ford said. "I go up to the welding shop and get the licence number off the Chrysler. That tells you who the owner is, the little old guy."

"For that," Locker said, "you're asking us to drop the charge against James Mortimer?"

"Whatever you do with the guy owns the Chrysler," Ford said, "that's your business. But I give you the licence number, you fix it for Jimmy."

"I can't guarantee anything here and now, Fred," Locker said. "Other people, the Department of Justice, have to be in on this."

"Well, for chrissake, you guys better make up your minds in a hurry," Ford said. "My sister's all over me about Jimmy, and this is a real good bargain I'm giving you."

"You get the licence number, Fred," Locker said. "We'll see what we can do for one another."

The white Chrysler was registered to a man named William De Ruiter. If he was a member of Doug Palmer's drug ring, he was an atypical member, neither young nor an East Ender. De Ruiter was a quiet, self-effacing man in his mid-fifties who lived in Richmond, a suburb south of Vancouver. He earned his living breaking down cars and selling the parts. Nevertheless, when Ford produced the licence number that identified De Ruiter, the Mounties welcomed the news. They began an investigation of De Ruiter and put a hold on the charge against Jimmy Mortimer. Fred Ford seemed to have struck a deal that got Mortimer out of jail and himself out of hot water with his sister. In the meantime, he kept quiet to Doug Palmer about his conversation with Sergeant Jim Locker and went on handling his job as a Palmer back-end man.

At two o'clock on the morning of October 20, 1972, less than two weeks after Ford had traded the information about Bill De Ruiter for his nephew's freedom, a dozen Mounties took up position outside De Ruiter's house at 2335 Westminster Highway in Richmond. The house was one-storey and humble. It had a front and a back door. The Mounties, waving shotguns, charged through both.

De Ruiter was alone in the house and emerged from a bedroom wearing long johns and hooking on his spectacles. The Mounties shoved shotguns in his forlorn face. They cuffed his hands behind his back, sat him on a sofa, and ransacked the house. Corporal Ron MacKay hoisted himself into the dusty attic through a trapdoor in the front hall. He shone his flashlight on a blue flight bag in one corner. The flight bag was conspicuously free of dust. The corporal opened it and, wearing gloves, inspected the items inside: one weigh-scale, one ten-pound bag of lactose, one bread bag containing 144 condoms which held capsules of heroin at the rate of fifty caps per condom, one bag of heroin in bulk form, one bag of fifty-five empty condoms, one metal flour-sifter. A flour-sifter? It was commonly used in the drug trade to mix lactose and heroin and thereby cut the drug.

The RCMP officers figured, with plenty of evidence at hand, including a total of forty-four ounces of heroin, that they had uncovered the paraphernalia of a thriving little capping-up operation. They couldn't establish conclusively that Doug Palmer was connected to the find in De Ruiter's house, but they were fairly certain they'd taken forty-four ounces of Palmer's heroin off the market. They charged Bill De Ruiter with possession of heroin for the purposes of trafficking.

One of the Mounties on the raid, Wayne Gadd, was a fingerprint expert. He dusted the bags and implements that came down from the attic. But Constable Gadd located only a single print. It was on the flour-sifter. And it wasn't Bill De Ruiter's.

Whether or not Bill De Ruiter, in his fifties and seemingly not qualified by age or personality to keep company with the East End guys, was a member of Doug Palmer's drug business, his arrest and the seizure of the heroin generated unease and anger among the Palmer group. Through the late fall of 1972 and into the winter, De Ruiter's fate was a subject of constant discussion around the tables of the Polynesian Lounge at the Waldorf. How did the Mounties pick up on the cache of stuff in the house down in Richmond? Someone had to have fingered De Ruiter. But who? Largely by the process of elimination, Doug Palmer arrived at a candidate for the role of snitch. He had no hard proof, but he suspected one member of his crew.

Fred Ford.

Palmer sent word that he wanted a special meeting with Ford. It took place on the evening of January 20, 1973, but not at the Waldorf. Palmer specified the Admiral's Lounge, a bar in a marginally more discreet hotel several blocks further east on Hastings Street in Burnaby. Doug Palmer had tough talk in mind and he wanted privacy in which to unload it.

"Hey, Dougie," Ford said when he arrived. "What's happening?"

Palmer wasted no time.

"I'll tell you what's happening, asshole," he said. "You're fired."

"*Fired*!?" Ford said. He put on a show of surprise at this stunning turn of events. "Fired? You're not gonna use me no more? This is crap, Dougie."

"Don't mess with me, man," Palmer said. "You're out as of right now."

"But everything's going smooth, Dougie," Ford protested. "I haven't screwed a single deal in however long I been with you. What? Year and a half?"

"What I think," Palmer said, eyes locked on Ford, "you're the guy set up Bill De Ruiter."

242

"Dougie, you gotta believe me," Ford said, "I don't know word one from what you're saying."

"You know who Bill De Ruiter is, right?"

"Guy I hear everybody talking about. Little old guy."

"You know the cops threw him in the bucket," Palmer said. "And from the talk around, maybe you knew the bust was going down before it happened."

"This is ridiculous, Dougie," Ford said. "I had nothing to do with the thing."

"You're fired," Palmer said. "This conversation's done."

"What about my money?" Ford said. "You owe me for buries I made the last couple weeks. Comes to twelve thousand, twelve-five."

"You're talking to me about money?" Palmer said, disdain weighting his words. "Man, you're lucky to be alive. If I find out for sure it was you set up De Ruiter's place, you better be looking over your shoulder even when you're sleeping."

Fred Ford was scared. The pressure was coming at him from two sides. On one side, Doug Palmer had cut him off from his source of income and had threatened to cut him off from his life. On the other side, the Mounties were hounding him for more information about the Palmer drug network.

If Ford thought the RCMP would settle for Bill De Ruiter in exchange for Jimmy Mortimer, he had committed another colossal blunder. Ford's indication to Sergeant Jim Locker that he belonged on the second tier of Doug Palmer's organization only whetted Locker's appetite for further revelations from Ford. During the last months of 1972 and into 1973, Locker bombarded Ford with phone calls, mixing promises and warnings in a tidy little package that he hoped Ford would find irresistible.

"Son of a bitch!" Ford said to Locker during one call. "You took De Ruiter when I give him to you, but you always knew you were gonna suck me for more, am I right?"

Locker said, "Fred, we appreciate what you did for us, but De Ruiter is just one small part of the machine."

Ford said, "He wasn't so damned small when I told you about him down at the station, the time you had Jimmy."

"We want to be sure we've got Doug Palmer, Fred," Locker said. "You can help us and help yourself at the same time."

"You kidding me?" Ford said. "Dougie'd have my ass if he knew I was even talking to you."

"We'll look after you, Fred," Locker said. "Take you into protective custody, you and the family. Relocate you."

"Big deal."

"Make it easy on yourself," Locker said. "We've already got Palmer and the rest of them on a preliminary hearing downtown."

"Right, I know," Ford said. "So how come you want me?"

"With you as a crown witness, Fred," Locker said, "we can put together a stronger case."

"I done time, Locker," Ford said. "I know what happens to guys that squeal."

"Fred," Locker said, "it could be a whole lot worse if you don't go along with us. You could get swept up with Palmer and his friends."

"Jesus, man," Ford said. "You're doing bad things to my head."

On January 24, 1973, four days after Ford's conversation with Doug Palmer in the Admiral's Lounge, the confrontation that gave Ford a shot of fear, he decided that his chances of survival might be stronger if he tossed in with the RCMP. He phoned Locker, who turned him over to Neil MacKay, another sergeant on the drug squad. MacKay had eighteen years on the force, long enough to have developed a smooth, ingratiating style with guys like Fred Ford. MacKay's new assignment was to hold Ford's hand.

Neil MacKay moved Ford into a downtown Vancouver

hotel with round-the-clock Mounties for company. To ensure that Ford was as thick with the Palmer gang as he claimed to be, MacKay asked him for physical evidence of his drug dealings. Easy, Ford said. He led MacKay to a house in the South Surrey neighbourhood. Ford said the place was one of his pickup locations for heroin, and inside, he pointed MacKay to a green garbage bag wrapped in black tape. When MacKay opened the bag, he found himself counting condoms. There were 326 of them, and each was filled with fifty capsules of heroin.

"You pass the test, Fred," MacKay said.

The two men got down to serious discussions about a trade, Ford's testimony against Doug Palmer even up for the RCMP's protective custody of Ford, his wife, and two children. Ford wanted details. Where would the Mounties find him a new home? How far from the East End? What part of the country? What about money? MacKay provided the answers.

"Y'know," Ford said, "this is the opposite of everything I oughta be doing. Ratting on guys I done business with."

Neil MacKay said, "I could tell you you're doing your duty as a good citzen, Fred."

"Saving my own neck."

"You could put it that way."

"There's one thing you gotta fix for me in this whole deal," Ford said.

"Well, we're going to relocate you and your family — "
Ford interrupted Mackay.

"Yeah, yeah," he said. "But you also gotta do something about my tattoos."

"Are you serious?" MacKay asked, half amazed, half amused.

"You can easy identify a person by the tattoos," Ford said, dead serious. "Everybody's got different pictures and words. Mine are like nobody else's I ever seen."

"Removing tattoos isn't a normal part of our relocation

program," MacKay said. "But I think we can probably look after your problem."

"I figure what I oughta do when this crap is all over is split to another country," Ford said. "England maybe."

"You'd be on your own in that case, Fred," MacKay said. "Our guarantee is to look after you and your wife and kids until you testify. After that, we'll move you some place inside Canada and set you up with a new identity."

"And a down payment on a house," Ford added.

"We'll carry you until you get yourself a job," MacKay said.

"I should live so long," Ford said.

The preliminary hearing for the men charged with conspiracy to traffic in heroin came before Provincial Court Judge D. D. Jones on November 14, 1972. With occasional time out for Judge Jones and the lawyers on the case to look after other scheduled cases, the hearing lasted on and off until late January of 1973. Ten men had been charged in the conspiracy, but only nine showed up for the preliminary. Bill Turner skipped out, and the Mounties were unable to find a trace of him. The nine remaining accused were represented in court by their lawyers, and the preliminary brought together for the first time the two principal counsel in the case. They were Arthur MacLennan, the crown attorney responsible for prosecuting the accused men, and Harry Walsh, the lawyer acting for Doug and Donald Palmer and the leader among the defence counsel in court.

About the only elements that MacLennan and Walsh had in common were their profession, lawyer, and their age, early sixties. In all other ways, visible and invisible, they were direct opposites. MacLennan was Wasp. Walsh was Jewish. MacLennan was tall and angular, built like an aging cowboy. He peppered his conversation, which was usually soft-spoken, with "shucks" and "golly" and with dry chuckles. Walsh was shorter and rounder, with the looks appropriate to a Roman senator. He had a magisterial way of holding himself and words flowed from him in stately rhythms. MacLennan wasn't particularly seasoned in criminal law. Walsh had been a defence counsel all his professional life. MacLennan had lived in Vancouver for forty years. Walsh was from Winnipeg, an out-of-towner on the Palmer case.

Arthur MacLennan went to law school in Alberta, where he was called to the bar in 1935, but he soon shook the Prairies for Vancouver. He formed a small firm with an old Alberta friend and built a busy practice with the emphasis on civil litigation. By 1972, MacLennan was ripe for a change — "I got tired of ordinary practice" — and he tapped his Liberal Party connections in Ottawa for an appointment to the Vancouver criminal section of the Department of Justice. His responsibilities took in combines cases, tax evasion, and drug offences. For MacLennan, the drug cases represented uncharted territory.

"When the Palmer case arrived on my desk, I knew hardly anything about narcotics prosecutions," MacLennan says today. "What made it even tougher was that the Palmer affair was incredibly complicated. Well, by golly, I just taught myself to handle it."

MacLennan's initial problem was that the evidence came at him in hundreds of memos and bits and pieces of paper from the RCMP. Each memo and each scrap of paper carried the details of a Mountie surveillance. The blizzard of documents called for a system, something that would keep confusion at bay. MacLennan's system began with several sheets of very large blank paper.

"I drew circles on the paper," MacLennan explains. "I made a circle for each RCMP report. Inside the circle, I wrote the date, the event, and the names of the Palmer people who took part in the event. I kept drawing, and eventually I had dozens of circles that were linked to one another by the names of the people in them. I knew who the accused were and what they did and where the unindicted co-conspirators fit into the picture, the people who were part of the conspiracy but hadn't been charged. By the time I went to court, I was pretty sure I had a grasp on the whole bunch of those characters."

Harry Walsh knew he had a grasp on the case for the defence from the very beginning. He had laboured for a whole career on such cases in the criminal courts. He was called to the Manitoba bar in 1937 and went into practice with a man named Jim McMurray, who was the wizard among Winnipeg defence lawyers. That was a title that Walsh came eventually to inherit. He defended scores of clients charged with murder and wrung from juries many astounding acquittals. His reputation spread beyond Winnipeg and he was summoned to represent accused people in distant Canadian cities. When Conrad Gunn and Dave Ponack were convicted in Vancouver of conspiracy to traffic in narcotics in the fall of 1970, Walsh was retained to argue the two men's appeals in both the B.C. Court of Appeal and the Supreme Court of Canada. Walsh's point on the appeals was that key evidence against Gunn and Ponack had been improperly admitted at the trial. Both courts rejected his argument, and Gunn and Ponack went away to do their time. Still, Doug Palmer was impressed by the word in the East End on Harry Walsh, and he hired Walsh to act for him and brother Donald at the preliminary hearing.

If Doug Palmer considered Walsh a splendid criminal lawyer, Walsh reciprocated the warm feelings. Walsh has never been a lawyer to pass social hours with his clients, but when he acts for them on a case, he brings with him a nicely developed partisan spirit.

"Doug Palmer was a clean-living family man," Walsh insisted years later. "Just because he knew people in the drug trade didn't mean he should be convicted of conspiracy to traffic. And, apart from what developed later out of the very suspect word of Fred Ford, that was the only real evidence the

248

crown had against Palmer — that he had drinks in a certain lounge with people who dealt in narcotics."

From the outset of the preliminary hearing in mid-November 1972, Arthur MacLennan felt beleaguered.

"Exhausting," he remembers. "The preliminary was as exhausting as anything I've ever done in court. Defence counsel, especially Mr. Walsh, kept trying to throw me off stride. They asked my witnesses impossible questions. They nibbled at my evidence. And it wasn't any help as far as I was concerned that Judge Jones let Mr. Walsh wander all over the place in cross-examination. Maybe Mr. Walsh's reputation impressed the judge."

Nevertheless, MacLennan was dogged in his presentation of the crown's case against Doug Palmer and his co-accused. He summoned a parade of RCMP witnesses to testify. Sergeants Beaulieu and Kilner and Welychka. Corporals Hart and Richert and Brown and Schafer. He called the men who went undercover into the Polynesian Lounge, the officers who staked out the homes of the accused men, and the Mounties who were in Ladner on the night when Tommy Duncan performed his drunken routine with the garbage bag of heroin. MacLennan withstood the happy gibes of defence counsel whenever the subject of the catastrophe at the bus depot surfaced. And steadily, relentlessly, through the sheer numbers of witnesses, all the members of the Vancouver drug squad, and through the cumulative weight of the testimony, he shaped an argument for committing the nine men to trial in a higher court on the conspiracy charge.

Judge D. D. Jones ruled that MacLennan was two-thirds right. Of the nine accused men, Jones held at the end of the preliminary hearing that six should be bound over for trial. On the other three, he ordered a discharge. Two of the three were Mike Watson, who, in Jones's view, had only a fleeting connection with the conspiracy, and Ed Stenson, about whom Jones wrote, "He may be blackened by the tar of suspicion arising out of his association with the others, but the totality of evidence against him is insufficient to bring him within the ambit of conspiratorial activity." Stenson looked on the discharge as a fair trade-off against the thirty-four ounces of plain white flour he'd been stuck with. MacLennan wasn't seriously concerned about losing Watson and Stenson, but he was distressed by the discharge of the third man. Donald Palmer.

"It was my mistake that cost us Donald," MacLennan says today. The error, as MacLennan explains, stemmed directly from Bill Turner's disappearance before the preliminary hearing began. "Not being too bright about such things," MacLennan says, "I just deleted Turner's name from the list of accused when he skipped out on his bail. I shouldn't have. I should have named him as one of the unindicted co-conspirators. But, shucks, I couldn't foresee that most of the strong evidence against Donald in the conspiracy, even allowing for the time he was found with the ten thousand dollars in the safe at his house, involved dealings that Bill Turner alone was also connected with. Since Turner was no longer listed as a conspirator or even an unindicted co-conspirator, I couldn't use that evidence. So Donald had to be discharged."

MacLennan was determined to reclaim Donald Palmer. "Even if he was a little simple, he was still central to the whole darned conspiracy," MacLennan says. And MacLennan was prepared to go to complicated lengths to get the job accomplished.

He plotted a secret tactic that would turn the case upside down. "The heck with it, I decided to lay a new charge against the entire gang of them, and that included Donald," MacLennan explains. "Naturally I didn't forewarn the defence counsel what I had in mind, but the plan was to just drop the old charge and start over again with a second charge that would cover a longer and continuing conspiracy. The Palmer fellows were still out on the street selling their drugs anyway. So I encouraged the RCMP to keep up their surveillance until we had enough evidence for this new and bigger conspiracy."

But MacLennan recognized one possible hitch in the plan. What if defence counsel pressed him to get on with the trial of the six men on the first conspiracy charge? MacLennan couldn't stall on such a request, and an early trial would rob the Mounties of the months they needed to put together the second conspiracy charge.

"That's where Mr. Walsh made a mistake of his own," MacLennan says today, the grin of a Cheshire cat decorating his face.

Walsh appealed Judge Jones's ruling at the preliminary hearing. He thought he had grounds to ask an appeal court to throw out the committal to trial of Doug Palmer and the other five accused. Much testimony at the preliminary, Walsh contended, had been improperly admitted in evidence. It was a point similar to the argument he raised in the Gunn-Ponack appeal. But this time, he looked for a win.

"Well, Mr. Walsh couldn't have known he was helping me," MacLennan says, softening the grin of pleasure at the memory of the small but crucial triumph his opponent inadvertently handed him. "But when Mr. Walsh brought his appeal, it gave the RCMP and me all the time we needed to gather evidence for the new charge. I didn't care whether I won or lost the appeal. Regardless of the outcome, I was going back to the beginning and start from scratch with a second conspiracy case."

Fred Ford changed his mind.

He stuck it out in protective custody with Sergeant Neil MacKay for ten days. The two men batted the deal back and forth, Ford's testimony in court in exchange for the RCMP's relocation of Ford and his family. At first Ford appeared anxious to cut an agreement and escape the streets of the East End, where, as Doug Palmer had warned him, his life might be in danger. But as the days passed, as the memory of Palmer's threat receded, Ford rethought his position. The East End was all he knew. He resisted the notion of moving across the country to a strange neighbourhood in an alien city. He wouldn't know the turf. And, what the hell, he told himself that Dougie Palmer wasn't going to hit on him. Dougie had other, larger worries. And this protective custody was a drag. Who needed it. Not Fred Ford. Better to be back on the street. Back in his own house.

On February 3, 1973, ten days after Ford checked in with Sergeant MacKay, he checked out. He returned to his home at 3475 Triumph Street in the East End and he returned to his pre-Doug Palmer employment. He dealt in drugs as a small-time private entrepreneur. The transactions didn't put him in the hundred-thousand-per-year category he'd enjoyed as a Palmer back-end man, but it was a living. And it seemed to be a safe living. Doug Palmer, as far as Ford could make out, had lost interest in punishing him over the De Ruiter incident. Everything, Ford decided, was cooled out.

Except that Neil MacKay was on his back. Ford may have walked away from MacKay's protective custody, but he couldn't stop the sergeant's telephone calls. It was like the old days with Sergeant Jim Locker. MacKay phoned once, a couple times, every week, and the message was invariably the same. Fred, MacKay would say, your neck is in a sling unless you come back and tell us what you know about Doug Palmer's drug operations. Ford resisted. He didn't know that Arthur MacLennan and the Mounties were building a fresh conspiracy charge against the Palmer group. He could hardly be aware that Sergeant Mackay wanted desperately to include Ford's testimony in the package of evidence for the new charge. All he understood was that MacKay was driving him nuts with the phone calls.

After the night of December 7, 1973, MacKay's message to Ford acquired a subtly different rhythm. On that night, someone knocked over Shore's Credit Jewellers in downtown Vancouver. The robbers broke into the store and scooped up two thousand dollars in watches and loose cash. The Vancouver police picked up a pair of rounders who admitted the robbery and fingered Fred Ford as the brains behind the enterprise. Police charged Ford with robbery and possession of stolen goods and sent news of the bust to the RCMP. The drug squad rubbed its collective hands and cooked up some behind-the-scenes machinations. Each time Ford's robbery and possession charges were called in court, the crown had them put over to a later date. It wasn't even necessary for Ford to appear in the courtroom. His case had entered a limbo. In Neil MacKay's regular calls to Ford, he made only oblique reference to the charges and to the seemingly endless delay in their disposition in court, but he let Ford know that just maybe Ford owed one to the RCMP.

"For chrissake, MacKay," Ford said. "Gimme a little space."

Ford knew he was between a rock and a hard place, but he still refused to commit himself as a witness against Doug Palmer.

Much later, Russ Chamberlain figured out that it was Doug Palmer who sent Bill De Ruiter to Chamberlain's law offices. But at the time, in the fall of 1972, when De Ruiter first consulted him, Chamberlain accepted De Ruiter as just another client who was charged with possession of heroin for the purposes of trafficking.

Russ Chamberlain was in his late twenties, a burly, confident man with a voice full of intimidation. He came out of the University of British Columbia Law School in 1968 with high grades and went to work in the office of Harry Rankin, the guru of Vancouver criminal lawyers. From the beginning,

Rankin steered tough and high-profile cases in Chamberlain's direction. Many of the clients Chamberlain represented were charged with drug offences. Chamberlain didn't care for drug clients. "These people want their profits," he says of traffickers. "But they can't take the heat when they're caught. And they don't pay their legal bills." At first Chamberlain thought Bill De Ruiter was another whining drug client, but he soon changed his mind. "De Ruiter was an ordinary working guy with dirty hands," Chamberlain says. "You looked at him and you thought, salt of the earth." Chamberlain never changed his mind about De Ruiter, not even when he discovered, years later, that De Ruiter's legal bills were being paid by Doug Palmer.

De Ruiter told Chamberlain his story. He talked about the RCMP's early-morning raid on his house, about the Mounties' discovery in the attic of the heroin and the drug paraphernalia. De Ruiter said he didn't know how all the stuff got up in his attic. He had nothing to do with drugs. He stripped down old cars and sold the parts. That was his business. Chamberlain accepted De Ruiter's story and set about the work of preparing a defence for his new client.

At the preliminary hearing on the charge against De Ruiter in the late spring of 1973, Chamberlain sniffed something fishy. The crown attorney put his RCMP witnesses on the stand. They described their search of De Ruiter's house and the finding of the blue flight bag and its contents. The flight bag, the weigh-scales, the bags of condoms, and the heroin and the flour-sifter were introduced as exhibits in evidence. Chamberlain took note of the particles of black powder on the exhibits. Okay, he thought, they've been dusted for fingerprints. And he waited for the other shoe to drop: whose fingerprints turned up on the weigh-scales and the bags and the sifter? But the crown attorney called no RCMP fingerprint expert as a witness. Nothing was said in evidence about prints. At the conclusion of the preliminary hearing, the judge held that there was enough evidence to send Chamberlain's client on for trial in a higher court. Chamberlain arranged bail for De Ruiter and went back to his office to brood over the mystery of the apparently non-existent fingerprints.

Jack Wismer was the crown attorney on the De Ruiter case, a veteran, a pro, a fair man, and when Chamberlain phoned him about fingerprints, he answered that, as far as he knew, no prints had been found. Chamberlain reasoned that Wismer was by nature incapable of holding out on a defence counsel but that the Mounties were capable of holding out on Wismer. He blitzed the RCMP drug squad with phone calls. Months went by before Chamberlain got the answers he was looking for. They came in a telephone conversation with Sergeant Jim Locker.

"We turned up something all right, Mr. Chamberlain," Locker said. "A fingerprint."

"Just one?"

"It was on the metal sifter."

"Whose was it?" Chamberlain asked, sucking in his breath.

"Not your client's."

Chamberlain breathed out.

"You got an identity on it?" he asked Locker.

"Duncan," Locker answered. "Print belongs to a man named Tommy Duncan."

The ubiquitous Tommy Duncan, a regular at the Polynesian Lounge, pal of Doug Palmer's, screw-up artist in Ladner.

Chamberlain went to De Ruiter and pieced together the rest of the story. Sure, De Ruiter told him, Tommy Duncan was a friend. He used to give Tommy the run of the house in Richmond. Duncan was in and out of the place, sleeping, eating, watching TV, even when De Ruiter wasn't at home. Chamberlain smiled. He had his defence.

De Ruiter's trial took place before a County Court judge and jury in mid-January 1974. The RCMP officers told the familiar tale about the search of De Ruiter's house and about the store of drugs and drug equipment they'd uncovered in the attic. In cross-examination, Chamberlain elicited testimony that revealed the owner of the fingerprint on the flour-sifter. The testimony paved the way for Chamberlain to offer the jury his version of events. It was Tommy Duncan, Chamberlain argued, who conducted the capping-up operation in Bill De Ruiter's house. Duncan waited until De Ruiter went out before he weighed, cut, and capped the heroin. When De Ruiter returned home, Duncan hid the drugs and the weigh-scales, sifter, and condoms in the attic. De Ruiter was an innocent victim of Tommy Duncan's crime. Just consider, Chamberlain underlined to the jury, that it wasn't De Ruiter's fingerprint on the sifter. The print belonged to Tommy Duncan, who already faced drug charges in another case.

"De Ruiter made a hell of a fine witness," Chamberlain says. "Here he was, a plain, taciturn, working guy, fifty-three, fifty-four years old, and he got up on the stand and stared through his glasses and said in a few monosyllables that he didn't know anything about drugs. Well, the jury were thinking to themselves, hey, this guy doesn't look like any kind of big-time heroin dealer."

The jury acquitted De Ruiter.

In the year and a half that began in late January 1973 with Judge D. D. Jones's decision in the preliminary hearing on the Palmer gang conspiracy charge and that ended in the summer of 1974, events in the case barrelled along on several fronts.

Doug Palmer and his associates, though they were aware that the Mounties must be keeping tabs on their activities, continued the lucrative dealings in heroin.

The Mounties, though they were certain that the Palmer guys had a weather eye out for the cops, went on with their undercover observations at the Waldorf Hotel and other Palmer hangouts.

Sergeant Neil MacKay maintained his pitch to Fred Ford to reveal everything about his past associations with Doug Palmer.

Ford waffled, promising to testify one week, rescinding the promise the next week.

Harry Walsh presented his argument to the appeal court that Judge Jones's decision to commit Doug Palmer and his five co-accused to trial should be set aside.

The appeal court mulled over Walsh's argument and rejected it.

Arthur MacLennan and the Mounties worked in secret to prepare a second conspiracy charge against all of the Palmer gang members including Donald Palmer.

In early August 1974, MacLennan at last announced that he was laying the new charge and dropping the old. The second alleged conspiracy covered almost five and a half years, from February 1969 to July 1974, and the named conspirators were eight men. Seven of them comprised the Palmer core group: Doug and Donald Palmer, Tommy Duncan, Bobby Porter, Cliff Luhtala, Johnny Smith, and the Montreal courier Walter Guay. The eighth conspirator was the odd man out — Bill De Ruiter.

The inclusion of De Ruiter's name in the list infuriated his lawyer, Russ Chamberlain. De Ruiter had already been acquitted on the substantive charge of trafficking in heroin. Now he was roped in on the lesser charge of conspiring to traffic. Chamberlain considered the second charge an abuse of the legal process.

"What it signalled to me about those guys," he said years later, speaking of the Mounties and the crown's office, "is that they were sore about getting beat on the trafficking charge, and to get even, they were going to play hardball. Well, so was I."

The information on the second conspiracy also named

eighteen unindicted co-conspirators. These were the people who fit into a middle category: they were, in the Mounties' view, part of the conspiracy to traffic in the heroin, but the Mounties lacked enough evidence to convict them as conspirators. By citing them as co-conspirators, the crown was permitted to introduce evidence at trial that centred on the co-conspirators but that, more important, might point the finger of guilt at the eight principal conspirators.

The eighteen unindicted co-conspirators included familiar names: Conrad Gunn, the veteran and already convicted drug conspirator; Allan Cressie, the money-changer; Ed Stenson, who'd been let off at the preliminary hearing on the first conspiracy charge; and the elusive Bill Turner, who had played a major role in the conspiracy and then gone missing before the first preliminary, a status he continued to maintain. The other co-conspirators were mainly men who were old hands on the Vancouver drug scene. The Mounties had observed them in occasional consort with the Palmer gang, and since many of them had been charged and convicted in past heroin conspiracies, the mention of their names and former drug associations at the Palmer trial would help to persuade the court that Doug Palmer and his pals were irretrievably wrapped up in illegal narcotics activities.

In the list of unindicted co-conspirators, there was one final name that belonged in a class of its own. It was not the name of a regular in the Palmer circle or of a veteran drug dealer. It was Fred Ford's name. In packaging Ford with the other conspirators and co-conspirators, Arthur MacLennan and the RCMP were going public with their pressure to induce Ford to testify for the crown. Sergeant Neil MacKay's blandishments and warnings hadn't got Ford on side. Scare tactics might do the job. Ford's inclusion as a co-conspirator was calculated to displease Doug Palmer. He'd wonder how much the RCMP knew of Ford's earlier part in the Palmer operation. Had Ford already opened his mouth to the Mounties? Was he likely to be called as a crown witness at the new preliminary hearing? And if he testified, would he spill what he knew about the drug ring? Where Ford was concerned, MacLennan and the RCMP had given Doug Palmer plenty to ponder, and in so doing, they'd tightened the squeeze on Fred Ford.

Ford's reaction was to pour himself a beer. Then a second, another couple, four or five more. He got the news of his status as an unindicted co-conspirator in the Palmer case when he read it in the *Vancouver Sun* on August 10, 1974. Sitting in his living-room, fretting, thinking over his options — take off to another country? ask the Mounties for protective custody? stay loose and hope Dougie Palmer didn't come after him? — he was working on his tenth or twelfth beer when his older brother Billy dropped by. Billy, a boyhood chum of Doug Palmer, was on an errand.

"What is this, Freddie?" Billy said. "I got this important message for you, and you're sitting here getting wasted."

"Lemme ask you a question," Fred Ford said. "What in fuck would you do if your name was all over the goddamn papers with Dougie Palmer and those guys?"

"Dougie's who sent the message."

"I'm asking you something," Ford said. "Wouldn't you have a couple drinks if the Mounties said you was in a drug conspiracy with Dougie Palmer?"

"Maybe."

"Fucking right."

"Dougie wants to talk to you," Billy Ford said.

"That's the message?"

"Over at the Waldorf."

"You shitting me?" Fred Ford said. "Me walk into the Waldorf?"

"All he wants is to talk," Billy said. "That's what he told me to tell you."

"Be like walking into the OK Corral."

"Freddie, it isn't all that serious," Billy said. "A little conversation is all."

"Think I got garbage for brains?"

"This is Dougie Palmer we're talking about," Billy said. "You hafta do something. I ain't going back and tell him you got no answer to the message I brought."

"Don't lean on it, Billy," Ford said. "You're gonna have an answer."

Ford pushed himself out of his chair and rummaged in a table drawer.

"What kinda answer?" Billy asked.

"Written," Fred answered. "Like, a memo."

He found a pad of letter-paper and a blue ballpoint pen in the drawer. Ford scribbled two sentences on a sheet from the pad, folded the sheet in two, and handed it to his brother.

"This's all?" Billy said.

"Tell Dougie I couldn't make it over to the Waldorf," Fred Ford said. "But say you got this, um, statement from me."

"Yeah?"

"It'll square me," Ford said. "No problem."

"Well," Billy said. "Your funeral."

"Y'know what, Billy," Fred Ford said. "You got a great way of putting things."

Billy Ford drove from his brother's house to the Waldorf Hotel. Doug Palmer, at a table in the Polynesian Lounge, was waiting for him.

"So, Billy," Palmer said, "where's your asshole brother?"

"Well, lookit, Dougie," Ford said. "Freddie's kinda lying low. Under the circumstances, y'know what I mean?"

"How come him and me got our names on the same information?" Palmer said. "That's the thing I want to know."

"Freddie's straight, I guarantee," Ford said. "He gave me this here note for you."

Palmer unfolded the piece of paper that Billy Ford handed across the table.

"'To whom it may concern,'" Palmer read out loud from the note.

Palmer stopped and looked at Billy Ford.

"You feature that?" he said. "It better fucking concern me."

His eyes went back to the note.

"'I, Fred Ford,'" Palmer read, "'have not ever conspired with one Douglas Palmer at any time. I know him of course, but I have never had any type of criminal activity with him.'"

Billy Ford said, "Couldn't be plainer, right, Dougie? Freddie even signed it."

"Your brother don't want to see me?" Palmer asked Ford.

"The note's instead," Ford said. "You show that to your lawyer, Dougie, and, hell, the Mounties can't make out nothing between you and Freddie."

Doug Palmer refolded the note and slid it into the breast pocket of his shirt.

He said, "Mounties make anything between him and me, your brother's in deep shit."

The preliminary hearing in the second conspiracy case was scheduled to begin in Provincial Court on September 13, 1974. By that date, Sergeant Neil MacKay was reasonably certain that Ford had come around and would testify as a crown witness. The crown was free to subpoena Ford and compel him to testify, but if Ford went into the hearing as an uncooperative witness, his testimony was unlikely to be frank and full and helpful to the crown's case. Sergeant MacKay knew nothing of the note that Ford had sent via his brother to Doug Palmer. As far as MacKay could gather from his conversations with Ford in late August and early September, Ford ought to make a friendly and valuable witness for the crown. Reluctant maybe, scared undoubtedly, but prepared to answer questions that stood to cinch the case against Doug Palmer.

Which explained why MacKay was more than a trifle upset when Ford vanished on September 13. Everyone connected with the case was primed to show up in the courtroom on the appointed date: the eight accused conspirators and their lawyers, Arthur MacLennan for the crown, and three or four dozen crown witnesses. But when MacKay discovered that Ford had skipped, he went into a huddle with MacLennan, who arranged to postpone the preliminary hearing until the following February.

Where was Fred Ford?

Somewhere on the American west coast.

That was the story he told Sergeant MacKay when he resurfaced back home in the East End later in the autumn. Got cold feet, Ford said to MacKay, and the off-again, on-again Ford remained uncooperative for the next several weeks. MacKay couldn't break through Ford's self-protective shell. No one could budge him until the dramatic events of January 5, 1975.

Fred Ford's house at 3475 Triumph Street was tidy and one-storey, built of cement and clapboard. Like all the houses on Triumph, it was set close to the road. The front yard had a small patch of grass overhung by a craggy old tree on the lawn of the house next door. Number 3475 was positioned at the crest of a steep hill that sloped down to the west, where it ended at a permanent barrier closing off the street. Triumph didn't attract much traffic apart from deliverymen and people visiting the street's residents. In the summer, sounds of the roller coaster and other rides drifted up the hill from the carnival in Exhibition Park on the other side of Cassair Road to the west. In the winter, the street was still and hushed.

On the night of January 5, at almost exactly nine o'clock, Ford stepped from the front door of his house. He walked the seven or eight steps that took him down his walk to the road. It was a dark night, and Ford didn't notice anyone on Triumph until a man stepped close to him. The man had a mask over his face and he was carrying a pistol in each hand.

"*Blam!*"

The blast from one pistol ricocheted through the quiet of Triumph Street.

"*Blam!*"

The man in the mask fired from the second gun.

"*Blam!*"

With the third shot, doors on Triumph flew open.

Ford's wife raced out of Number 3475.

"Oh my God!" she screamed. "There's *blood!*"

Ford lay on the sidewalk face up. His wife cradled his head. Ford was conscious but seemed to be bleeding from his legs, torso, and cheek. Neighbours surrounded him, and in the commotion, no one noticed the masked man with the two pistols slip away.

A neighbour phoned for an ambulance and a police car, and within ten minutes, both screeched on to Triumph Street.

Sergeant Gil Steer of the Vancouver City Police was the senior man on the scene.

"Who shot you?" he asked Ford. "Can you speak? Who shot you?"

Ford's voice was low and weak, but Sergeant Steer had no trouble making out his words.

"Pick up Doug Palmer," Ford said.

"Did this Palmer shoot you?" Steer asked.

"Just pick up Doug Palmer."

"Okay, officer," an ambulance attendant broke in. "We gotta take this guy to the hospital."

The ambulance, siren squealing, sped south and west to Vancouver General Hospital at West 12th and Heather Street. Within an hour, not much after ten o'clock, a Vancouver Police detective named Bill Garos was standing at

Ford's side in the hospital's emergency section. Nurses and doctors were preparing Ford for surgery, but they allowed Garos a short interview with their patient. Garos had already talked to Sergeant Steer and he had a head start in his questioning.

"Who shot you, Mr. Ford?" Garos began.

"I don't know," Ford answered.

"You mentioned a man at the scene of the shooting."

"Yeah, Doug Palmer," Ford said. "He didn't do it. He's too chicken. He hired someone."

"Why did he do it?"

"Guess he didn't like me."

Garos jotted Ford's answers on his pad.

"How many men involved?" he asked Ford.

"One."

"Did he have two guns?"

"Yeah."

"Did you see a car?"

"No."

"What did he look like?"

"He had a dark mask on and a toque and a dark coat."

Ford was running low on stamina.

Garos tried a final question.

"Did you know the man who shot you?" he asked Ford.

"No."

Two nurses wheeled Ford to surgery.

Fred Ford didn't die. In fact, he wasn't even close to being mortally wounded. He had bullet punctures in his legs, stomach, and head. He lost a couple of pints of blood and he felt lousy. But he was alive and frightened and talking his brains out to Sergeant Neil MacKay.

MacKay summoned the troops and enclosed Ford's hospital room in twenty-four-hour RCMP protection. Ten days later, when the patient's strength edged back, MacKay moved him and the round-the-clock Mounties out of Vancouver General and two blocks east to a suite in the Plaza 500 Hotel, a stolid fifteen-storey cement building that wouldn't have looked out of place in downtown Leningrad.

"Twelve hundred dollars," MacKay said to Ford. "You got that straight, Fred?"

Ford said, "First of every month, you pay me the twelve."

"Right," MacKay nodded to his prize pupil.

"And you look after my old lady and kids."

"Strict security for the whole family."

"That's for me testifying against Dougie at this thing in a couple weeks."

"Preliminary hearing," MacKay said. "And later you testify at the trial."

"The part I don't get," Ford said, "how come I can't do my number in court the one time and then I split?"

"We've been over this, Fred," MacKay said. "After the preliminary hearing, unless something goes haywire, which it won't, the Palmer people'll be committed to trial and you give the same evidence at the trial that you give on the preliminary."

"Then it's over."

"We relocate you and the family," MacKay said. "New identity, new home, new part of the country."

"That's when you stop paying me the twelve hundred?"

"Come on, Fred," MacKay said. "It'll cost us a whole lot more than twelve hundred a month to cover the relocation."

"Lemme ask you something else."

"Not the tattoos again."

"Forget them," Ford said. "Suppose after I say all this stuff in court, I just take the money instead, whatever it'd cost you guys to pay for the relocating. Suppose I do that and I look after the relocating myself."

"Accept a lump-sum payment?"

"Yeah."

"I guess it's possible," MacKay said. "But hardly advisable under the circumstances."

"It's what I'm thinking about."

"Think about this, Fred," MacKay said. "Someone in Vancouver's tried to kill you once. Maybe next time they'll get it right."

"The way things are, nothing's right anyway," Ford said. "Those pills the doctor gave me, they make my stomach feel like shit. I can't eat or sleep or nothing."

"Who's responsible for that?"

"Hadda be Dougie Palmer," Ford said. "There's other guys out on the street hate my guts, but I can't see any of them taking a blast at me. Dougie, I can see it, him sending a guy to do it."

Neil MacKay shared Ford's view of Doug Palmer as the man behind the shooting on Triumph, and so did his colleagues in the drug squad. But later an alternative theory made the rounds among street people and defence lawyers. Maybe, as Russ Chamberlain for one speculated, there was another candidate for the role of shooter.

"What about a policeman?" Chamberlain said. "I have no evidence, but I can imagine a scenario. The police tried everything to get Ford to testify — money, inducements, warnings — and Ford never rolled over. So they put some bullets in him, not enough to kill him, just enough to scare him into taking the stand in court."

One element in the attack on Ford, Chamberlain postulated, supported the notion of a policeman as assassin.

"When it was over, Ford was still alive," Chamberlain said. "That's crazy. Everybody knew the Palmers had access to a hit man, a guy who later went to prison for another killing, and this hit man didn't leave guys breathing on the street. When he was sent out on a hit, the victim was a sure dead man. If it was him, if Doug Palmer told this guy to do Fred

Ford, Ford wouldn't have been around to testify at the preliminary."

The preliminary hearing on the second conspiracy charge was largely a formality. True, from Arthur MacLennan it called for slogging, detailed, mind-numbing dedication. But he didn't have to establish the guilt of the eight accused conspirators. It was only necessary for him to satisfy the presiding judge that the eight should be passed on to a higher court where their guilt or innocence would be decided. And with the years of surveillance evidence from the Mounties and with Fred Ford's testimony of first-hand experience with Doug Palmer, it looked as if MacLennan had a lock on the preliminary. The hearing began in mid-February before a Provincial Court judge named Johnson, and from the start, as the crown plodded relentlessly through the roster of witnesses, MacLennan felt he had Johnson and everything else under control.

But there was one episode that got Arthur MacLennan's dander up. It came along early in the hearing, about the fourth or fifth day. Sergeant Neil MacKay was sitting beside MacLennan at the crown's table in court. MacKay's job was to direct traffic. Since MacLennan planned to use forty or fifty witnesses, most of them RCMP officers, someone had to take charge of the logistics involved in keeping the witnesses on call and running them in and out of the courtroom in the designated sequence. The chore fell to Neil MacKay.

On that fourth or fifth day of the preliminary, during a break in the proceedings, MacLennan grasped MacKay's arm and pointed out a man sitting in the courtroom's public seats. The man, who'd been in court each day, was making notes on a yellow legal-sized pad.

"I know that fellow," MacLennan said.

MacKay studied the man.

"He's a lawyer," MacKay said. "I've seen him around the courts."

"Not just any lawyer," MacLennan said. "He looks after civil work for the Palmer brothers."

"I can tell you something else about the guy," MacKay said.

"What?"

MacKay turned toward the dais at the front of the courtroom.

"That woman up there?" MacKay said. "Your Palmer lawyer lives with her."

MacKay was talking about the woman court reporter who was keeping the transcript of the testimony at the hearing.

"She can't sit on this case," MacLennan sputtered.

MacKay shrugged.

MacLennan said, "I could get a 'yes' from a witness and it might come out 'no' in the transcript."

At the end of the day, MacLennan telephoned the chief court reporter and demanded that he remove the woman reporter from the Palmer preliminary hearing. Next morning in court, a new reporter showed up for duty. A week later, MacLennan received two letters in the mail. One was from a lawyer representing the woman court reporter and the other was from a lawyer representing the reporter's lawyer boyfriend. Both demanded the MacLennan issue apologies to the aggrieved parties. MacLennan wrote back notes that he later described as "innocuous, along the lines of my hoping there were no hard feelings." That was good enough for the court reporter but not for her boyfriend. He commenced an action for slander and named MacLennan, Neil MacKay, and the federal government as defendants.

The slander action hung in the air through the Palmer preliminary hearing and was still around to bug MacLennan two years after the hearing ended. But it never reached the trial stage. The action had been filed at the outset in the British Columbia Supreme Court. That was where the tech-

nical goof came in. Since the federal government was a
named defendant in the suit, the only court that had jurisdiction was the Federal Court. The action was struck out in the
B.C. Supreme Court and never resumed in the proper court.

MacLennan saw something machiavellian in the lawsuit.

"I think somebody among the Palmer defence lawyers
might have had a hand in it," he said. "I was in the middle of
a tense preliminary hearing, and all of a sudden I had to fend
off a lawsuit in slander. I had the suspicion it was a plot to
rattle me."

MacLennan didn't rattle. He had Prairie tenacity, and he
trudged through the seven weeks of preliminary hearing.
The defence counsel took their whacks at the crown witnesses, particularly at Fred Ford, and they ferreted out useful
bits and pieces of information about MacLennan's case, a
possible weakness here, the trace of a flaw there. But everyone in the courtroom, crown and defence, understood that
the preliminary was a gavotte. A formality. They knew there
was enough evidence, with plenty left over, to have the eight
accused conspirators committed to trial.

Which is what, after the seven weeks of testimony, Judge
Johnson ruled.

In all, the judge had three counts to deal with in the
indictment before him.

Count One was the conspiracy to traffic in heroin and it
took in the Big Eight: the Palmer brothers, Cliff Luhtala,
Johnny Smith, Tommy Duncan, Bobby Porter, and the two
elderly parties, dapper Walter Guay and baffled Bill De Ruiter.

Count Two was confined to Tommy Duncan. It covered a
charge not merely of conspiring to traffic in heroin but of
possession of heroin for the purpose of trafficking. Which
heroin was that? The stuff that he so cavalierly tossed around
in Doug Manuel's crew-cab truck on the night of January 25,
1971.

Count Three hit Walter Guay with the same charge of

possession of heroin for the purpose of trafficking. The heroin in question was, of course, the thirty-four ounces that he more or less escorted from Montreal to the Vancouver train station in the green Lucerne suitcase in April 1971.

Judge Johnson held that the various accused men should stand trial in the B.C. Supreme Court on all three counts.

Russ Chamberlain told Bill De Ruiter that the best strategy at the upcoming trial was to elect to be tried by a jury.

"Jury acquitted you the first time around," Chamberlain said to De Ruiter in his office. "They'll do it again."

"Whatever you say, Russ," De Ruiter agreed.

"I'll explain it to you another way," Chamberlain went on. "If you go to trial in front of a judge sitting alone, you're going to be in danger of riding down with all those other guys, the Palmer brothers and the rest of them. You understand why?"

"Comes to the courts," De Ruiter said, "I don't understand shit."

"The crown's coming to court with a ton of surveillance evidence," Chamberlain said. "A whole regiment of Mounties is going to testify about seeing certain guys doing certain things, and somewhere in there you're gonna get lost. The judge'll tie everybody up in the same bag and convict the bunch. You included."

"What's different with a jury?" De Ruiter asked.

"Human element," Chamberlain answered. "I put you on the stand and it's the same as last time. Jury says no way this guy's a dope dealer."

"Do what you think, Russ," De Ruiter said.

Chamberlain filed a notice with the B.C. Supreme Court electing that his client be tried by a jury. The notice had an automatic effect on the other seven men accused in the conspiracy. They, too, had to be tried by a jury. When one person on an indictment elects a jury trial, then everyone on

270

the indictment must be tried in the same way.

Russ Chamberlain's election immediately brought him into conflict with one of his fellow counsel, who, as it happened, held an almost diametrically opposite view of the workings of judges and juries in conspiracy cases. Or, at any rate, in *this* conspiracy case.

"I want a judge sitting alone on your case," Harry Walsh said to his client, Doug Palmer.

"Sounds good," Palmer said. "Tell me about it."

"A jury's more likely to be impressed with the mass of RCMP evidence that the crown will present," Walsh elaborated. "A judge is better qualified to cut finely on that type of evidence. Do I make myself clear, Douglas?"

Palmer said, "This kind of stuff's what I'm paying for."

"With a jury," Walsh said, "you could get convicted just because you fly with the crows."

"Huh?"

"Maybe the crown can show that you associated with drug dealers," Walsh said. "But that doesn't mean it follows that you *are* a drug dealer."

"And a jury might not figure that out?"

"Douglas," Walsh said, "my experience is that a judge alone is a better bet."

"What about Fred Ford?" Palmer asked. "Him and his story?"

"My reading from Ford's appearance at the preliminary hearing," Walsh answered, "is that no one would convict a dog on his evidence alone. But, as I say, with a jury, when you put Ford's evidence in a setting of fifty other witnesses, all this talk about capping up and stuffing things in condoms, the exchanging of small bills for large bills, and so on, the jury might become more swayed than a judge."

"No jury," Palmer said.

"As I say, Douglas," Walsh said.

Russ Chamberlain's first hint that someone in the Palmer

case disagreed with his jury election came when Bill De Ruiter telephoned him with a request that he withdraw the jury notice.

"The hell I'll withdraw it, Bill," Chamberlain said. "I already told you why we need a jury."

De Ruiter said, "I want to re-elect for a trial by a judge."

"'*Re-elect*'?" Chamberlain shouted down the line. "Where'd you suddenly get the legal education?"

"Just do what I'm saying, okay?"

"Bill," Chamberlain said, "under no circumstances should you re-elect. That's my advice as your counsel."

"I got no choice."

"If you want to re-elect," Chamberlain said, "you'll have to bring me instructions in writing saying exactly that."

Chamberlain hung up his phone.

"Until that moment," he said many years later, "De Ruiter had always listened to me. The only conclusion I could draw from his phone call was that somebody else was pulling the strings for De Ruiter all along. In fact, after the trial, the rumours on the street came back to me that the money I got paid on the case was Doug Palmer's money. But the first indication I had of the way the wind was blowing, of who was really running the case, was over the jury election."

A few days after Bill De Ruiter's telephone conversation with Russ Chamberlain, De Ruiter walked into Chamberlain's office with an envelope. Inside was a formal direction that Chamberlain file a notice with the court re-electing for a trial by a judge sitting alone. De Ruiter had signed the document.

"If that's what you want, Bill," Chamberlain said. "But I'll predict one thing for sure. If this's going to be a trial with just a judge, the Chief Justice will assign one of two judges to hear it. McKay or Macfarlane. Both those guys are the same on drug cases, very tough. I'm not saying unfair. I'm saying hard-nosed. And that's the way either guy's gonna be on this case, because it's the biggest damn drug trial we ever had in B.C. McKay or Macfarlane. Remember the names, Bill."

In dress and style, Francis Mawson Rattenbury was at least as much of a swell as Walter Guay. It helped that Rattenbury had more money than Guay, *honest* money, and lived in an era that permitted men more of a peacock look. Rattenbury was born in 1867 in Leeds, England, where he took training as an architect. He emigrated to Canada, travelling as far across the country as he could go before settling on Victoria as his new headquarters. At the precocious age of twenty-five, he won a competition to design British Columbia's new Parliament Buildings. The buildings, as elaborate as a Liberace suit, were deemed a great success, and Rattenbury's architectural career zoomed. He did numerous rich people's mansions, railroad terminals, and the Empress Hotel in Victoria. He grew wealthy, cut a chic figure in B.C. society, and drank more than was good for him. The flaw in his life was an unhappy marriage, but that was taken care of, Rattenbury thought, in 1922 when he met a beautiful young woman with the voice of a nightingale. Her name was Alma Pakenham. Rattenbury jettisoned his first wife — they'd been living in separate wings of his large house for years — and married Alma, who gave up her career as a singer of light songs. Rattenbury was fifty-eight, and lovely Alma was thirty. The age difference didn't seem to matter to either of them.

The Rattenburys left Canada and moved into a white cottage called Villa Madeira that sat in a gorgeous setting near the sea on the Hampshire-Dorset border in England. A son was born to Alma, and all was blissful at Villa Madeira until two events occurred. Rattenbury lost his urge for sex and reacquired his taste for liquor. Alma, apparently a woman of lusty desires, remained faithful to Rattenbury until George

Stoner, whom the Rattenburys hired as a chaffeur-handy-man, swept her off her feet. Or maybe it was the other way around, since George was only eighteen. George may also have been a touch unstable. On the night of March 24, 1935, without saying a word about his intentions to Alma, George crept into Rattenbury's sitting-room and bashed him over the head with a carpenter's mallet. Rattenbury, drunk at the time, probably didn't feel a thing, but the bashing left him dead.

The crown charged both Alma and George with murder. At their joint trial, the jury acquitted Alma and convicted George, who was sentenced to life imprisonment (he served seven years, joined the army after his release, took part in D-Day, and thereafter lived a model life). Alma passed the days immediately following the trial in sorrowful contemplation. She wrote several notes complaining of the cruel press treatment during the trial and expressing the pain she felt for her son. Then she walked out beside a river in the countryside not far from Villa Madeira and stabbed a long knife into her breast six times. She hit her heart with three of the stabs and died.

Of all the buildings that Francis Rattenbury left as his legacy, the Vancouver Courthouse was probably the most celebrated. He worked on it from 1907 to 1911 and it boasted the intricacies and curved lines, the flourishes and frills and furbelows, that Rattenbury favoured in public buildings. Rattenbury and Frank Lloyd Wright may have been contemporaries in age, but they were light years apart in artistic vision. The courthouse stood on the south side of Georgia Street in downtown Vancouver, set far enough back to allow for appreciation of its flaming neoclassical style. Rattenbury constructed it of grey limestone and set off the main façade with four Ionic columns. There was a cupola on top, and inside there were enormous staircases, lots of moulding and wainscoting, decorative window frames, and great echoing high ceilings. It fit firmly in the tradition of courthouses that made judges and counsel feel right at home and thoroughly intimidated the members of the public who had to look to it for justice.

By January 12, 1976, a Monday, when the trial of the Palmer gang got under way, Francis Rattenbury's courthouse was developing creaks and groans. Cold drafts swept through it in winter, and in all seasons it never seemed quite clean. It had also become too small to satisfy the city's increasing need for court space; many Supreme Court trials took place in makeshift courtrooms in the nearby Board of Trade Building. Still, the lawyers who gathered for the Palmer case in courtroom 515 on the courthouse's upper south side welcomed the chance to perform once again in the dramatic setting that Francis Rattenbury had designed for them.

The line-up of counsel went like this:

For the crown, Arthur MacLennan, assisted by another attorney from the Department of Justice, Frank Haar, and by RCMP Sergeant Neil MacKay.

For Douglas and Donald Palmer, Harry Walsh.

For Bill De Ruiter, Russ Chamberlain.

For Tommy Duncan and Cliff Luhtala, Josiah Wood. Known to everyone around the courts as Joe, Wood graduated from UBC law school in the class of '68 with Russ Chamberlain. The two were marked out as their year's star orators — aggressive, fast on their feet, stuffed full of the law. Like Chamberlain, Wood was large in presence and voice. He wore his hair in a longish cut and buzzed around town in a sporty MG. Wood practised with one of Vancouver's sharpest and most enterprising criminal firms, Deverell, Harrop & Company. Wood's partner, Bill Deverell, was stoking himself for a second career as a novelist; his first book, a speedy, authentic thriller called *Needles*, dealt with Vancouver lawyers and low-lifes and won the first $50,000 Seal Book Award. Deverell, Harrop's offices were in a building in the ancient Gastown neighbourhood. A refurbished haven of sand-blasted brick, red cedar trim, and jungles of greenery.

275

As well as acting for Duncan and Luhtala, Joe Wood served as Harry Walsh's point man in Vancouver; he organized defences and plotted law while Walsh attended to other cases back home in Winnipeg.

For Walter Guay, Larry Hill, a hard-drinking veteran of the criminal courts. Hill had an edgy, compulsive sense of humour. He cracked jokes during the trial that no one laughed at. His health was on a roller coaster, putting him in reasonably fine fettle one day, leaving him weak and unfocussed the next. Off and on through the trial, he was pestered by a bleeding of the retina in one eye, and some afternoons his fellow counsel noted that he was operating on a liquid lunch. As a student many years earlier, Hill had articled with Arthur MacLennan's firm. "That may be the starting-point where I got badly off the track," he quipped one afternoon. The other lawyers rolled their eyes. *There goes Larry again*.

For Johnny Smith and Bobby Porter, David Gibbons, the junior member of the defence team. A short, amiable, self-contained man, Gibbons had been in practice for only four years at the time of the trial and he looked at the case partly as a chance to soak up a little legal wisdom from his seniors. "What I learned from Harry Walsh," Gibbons said years later, "was how to calm things down to a sensible pitch in court. The Palmer case had so much pressure from outside, so much media attention, so much built-in excitement, that it would have been easy to lose track of the real issues. Harry showed me the value of staying cool."

On the bench for the trial, His Lordship, Mr. Justice Alan B. Macfarlane. "Did I tell you?" Russ Chamberlain said to Bill De Ruiter. Macfarlane was a handsome, brown-haired man in his early fifties. He ran a tight ship in court, but, unlike other judges whose strict ways stemmed from arrogance or crankiness, Macfarlane backed up his rulings and opinions with a good legal brain. As a judge, he was much learned in the law, and he had made it clear in earlier trials that he didn't care for drug offenders.

Arthur MacLennan signalled the beginning of the trial with the good old reliable RCMP March Past.

Sergeant Hartley Dillworth led off as the first Mountie witness on the first day. He talked about a stake-out where he observed Donald Palmer getting together with Conrad Gunn. And following Sergeant Dillworth in straight-backed, chin-up, chest-forward parade came Sergeants Harry Wallace and Bill Hacock and George Ripley. Corporal John Grady. Sergeant Don Wilkie. Stake-out men, every sergeant and corporal of them. In formation, the squad from the Ladner detachment made its appearance on the stand, Corporal Terry Hart and Constable Fred Hammond and others from the ranks who knew what Tommy Duncan and Bobby Porter had been up to. The bus-depot detail: Welychka, Brown, Schafer, Paterson, Richert, Chan, and Domansky. The brass: Sergeants Frank Kilner and Emil Beaulieu and, rising from his seat beside Arthur MacLennan, Neil MacKay. Before the presentation of evidence ended on February 26, MacLennan marched thirty-seven members of the drug squad, past and present, to the witness stand. Some testified for hours at a stretch. Some gave their evidence and were recalled weeks later to present more evidence. All were resolute and unswerving. Mounties on parade.

MacLennan also summoned as witnesses three Vancouver City Police detectives who had assisted the RCMP on stake-outs. Three bank clerks who'd exchanged small bills for large. Fingerprint experts from the laboratories of both the RCMP and the Vancouver Police. An RCMP chemical analyst who knew the difference between heroin and flour. Desk clerks and managers from hotels, motels, and bars around Vancouver. Yves Gascon, a member of the RCMP's Quebec drug squad, who watched Walter Guay transact a tricky exchange at the Green Garden Café in Montreal. And, among a dozen other crown witnesses, Doug Manuel, the ferry-master from Vancouver Island who began an innocent evening in January 1971 playing shuffleboard with Tommy Duncan.

The crown's case assumed shape. No surprises. Eight men conspired to deal in heroin. The drugs arrived from Montreal and were parcelled out, businesslike, to peddlers and addicts in Vancouver. Sometimes, unbusinesslike, the heroin dropped into the hands of the RCMP watchers. Heroin from Bill De Ruiter's attic, from Doug Manuel's truck, from a back alley that Cliff Luhtala had recently visited. The eight men ran an expeditious enterprise, and head office was situated in the little corner of Hawaii at the Polynesian Lounge of the Waldorf Hotel.

In cross-examination of the Mountie watchers, surveillants, and note-takers, the defence counsel were remorseless in their insistence on details. They wanted specifics in identification. Was that *really* Cliff Luhtala who went up the alley on the pitch-black night? The counsel made the witnesses dig hard to establish, if they could, connections between the accused men and the loose heroin. And, as for the hundreds of sightings at the Waldorf, so what? The defence lawyers took a consistent tack in the cross-examinations of the cocktail-bar undercover Mounties: seven accused, all except De Ruiter, may have enjoyed an inordinate number of happy hours in the Polynesian Lounge, but don't most men relish the sanctuary of a clubhouse? Was it strange for old East End buddies to reunite over a brew? What did the Mounties observe at the Waldorf that was so incriminating anyway?

"The lounge was in a dimly lit state, wasn't it?" Harry Walsh asked Corporal John McConnell.

Walsh's cross-examination of McConnell came on the third day of the trial, January 15, after McConnell had testified that he and Corporal Karl Richert had spent a smoky evening in December 1969 at a table in the Polynesian watching Doug Palmer, the brothers Johnny and Andrew

Smith, and a fourth, unidentified man at another table twenty feet away.

"Dimly lit," McConnell answered Walsh. "A lot dimmer than this courtroom. Typical lighting for a lounge."

"Not a place where one could sit and read a newspaper?"

"One could, I presume."

"You observed a number of tables in the lounge?"

"Yes."

"You observed a number of patrons in the lounge?"

"Yes."

"And you observed that there were some tables at which one person sat alone, other tables at which there would be more than one person, and so on?"

McConnell wasn't about to give much away, not to a counsel as cagey as Walsh, not on a question that — who could know? — might lead to trouble, not on anything that McConnell might avoid.

"I don't recall if there were or not," McConnell answered.

"In any event, you saw Douglas Palmer at the same table with John Smith. Is that correct?"

"Yes."

"And there were drinks in front of them?"

"Yes."

"And when Andrew Smith came up, he ordered a drink?"

"I don't recall if he did."

"Well, did there appear to be a drink in front of him?" Walsh asked, willing to pull teeth if that's what it took.

"There were drinks on the table," McConnell answered. "I don't know if he had a particular drink or not."

"Then an individual whom you don't know came to the table. Is that correct?"

"That is correct."

"Did you see him do anything when he sat down at the table?"

"He shook hands with Doug Palmer."

"Now, during this whole period of time that you had the

279

table under observation, there was general conversation going on at it?"

"Yes."

"And there was drinking going on?"

"Yes."

"And a general chatter, isn't that right?"

"Yes."

"And you didn't see anything of an unusual nature of any kind whatsover, did you?"

"No."

"And the persons around the table, Douglas Palmer, John Smith, Andrew Smith, the unidentified person, you didn't see them do anything that was improper or illegal or unusual, did you?"

"I did not."

"You didn't see them act in a furtive or surreptitious manner, did you?"

"No."

"This was the kind of thing, I put it to you, Corporal McConnell, that you could observe in any cocktail lounge. Isn't that so?"

"Yes," Corporal McConnell answered.

Walsh and the other defence counsel felt they were chipping away at Arthur MacLennan's case, casting small doubts on the accuracy of the Mounties' observations, stirring questions as to whether MacLennan could satisfy Mr. Justice Alan Macfarlane that the accused men were guilty beyond a reasonable doubt of the conspiracy charge.

Each defence counsel had some interests that dovetailed with the interests of other counsel and some that slid off on a unique and exclusive tangent. It was Larry Hill alone who had to distance his client from the heroin in the green Lucerne suitcase, since, along with the conspiracy charge, Guay faced a count of trafficking in the heroin from the suitcase. In the same way, Joe Wood had to combat the evidence of the events in Ladner that appeared to damn his client, Tommy Duncan. Russ Chamberlain had to show Justice Macfarlane that his client, Bill De Ruiter, had no connection at all with heroin or the Palmer guys or anything illegal except his sneaky sometime lodger, Tommy Duncan. And, most threatening of all on the defence side, Harry Walsh had to demolish Fred Ford, since it was only Ford who could pin Walsh's client, Doug Palmer, as the head honcho of the whole busy, rich drug conspiracy.

Walsh and everybody else including Arthur MacLennan had trouble getting off the pad with Ford. He cut a shadowy figure at the beginning of the trial, reluctant and jittery and, worse, apparently sick. MacLennan scheduled an interruption in the parade of RCMP witnesses in order for Ford to take the stand on the second Monday of the trial, January 19. Mounties escorted him into the courtroom. Ford eyeballed his boyhood pal Doug Palmer, who fired one of his laser glares from the prisoners' box. The newspaper, radio, and TV reporters poised pens over notebooks to record what they knew would be the trial's most telling testimony. Defence counsel edged forward in their chairs. And Arthur MacLennan cleared his throat.

"Mr. Ford," he asked, "where do you live?"

"Nowhere right now."

"What do you mean by 'nowhere right now'?"

"I'm in the custody of the RCMP."

"Are you in their protective custody?"

"Yes."

And that was as far as Arthur MacLennan got on January 19. Before he asked Fred Ford another question, Ford turned to Mr. Justice Macfarlane.

"Your honour," he said in his smallest voice, "I don't feel like answering any questions today. I'm not feeling very well."

The courtroom erupted in a babble of voices. Amid the

hugger-mugger, MacLennan squeezed out a detail of update on Ford's health.

"I got stomach flu," Ford said on the witness stand. "Been throwing up all week."

"Have you been to a doctor?" MacLennan asked.

"No."

MacLennan looked at Macfarlane, shrugged his shoulders, and asked that Ford's testimony be put over to Wednesday.

Macfarlane, annoyed, clipped off his own questions for Ford.

"Do you *want* to see a doctor?" he asked.

"Yes, I would."

Macfarlane asked, "Do you want to remain in the protective custody of the RCMP between now and Wednesday?"

MacLennan didn't much care for that question.

Ford answered Macfarlane, eagerness showing all over his round face, "I'd like to be able to come and go as I please to."

MacLennan liked the answer even less than Macfarlane's question. He leaped into the exchange between judge and witness and explained to Macfarlane, speaking fast, that Fred Ford was a prize witness and that the Mounties had been baby-sitting him for almost a year, ever since the preliminary hearing the previous winter.

MacLennan said, "The witness has been kept in a location, a *secret* location, and he was just recently brought back to the city to testify."

Ah, of course, Macfarlane understood.

He said to Ford, "You will return here at 10 a.m. on Wednesday, January 21, 1976, and in the meantime, the RCMP will be asked to — "

Ford, seeing his chance at the outside world that had so suddenly crept within reach being even more rapidly whisked away, interrupted.

"Does that mean I can't go anywhere or do anything?" he asked Macfarlane.

" — to get a doctor," Macfarlane finished.

"Your honour," Ford started again.

Too late. Macfarlane shuffled papers in front of him, paying no attention to Ford, who was peremptorily escorted through the courtroom's side door by a Mountie contingent.

David Gibbons stood up before anyone could get in another word.

"My lord," he said to Macfarlane, "may it please the court, I have an application to make."

"Does it pertain to this witness?" Macfarlane asked, meaning Fred Ford.

"It does, my lord."

David Gibbons, while he'd been looking at Ford in the courtroom, had come up with an idea. Gibbons was the junior member of the defence team, the least experienced in trial work in general and, more to the point, in the Palmer case in particular, since he hadn't represented his clients, Porter and Smith, at the preliminary hearing. He had been brought into the case late, and that morning was the first and only time he'd laid eyes on Fred Ford. Gibbons wanted to see more of the crown's star witness.

"My lord," he said to Macfarlane. "I would like the opportunity to speak to Mr. Ford, if he might choose to speak to me, now that he seems to be available. You see, my lord, since I came on the case, I have been asking my friend Mr. MacLennan when Mr. Ford would be brought to court and my friend wouldn't tell me. All I want, my lord, is the freedom as a barrister to be able to interview the crown's witness."

MacLennan, resisting, said, "Well, my lord, it isn't as if Mr. Gibbons is going to be taken by surprise by Mr. Ford's testimony. He can read in the transcripts what Mr. Ford said as a witness at the preliminary hearing."

Joe Wood chimed in on Gibbons's side. "The crown," he said to Macfarlane, "has no property in a witness. The only restriction on Mr. Gibbons is if Ford refuses to talk to him."

"Mr. Ford is ill," Macfarlane said. "Or so he says."

Gibbons said, "I don't want to talk to him if he's too sick, but I *do* want to talk to him when he's able."

Macfarlane thought over Gibbons's submission.

"All right," he said to Gibbons. "I don't wish to put you in a position where the proper defence of your clients is prejudiced. You're entitled to talk to Mr. Ford before he testifies."

"Thank you, my lord," Gibbons said.

Macfarlane said, "I'll leave it to you and the crown to work out an appropriate time."

Gibbons thought he'd scored a small tactical win for the good guys.

Harry Walsh didn't.

"David," he said to Gibbons in the barristers' changing-room at the courthouse after court ended for the day, "I doubt that it's wise."

"What's that, Harry?"

"Speaking to Fred Ford on your own."

"Harry, Macfarlane's willing," Gibbons said. "You're more experienced about these things than me, but I like to find out in advance what a crown's witness is going to say on the stand."

"There's another imperative consideration, David."

"I'm willing to learn, Harry."

"You might have your interview with Fred Ford," Walsh said. "But you might be shocked to find that when Ford takes the stand, he tells a series of lies about the subjects the two of you discussed."

"I *would* be shocked, Harry."

"It's not unknown for a crown witness of the calibre of Ford's sort of person to fabricate what a defence counsel has said to him."

"Obviously you think I should leave Ford alone."

Walsh nodded sagely.

Gibbons withdrew his request to interview Ford. But many years later, long after Ford's testimony at the trial, after

the case was done and judgments had been rendered by Mr.
Justice Macfarlane and by the B.C. Court of Appeal and by
the Supreme Court of Canada, in the years following the
astounding turn in events that Fred Ford precipitated with
actions and statements he made public in the case's after-
math, Gibbons had second thoughts.

"The one regret I still carry about the trial," he said, "was
not following through on my idea of talking to Ford. Maybe it
was a long shot, looking back, but what if Ford had given
away something to me that I could have picked up on for my
cross-examination of him in court? Who knows? Harry
Walsh might've been right in the advice he gave me, but on
the other hand, I could conceivably have developed a line of
questioning that would have headed off the royal mess we got
into after the trial."

On Wednesday, January 19, the day Mr. Justice Macfarlane
had stipulated for Fred Ford's testimony, Ford was nowhere in
sight in the courthouse. He sent an excuse note instead.
MacLennan read it to the court:

"To whom it may concern:

Re: Fred Ford.
The A/M patient has acute gastroenteritis (stomach
flu). He should be fit to appear in court by January 26/76.
Yours sincerely,

T. W. Acheson, M.D."

"What," Larry Hill asked, "is A/M?"
"Above-mentioned," MacLennan answered.

Ford passed his convalescence in the tacky splendour of the
Plaza 500 Hotel on West 12th. For company, not to mention

protection, he had RCMP Corporal Art Hoivik.

"Something I gotta work out with you guys," Ford said to Corporal Hoivik. "With you Mounties."

"Only thing you work out with me is keeping your ass covered," Hoivik said. "That's what we're around for, me and the other officers."

"This here protective custody's probably what's making me sick," Ford said.

"You're looking not so pale as before," Hoivik said. "All you have to do's hang in a couple days, give your testimony in court, and you're out of here. Go into relocation and you never see another Mountie in your life, long as you stay clean."

"That's what I don't want," Ford said. "Relocation."

"What're you talking about?"

"I got promised I could take money in place of it, the money it'd cost to pay the relocating."

"First I heard of it."

"Take the money and disappear, whatever, on my own."

"Who promised?"

"I talked about it a year ago."

"You want to discuss this," Hoivik said, "I'm not the guy. Almrud's in charge of that kind of stuff."

"So tell Almrud I needa see him right away."

Ford's conversation with Corporal Hoivik took place on the morning of January 26 — Ford's testimony had been put over yet again to January 28 — and that evening, after Hoivik had briefed his superior, Staff-Sergeant Harold Almrud, Almrud dropped into Ford's room at the Plaza 500.

"What's this I hear about you and relocation, Fred?" Almrud asked.

"What you hear's I don't need it," Ford said. "I want the money, like MacKay told me."

"I'm not getting into any conflab about something Sergeant MacKay may or may not have told you," Almrud said. "Neither one of us, Sergeant MacKay or me, can speak for the government, and they're the people who pay the bills in these matters. All I'm telling you is recommendations can be made."

"Jesus, Almrud, I'm sick, right?" Ford said. "I'm in bed and I'm swallowing about a hundred pills a day the doctor gave me and I gotta go into court and you're talking to me about fucking *recommendations*?"

"You want money?" Almrud said, switching to his man-of-decision posture. "Okay, Fred, you tell me right now how much."

Ford didn't expect *that* question, not so soon.

He said, "Well, hey, you're asking me, like, flat numbers?"

"You're the man making the commotion, Fred," Almrud said. "You must have a figure."

"Ah, yeah, what's fifty thousand, somewhere in there, sound like?"

"Don't *ask* me. *Tell* me."

"Fifty grand," Ford said. "That's my number."

"Thank you," Almrud said. "I'll pass on your request to the people upstairs, you understand me? I don't decide these matters. Other people do. They'll get back to you."

"You're not putting me on?"

"Look after your flu, Fred."

The following morning, before Sergeant Neil MacKay went into court to assist Arthur MacLennan at the trial, Staff-Sergeant Almrud pulled him aside and told him about Ford's state of mind.

"Fifty thousand?" MacKay said.

"Sounded on the high side to me," Almrud said. "Ford claims you promised he could trade relocation for cash."

"Didn't promise him a thing," MacKay said. "But actually fifty thousand's a little low, considering what we'd pay to set up him and Mrs. Ford and the family. Sixty thousand's more like it."

"We can't authorize *any* sum of money."

"Hell, no," MacKay said. "But the other point is, right

now, this very minute in the trial, we don't want to antago-
nize Mr. Fred Ford."

"Well, what?"

MacKay said, "We'll play fair with the bugger."

MacKay telephoned Corporal Art Hoivik at the Plaza 500.

"Uh-huh, uh-huh, yes, sir," Corporal Hoivik said into the
phone, absorbing his marching orders.

"You ready for this?" Hoivik said to Fred Ford after he
hung up the phone.

"You gonna give me the gears some more?"

"Sixty thousand?" Hoivik said. "That sound like the
gears?"

"MacKay says pay me sixty thousand?"

"Here's what I'm supposed to tell you, Fred," Hoivik said
in his finest formal tones. "Authorized to tell you. Sergeant
MacKay will make representations to Ottawa, Department
of Justice, to obtain sixty thousand dollars, payable to you, in
the place of any and all relocation arrangements for you and
your family."

"Sixty is good."

"You get the whole picture?" Hoivik said. "This is no sure
thing. This is what the RCMP is representing to the government people that they oughta do."

"Sixty'd set me up nice."

"The government people don't have to do what MacKay
says."

"Probably worth more than sixty, my testimony," Ford
said. "But, okay, sixty."

"That's settled," Hoivik said.

It wasn't settled. A few weeks later, the round robin of
conversations — Ford to Hoivik to Almrud to Ford to Almrud
to MacKay to Hoivik and full circle back to Ford — would
return to haunt the RCMP and threaten to topple the entire
case against the Palmer drug ring.

By January 27, nerves were fraying in courtroom 515. Counsel became testy over the wait for Ford, and even without him, the trial made demands on stamina and patience. The pushy media accounted for part of the tension. The press table, occupied during less high-profile trials by Larry Still of the *Vancouver Sun* and a couple of other print people, overflowed into the aisle with men and women from radio and television, mostly young, mostly inexperienced, who asked counsel gauche questions in the recesses. Out in the hall, daily war was waged between TV cameramen and husky lads from the East End. The cameramen were aiming for footage of Doug Palmer entering and leaving the courtroom, which was what the East Enders were on assignment from Doug to prevent. The cops guarding the courtroom, searching everyone who entered for concealed weapons, got a kick out of the civilian skirmishes.

Even inside the courtroom, Doug Palmer exercised a hint of intimidation.

"What I'd appreciate from you guys," he said to the people at the press table one morning, "maybe you won't mention the name of my trucking company."

"Sure, Doug," Larry Still answered. "No problem."

Later, Still explained his reasoning: "Why mess up the guy's legitimate business? Besides, I didn't want to get on the wrong side of Doug Palmer."

On the morning of the twenty-seventh, tempers broke. The tempers belonged to defence counsel, and the man who fractured them was Arthur MacLennan. He announced that Fred Ford would be due on the witness stand at any hour, and, as a precaution, out of concern that a diabolically sneaky assassin might take another run at Ford, a phalanx of plainclothes armed guards was being introduced to the courtroom. "These so-called sharpshooters looked to me like recent graduates of police school," David Gibbons later recalled. "Just kids. And where were we defence counsel sitting? In a direct line between the witness stand and the pistol-packers. I was kind of worried." More than worried, the normally placid Gibbons was mad, and he didn't conceal his rising anger.

"The only time anybody gets shot," he said in court to Mr. Justice Macfarlane, "is when there are weapons around. If there're no weapons, nobody gets hurt. It's common sense — no guns in the courtroom."

"Matters of security," Macfarlane said, "are not within my province. They are the sheriff's responsibility."

Russ Chamberlain blew his stack.

"In my respectful submission," he said, sounding not at all respectful, his voice doing its imitation of thunder, arms wheeling like windmills, "I would feel a lot more secure if the armed officers were standing outside *that* door" — Chamberlain's finger poked in the direction of the court-room's side door — "and *that* door" — finger aimed at main courtroom entrance — "and outside *both* windows" — arm sweeping toward the sunlight — "than inside the courtroom. There is no need for weapons if nobody else has weapons."

Macfarlane said, "There's no cause to become hysterical, Mr. Chamberlain."

"I don't think I'm becoming hysterical," Chamberlain shot back.

"You are sounding very much like it," Macfarlane said. "If there are armed guards present in the courtroom, it wouldn't be the first time armed officers were ever in a courtroom."

"What if something goes wrong?" Chamberlain asked.

Macfarlane said, "Oh, do not speculate, Mr. Chamberlain."

"In plain clothes, we don't even know who the police officers are," Chamberlain said.

Macfarlane said, "I can only label your remarks as verging on hysterical, Mr. Chamberlain."

"Thank you, my lord, for your comments," Chamberlain said, spitting sarcasm.

In the end, after several minutes' more wrangling, the police kids with the guns remained in place.

"At first," Gibbons remembered, "I adjusted my seat to get slightly out of the line of potential fire. After that, I put the armed guards out of my mind."

That evening, January 27, Arthur MacLennan and Neil MacKay went calling on Fred Ford at the Plaza 500. They didn't have money on their minds, not the sixty thousand dollars that had been batted around by Ford and the Mounties earlier in the day. The two men were exclusively concerned that night with ensuring that Ford would be up to scratch for his court appearance.

MacLennan said to Ford, "I've brought homework to keep you busy, Mr. Ford."

"You're not even gonna ask how I'm feeling?" Ford grumped.

"We can see you're in discomfort," MacLennan said. "I'm sorry for that, but I'd like you to try and pay attention."

Ford said, "Feel like I'm dying, you want to know the truth."

"Listen up a minute, Fred," Sergeant MacKay said.

MacLennan said, "I'm going to leave with you a transcript of the testimony you gave at the preliminary hearing last year. You recall that?"

"Think I'm gonna forget something screwed up my whole life?"

"Fred," MacKay said, "you want to relax, all right?"

MacLennan said, "Read your testimony in the transcript, this is all I'm asking, and let me know if it contains any errors."

"Any errors in there," Ford said, "they aren't mine."

"It doesn't matter whose they are," MacLennan said. "I want to be made aware of them if they exist."

MacKay said, "Simple, okay, Freddie?"

"Nothing's gonna be simple till I get out of this goddamn hotel," Ford said.

"Thank you for your co-operation," MacLennan said.

He and MacKay left the room. MacLennan later estimated that the audience with Ford lasted no longer than three or four minutes and dealt with nothing more than the transcript from the preliminary hearing. Ford told another, more sinister version of the meeting.

There should have been a roll of drums. There wasn't. There was only fussing by cautious sheriff's officers who delayed the grand entrance by five minutes and a false start by Arthur MacLennan, who got the star's name wrong.

"I call as the next witness Thomas Frederick Ford," MacLennan said at five minutes past ten on the morning of January 28. "Oh, I think I misplaced the names. It's Frederick Thomas Ford, my lord."

At last Fred Ford was on the witness stand.

"Mr. Ford," MacLennan began, "do you ordinarily reside in the city of Vancouver?"

"Yes, I do."

"At what address?"

"None right now."

"In the year 1971, did you reside in Vancouver?"

"At 3475 Triumph Street."

"Mr. Ford, how long have you lived in the vicinity of Vancouver?"

"Thirty-three years."

"How old are you?"

"Thirty-three."

"Do you know a person called Douglas Palmer?"

"I grew up with him in East Vancouver."

"Do you recall around the month of June 1971?"

"Yes."

"Did you have occasion to see Mr. Palmer around that time?"

"Well, I went up to 22nd and Renfrew where he had this trucking outfit and I asked to talk to Doug Palmer and we went for a walk and I asked him for a job in the drug business."

If Ford was feeling ill on the witness stand, he kept it concealed. He wore a poker face and talked in a flat monotone. He listened to MacLennan's questions, and when he answered them, he unravelled to the court the long, crazy, crooked tale of his fling in the heroin trade with Doug Palmer. He described his initiation as a back-end man, the logistics of drug buries, the telephone instructions in code, the maps and descriptions on cigarette paper. Okay, Ford seemed to be conveying to MacLennan and, beyond him, to the RCMP, I'm delivering on my end of the bargain. Ask the questions, because I got the answers.

"What were you getting for your part in this drug business?" MacLennan asked.

"Money," Ford answered.

"From whom?"

"Doug Palmer and sometimes from Bill Turner."

"What was your pay scale?"

"I used to get two-fifty for a jar, to bury it like, you know?"

"For each time you buried a jar?"

"Well, for a bigger jar, and a couple hundred dollars for a smaller jar."

"And where would you go to receive payment?"

"Different places. A couple times, it was the house on Empire Drive out there in Burnaby."

"Whose house?"

"Doug Palmer's."

Ford told of driving Tommy Duncan and Johnny Smith, on Palmer's instructions, to motels where they capped up bulk heroin. He told of Jimmy Mortimer's arrest and the other events that led to the RCMP raid on Bill De Ruiter's house in

293

Richmond. And he tossed in a tantalizing item about Bill Turner, the missing conspirator.

"One time, June or July '72, I had to go out to Coquitlam to see Bill Turner," Ford testified.

"Why Coquitlam?" MacLennan asked. Coquitlam is a community east of Burnaby.

"He had a house out there."

"How did you know?"

"I rented it for him."

"And how did you happen to rent it?"

"He got ahold of me and said he's on the run and needs a place to stay and I should get him the place."

"He told you he was on the run and needed a place?"

"To hide out."

"Did you ever have occasion to go back to this place you rented for Bill Turner?"

"Every day nearly. I always drove Doug Palmer out there and he and Turner used to go in the other room, by themselves like, and talk about I don't know what."

"How long did Turner live in the house in Coquitlam?"

"It was until just after De Ruiter got arrested. Then he disappeared."

"Turner disappeared?"

"Dougie Palmer told me Turner was gone and I should go out to the place in Coquitlam and clean it out."

"What happened to Turner?"

"Gone."

It was the last anyone — at least anyone who was talking — saw or heard of Bill Turner.

From the witness stand, Ford carried the story down to his final moments in Doug Palmer's employ, to the interview at the Admiral Lounge on January 20, 1973, when the angry Palmer dismissed the panicky Ford.

"You went out to the lounge," MacLennan asked, "and what happened?"

"Doug Palmer laid it on me."

294

"Yes?"

"He said he thought I was the one set up De Ruiter for the bust and I was fired."

"He terminated your services?"

"He said if he finds out for sure it's me, I am in big trouble."

"Anything further?"

"I am lucky to be alive. That's all."

MacLennan finished his examination-in-chief at 11:35 a.m., an hour and a half of questioning, and he sat down beside Frank Haar, the assistant crown counsel.

"How was it?" MacLennan whispered to Haar.

"Very tidy," Haar said. "Very thorough."

"Enough to make Harry Walsh worry?"

"Plenty."

MacLennan gave one of his cowboy chuckles.

Harry Walsh lived monastically for the seven weeks of the trial. "Maybe a symphony concert or two, weekend trips to the art gallery," he later remembered of his time in Vancouver. "There's not much else when I take a case away from home. I'm a simple eater, don't drink much, and never socialize with clients." So he worked. He took a suite at the downtown Holiday Inn not far from the courthouse. The bedroom was his retreat, and the sitting-room, with transcripts, case books, affidavits covering every available surface, served as his Palmer brothers war room. It was in there that Walsh hatched his crucial cross-examination of Fred Ford. He decided on a two-pronged assault. He would demonstrate that Ford was at all times an untrustworthy character and that he was especially devious when the subject was Doug Palmer. The Mounties, Walsh planned to show, had given Ford persuasive motivation in money and promises to commit outrageous perjury at the Palmer trial.

At noon on January 28, after a brief recess following

Arthur MacLennan's examination-in-chief, Walsh's first question on cross-examination knocked Ford into a defensive stance.

"You have served time in the penitentiary, haven't you, Mr. Ford?" Walsh asked.

Ford's eyes flicked around the courtroom.

"Yes," he answered.

"How much time and when?"

"I've been in the penitentiary twice, five years once and two and a half or something."

"You got a five-year term. For what?"

"Wounding with intent."

"And in what penitentiary did you serve?"

"British Columbia Pen in 1963 or '64."

"And then you were sentenced to another term of two and a half years?"

"That was before, 1960 or '61, something like that, for theft, stealing stuff, like that."

"Mr. Ford, you have given evidence in court before, under oath?"

"Yes."

"And on that occasion you lied? You were convicted of perjury?"

The question blindsided Ford. He knew Harry Walsh would have checked into his seamy history, but the *perjury* thing!? Wow, Ford thought, he was only a kid when that happened.

"Yes," Ford answered Walsh's question.

"How long ago was it you perjured yourself? You *do* understand the meaning of the term perjury?"

"It means to lie."

"Under oath?"

"Under oath or at any time."

"How long ago was that, Mr. Ford?"

"Seventeen years ago. I was only sixteen."

"And you wouldn't be averse to lying under oath if it would save your skin, would you?"

MacLennan tried to run interference for Ford.

"My lord," he said to Macfarlane, "I object to the question."

Walsh said, "It's a proper question, my lord."

Macfarlane said to MacLennan, "I think I have to give some latitude in cross-examination."

Ford said to Walsh, "I don't understand your question."

"Well," Walsh said, "you wouldn't have any particular conscience qualms about lying under oath if it would save your skin, would you?"

"I haven't told a lie since seventeen years ago," Ford said. He paused. Then he said, "In court."

"Ah," Walsh said, "you added 'in court'."

As Walsh's cross-examination of Ford moved through the day, taking time out for lunch and a short afternoon breather, it segued from the general to the particular. The subject remained Ford's capacity for the truth, which Walsh was trying to show was minimal, but it got down to the nitty-gritty of Ford vis-à-vis the Mounties and their pursuit of Doug Palmer.

"Mr. Ford," Walsh asked, "are you presently facing a charge that you did, at the city of Vancouver on the seventeenth day of December 1973, commit robbery of Shore's Credit Jewellers of a quantity of watches and jewellery and a sum of money?"

"Think I'm just charged with possession of stolen property," Ford answered. He *knew* Walsh would drag in that stupid damned jewellery job to make him look bad. "I'm not sure of the charge."

"And you have been told you would be given protection on that charge, haven't you?"

"They just said they'd try and look after it. That's all."

"Who told you it would be looked after?"

"The RCMP. Sergeant Locker and Neil MacKay."

"It would be looked after. How do you mean?"

"I don't know. Maybe get two years suspended sentence. I don't know what they're going to do."

"Sergeant Locker had already told you he wanted Doug Palmer, isn't that right?"

"He wanted him pretty badly, yes."

"So when you say you were told the jewellery-store charge would be looked after, what did that arise out of? If you gave evidence in this case?"

"Yes."

"So that's a payment to you, isn't it?"

"Well, I hope so."

Ford was developing an insouciant style on the witness stand. Walsh was scoring points off him, showing him up for a guy who'd cut a deal to get himself off the hook. But, hell, it was all true, the stuff Walsh was hitting him with. So why not let everything hang out? What was there to lose?

"Now," Walsh asked, "since January 1973 you have continued in the drug-trafficking business, haven't you, witness?"

"Yes."

"With a number of other persons?"

"Quite a number."

"Have you discussed with the police whether there would be any chance of charges in connection with these drug activities of yours?"

"I haven't discussed it. I just assumed they must know what I was doing."

"And you're *assuming* nothing will be done in that connection?"

"I haven't been charged. So I assume there isn't."

"Since you haven't been charged," Walsh asked again, trying to arrange all the assumptions in a straight row, "you are assuming there will be no charge laid against you, is that it?"

"Yes."

"And that's part of the idea in your giving evidence here today, isn't it?"

"I wasn't worried about that."

"You weren't worried?"

"Well, I wasn't charged, so why should I worry?"

Walsh liked that answer. Ford was a liar, and his responses were revealing to Mr. Justice Macfarlane where the incentive for the lies about Doug Palmer originated. The cross-examination, Walsh thought, was proceeding according to plan. Now it was time to clobber Ford with another stream of questioning that would unveil him as the two-faced witness he was.

"I'm going to show you a little piece of paper," Walsh said, at the same moment removing from a file on the counsel's table a folded sheet of letter-paper.

Ford looked at the sheet and recognized it.

"Is that your handwriting?" Walsh asked.

"Yup."

"All in your handwriting?"

"Yup."

"Read it out."

" 'To whom it may concern,' " Ford started. It was the note Ford wrote on August 10, 1974, the note that his brother Bill took to Doug Palmer at the Waldorf Hotel. Palmer must have held on to it for all those months.

" 'I, Fred Ford,' " Ford read, " 'have not ever conspired with one Douglas Palmer at any time. I know him of course, but I have never had any type of criminal activity with him.' "

"Signed?" Walsh asked.

"Signed," Ford answered.

"How?"

"My name. Fred Ford."

"And," Walsh said, "that was before you were shot, some months before, wasn't it?"

"Five months or so," Ford said. "Four months."

No need to push further, Walsh thought. He'd chalked up his point. Couldn't be more transparent. Ford had gone on written record in the summer of 1974 as being clean of drug-dealing with Doug Palmer. Six months later someone plugged him. Why would the shooting, *after* he'd cleared Palmer's name, push him into changing his tune and implicating Palmer in heroin-trafficking? It would only have been the Mounties who pressed Ford to testify at trial with his cockamamie story. And that was a topic — the RCMP influence on Ford — that Walsh got right back into with his cross-examination.

"It was in 1975 that you decided to give evidence in this case," he said. "Isn't that right, Mr. Ford?"

"Yes."

"You didn't decide that on your own, did you? You were approached by the police and given a proposition, weren't you?"

"Well, they were at the hospital when I was shot."

"Weren't you given a proposition?"

"They just told me I was crazy if I didn't testify after getting shot."

"You were crazy if you didn't testify against whom?"

"Against Doug Palmer."

"You were visited numerous, numerous times by police who were exhorting you to testify against Douglas Palmer?"

"Well, I was in their custody."

"When did these exhortations start?"

"About a couple of weeks after I was shot."

"Did they keep insisting you take the stand?"

"They kept saying, you know, I'm lucky to be alive and to do it, yes."

"Now, Mr. Ford, you haven't been giving this evidence out of any prick of conscience, have you?"

"No."

"That is, you are giving it pursuant to the arrangement that you have, isn't that so?"

"What arrangement?"

"Getting the charges against you dropped, getting protection—"

Ford broke in on Walsh.

"Yes," Ford said.

"Just let me finish," Walsh said. "Getting relocation. Isn't that right?"

"Do you want me to answer now?"

"Yes."

"Yes."

"Yes," Walsh said. "And the relocation, that's part of the deal. It would be for yourself and your family. Isn't that right?"

"Yes."

"And you couldn't look to the police for any protection unless you, in effect, turned in Doug Palmer. Isn't that right?"

"Testified at a trial, yes."

"And that was a pressure on you, wasn't it?"

"In a way."

Walsh used another hour of his cross-examination to waltz the subject around the floor, coming at Ford with the same questions at different angles, rephrasing, restructuring, but sticking to the reasons behind Ford's presence on the witness stand. Promises, promises. The Mounties promised they *wouldn't* prosecute Ford for the jewellery robbery or on the narcotics-dealing. That was on one side, and on the other side, the Mounties promised they *would* protect Ford and pay him expense money — the $1,200 a month — and take care of his wife and kids.

"Who promised to relocate you?" Walsh asked Ford.

"Neil MacKay."

"The relocation would indicate to you that you weren't

going to a jail, wouldn't it?"

"I would hope not."

"And that would be a promise to you that you would be relocated as a free citizen?"

"Yes."

"And that would be very interesting to you?"

"Staying alive would be."

Walsh looked up at Mr. Justice Macfarlane.

"That's all I have to ask, my lord," he said.

Walsh's cross-examination carried the trial until almost the end of the day, January 28, and the next morning, after the other defence counsel had conducted their own short cross-examinations, Arthur MacLennan used his re-direct examination of Ford to effect a little damage control. He was concerned about the note of the summer of '74. When Walsh sprang it on Ford, that was the first MacLennan had heard of any note. And he thought it could be troublesome.

"Mr. Ford," MacLennan said, "Mr. Walsh put to you a note in your handwriting of August 10, 1974. Would you tell the circumstances under which that arose?"

"I really don't even remember the circumstances. It was just because I was scared, I guess."

"Are the contents of the note true?"

"No, it's not true."

"Do you recall what you did with it after signing it?"

"I gave it to somebody, but I don't even remember who."

The "somebody" was Ford's own brother. Good old Billy. Ford didn't remember it was *him* who took the note? That was Ford's story, and he had an explanation for his forgetfulness.

"At that time," he said to MacLennan, "I was drinking quite a bit, and I don't remember exactly who I gave the note to. I believe it was . . ." Ford's voice drifted off. "No, I don't know. I can't swear to it, who it was."

"All right," MacLennan said.

"As a matter of fact, until I saw it yesterday, I forgot I even wrote the note."

MacLennan was finished, and so was Ford.

"My lord," MacLennan said to Mr. Justice Macfarlane, "the police have no desire now to retain Mr. Ford in protective custody. But my impression is he'll want to be in the company of the RCMP for some little time. He wants, however, to do it voluntarily."

Macfarlane turned to Ford on the witness stand.

"You can make your own decision as to what you think is best," Macfarlane said.

"Is that it?" Ford asked.

"You may go," Macfarlane said.

Ford walked from the courtroom, minus his RCMP guard, and kept on going all the way back to the East End and out of protective custody.

The counsel on the Palmer case, both crown and defence, read the impact of Fred Ford's testimony in contrasting ways. Their differences were hardly surprising, since the case against Doug Palmer hinged almost entirely on Ford's evidence.

"He didn't look like a believable witness," David Gibbons said. "And the story he told, it didn't have the ring of truth to me."

"I was very content with Ford's examination-in-chief," Arthur MacLennan said. "There was no doubt in my mind that the story he told on the stand was the truth. It was the same story he'd been telling from the very beginning. It must have been true."

"The point about a liar, which is what Fred Ford was," Harry Walsh said, "is that he forms his lie and commits it to memory. That was what Ford did and that explains why he was consistent throughout in his story. He also had the assistance of reading the transcript from the preliminary hearing. That helped him to maintain consistency. But his demeanour gave him away on the witness stand. He was terribly shifty-eyed."

"I wouldn't trust a whiner like Fred Ford," Russ Chamberlain said. "He was worse than a whore as far as whining went. But he gave me the impression he was telling the truth in the courtroom. He knew too much. He couldn't have put together the stuff he testified to out of whole cloth."

Arthur MacLennan lived in a townhouse in a green and secluded section of Burnaby across the street from a gently rolling golf course. On trial days, MacLennan left the townhouse about seven-thirty in the morning and drove a route that took him west along First Avenue past the intersection of Boundary Road. One morning midway through the trial, as he passed the corner of First and Boundary, he caught a glimpse of someone waving a friendly arm in the direction of his car. He slowed speed, studied the man with the waving arm, and vigorously returned the greeting. MacLennan chuckled the rest of the way to the courthouse.

"By golly, it was Doug Palmer," he explained. "That's where he'd moved his trucking business, somewhere near Boundary and First, and he'd evidently found out my route to work. Nervy fellow, Doug Palmer was, or maybe he just had an interesting sense of humour."

Doug Palmer got a chance to demonstrate his nerve, if not his interesting sense of humour, on February 20, when Harry Walsh called his client to the witness stand.

After Fred Ford's testimony, Arthur MacLennan had

resumed his parade of RCMP witnesses, and it had taken MacLennan almost four more weeks to complete the crown's case against the eight accused men. That put the ball in Harry Walsh's court. Should he summon Doug Palmer as a defence witness? The risk lay in exposing Palmer to Arthur MacLennan's cross-examination. MacLennan might ferret out testimony that would damage Palmer's defence. But Walsh brushed aside the notion that he was taking a chance. He barely considered it. He'd pit Doug Palmer against Fred Ford any day.

"My lord," Walsh said when court opened on the morning of February 20, "I'm calling the accused Douglas Palmer."

Palmer walked across the courtroom from the prisoners' box to the witness stand. He looked composed. He might have been sitting behind a table at the Waldorf, in charge, eyes fixed on Harry Walsh, ready to handle whatever came his way.

"What is your occupation, Mr. Palmer?" Walsh asked.

"I manage a trucking line."

"And before that, what type of occupation were you in?"

"After I got out of school, I worked in the tugboats for roughly seven, eight years, and then I drove cab, I worked in a cannery, and I worked as a bartender at the Waldorf."

"Have you a criminal record of any kind?"

"I have a dangerous-driving charge or driving with undue care and attention about ten years ago."

"Other than that particular traffic charge, have you any other convictions?"

"None."

"Now," Walsh said carefully, "you are charged, as I'm sure you are well aware, in an indictment with a number of other persons as participating in a conspiracy to traffic in narcotic drugs. You are aware of that?"

"Yes."

"What have you to say, if anything, generally in connection with the charge?"

"I have never ever in my life had any transaction to do with narcotics of any kind."

There it was, Doug Palmer's defence. A flat-out denial that he had dealt in heroin. Simplicity itself. No frills. Maybe the other guys in the prisoners' box had been peddling drugs, but not Doug Palmer. The Mounties were mistaken, and Fred Ford was lying. There was nothing fancy about the defence. Take my word for it, Palmer was saying from the witness stand, I just didn't deal drugs.

Walsh led Palmer through the list of his seven co-accused and asked about his associations with them. Walter Guay? Never met him, Palmer said, until the two men, Guay and himself, were arrested on the first conspiracy charge back in 1972. Johnny Smith? Knew him since Grade 3 in the East End. Tommy Duncan was another boyhood pal, and Cliff Luhtala was a guy Palmer met through a mutual friend in 1960. He didn't know Bobby Porter until, oh, the early 1970s. And Bill De Ruiter fell into the same category as Walter Guay, a guy Palmer never heard of till the day De Ruiter was named in the second conspiracy indictment in 1974.

Did Palmer ever conspire with these seven men to deal in drugs?

Not a chance.

And what about the boyhood pals? What were Palmer's connections over the years with Smith and Duncan and Luhtala?

"Well," Palmer answered, "if I seen them at the Waldorf, after I started drinking there, I'd have a drink with them. Just sit down. Order a drink. Whatever. Be social."

Walsh directed Palmer to the unindicted co-conspirators. Conrad Gunn, Allan Cressey, Edward Stenson, and so on. Walsh named all eighteen co-conspirators. Gunn, Palmer said, was just a guy he'd met around the Waldorf maybe a dozen times in all the years he'd been dropping into the place.

Cressey was someone he grew up with in the East End. Stenson? Palmer had seen him around, him and his flower girls, at the nightclubs. Many of the names on the list, Palmer said, belonged to people who, as far as he was concerned, didn't even exist until he got his name mixed up with theirs in this trial. Bill Turner? He was a friend of Ray's, the older Palmer brother, and Doug had naturally been bumping into him for years. There was nothing illegal in their relationship. As far as that went, there wasn't anything that went contrary to the law — for sure, nothing to do with heroin — in his friendships or acquaintanceships with any of the people named as conspirators or co-conspirators.

Now, Walsh calculated, it was time to match Palmer against his principal nemesis.

"Do you know a Frederick Thomas Ford?" Walsh asked Palmer.

"Yes."

"How long have you known him?"

"I would say maybe twenty-five years."

"What has been your relationship with Frederick Thomas Ford over those years?"

"I have had no relationship with Frederick Ford other than if I seen him, I nodded or he nodded. I know his older brother quite well, Bill Ford."

"Have you ever had a conspiracy or agreement with Frederick Thomas Ford to traffic in narcotic drugs?"

"Not ever."

"You've listened to the evidence of Frederick Ford as he gave it on the witness stand. What have you to say about that?"

"It's a complete lie."

"Ford testified that on January 20, 1973, you met with him and told him he was fired and he was lucky to be alive and so on. What do you say about that?"

"I have never in my life met with Fred Ford except to bump

into him. I have never ever had a premeditated meeting with this fellow."

Walsh said, "Ford says it took place at the Admiral Lounge, this conversation about being fired, and it was some time after eight-thirty or nine o'clock at night."

"There's a possibility I could have bumped into Ford at the Admiral," Palmer said. "I don't recall seeing him there, but it's possible. I live in Burnaby. I go by the Admiral. I have a drink."

"Is it possible there was such a conversation about him being fired?"

"There was definitely never any conversation with this person in regards to anything related to drugs."

Palmer was on a roll of denials. Perfect, Walsh thought, just what was needed to counter Ford's evidence. But it was time to allow Palmer to slide into a positive stance. Walsh produced Ford's note of August 10, 1974.

"What do you know about this note?" Walsh asked.

"It was given to me by Fred Ford's brother Bill."

"Under what circumstances?"

"It was shortly after we'd been arrested on this charge," Palmer answered. "And Fred Ford's name appeared on the indictment and I was having a few drinks with Bill one day and I asked him to ask Freddie to come down and have a talk with me. I wanted to know why his name was linked to mine. Anyway, he never come down, but his brother brought this note later. That's all."

The origins of the famous note had now been revealed in court. But Walsh and Palmer weren't finished with Fred Ford and his messages.

Walsh asked Palmer, "Did you get any other communication on behalf of Ford?"

"After the preliminary hearing in 1975," Palmer said, "a fellow named Rick Bezanson came into the Waldorf and handed me a note. It was signed 'FF', and it said if I could get together ten thousand dollars, he wouldn't testify at the trial."

"Did you ever pay money to Ford?"

"No."

"What happened to the note?"

"When I got it, I had to go over to the bar to read it because there's a light that runs under it, fluorescent light, and I held it there and read it. Rick Bezanson was standing right beside me. And then I ripped up the note and threw it in the pail at the bar. It said on the note, 'Rip up.' But that isn't why I ripped it. I ripped it because it was pretty hot, the note."

That wrapped the defence for Walsh. In the department of veracity, he thought, Palmer's testimony put Palmer in exact contradiction to Ford, and Walsh was betting that Mr. Justice Macfarlane would opt for his man over the crown witness. "Douglas was plausible and credible as a witness," Walsh said later. "He appeared strongly to me as the witness who was forthright as opposed to Ford who was evasive." Walsh turned Palmer over to Arthur MacLennan for cross-examination.

MacLennan asked, "Why do you suggest that Frederick Ford should fabricate the story he told this court?"

"I've thought about that," Palmer said. "I think you should ask him the question. He's the one who done it."

"You have no answer?"

"Other than to get himself out of trouble."

"You say Fred Ford's testimony is a complete lie?"

"That's it."

"Not quite a complete lie," MacLennan said. "You don't deny he was shot in January 1975, do you?"

"It was in all the papers. I know he was shot from what I read."

"So you don't say the shooting was a lie?"

"I had nothing to do with the shooting."

MacLennan trotted out the August 10 note.

"What do you know about the note?" he asked. "How did it come about as far as you're aware?"

"Like I said, I received it from his brother Bill at the Waldorf Hotel."

"And did you ask Fred Ford for it?"

"No, I asked Billy to get hold of Fred and have him come and see me. And later Billy came walking in and handed me this note."

"So obviously Ford was concerned that you might think he might spill the beans and the note was the answer."

"I don't know what Ford thought," Palmer said. "I know one thing — I never have had any dealings with him of any kind."

Palmer didn't budge off his story. MacLennan took runs at different aspects of Palmer's testimony, but Palmer held to his version of events, which struck MacLennan as a non-version. Palmer insisted, take it or leave it, never mind what other witnesses might tell the court, that he was innocent of drug-dealing.

"I swear on it," Palmer said in his last words to MacLennan's cross-examination.

MacLennan gave up the chase and sat down. And Doug Palmer walked back across the courtroom floor from the witness stand to his place in the prisoners' box.

Harry Walsh called no other witnesses for his defence of Palmer. And of the other defence counsel, only Larry Hill for Walter Guay summoned witnesses. Hill had two of them, a woman named Liz Harnois and a man named Rolly Trudell. Liz was a retired topless dancer and Rolly was a thief, a break-and-enter man, and a drug dealer whose current address was the Matsqui Correctional Institution in British Columbia. And between them, under Larry Hill's questioning, the odd couple of Liz and Rolly told an intricate and fabulous story.

According to them, Walter Guay, innocent dupe, didn't

have a clue that the green Lucerne suitcase the Mounties observed him with held a cargo of heroin. It seemed that in April 1971 Liz had run into Rolly at Ruby Foo's Restaurant in Montreal. Liz and Rolly went way back together to the days when Liz used to shake her breasts at a nightclub in Vancouver called The Factory and Rolly was doing burglaries and one thing and another around town. When Rolly heard at Ruby Foo's that Liz was visiting from Vancouver and was about to catch a train back to the coast, he asked her to take along a suitcase for delivery to a Vancouver guy named Joe Scott. Sure thing, Liz said, not knowing, because Rolly had omitted this detail, that the suitcase contained heroin which an Italian named Gene was paying Rolly $3,500 to ship to Joe Scott in Vancouver.

Liz boarded the Supercontinental with Rolly's suitcase, the green Lucerne number, and she was joined by Walter Guay, another of her old bosom buds. Walter was riding west to visit his sister, who was married to a Vancouver lawyer named Jack Rossi. The reason that the Mounties connected Walter with the green suitcase, Liz said in her evidence, was because she was travelling with so many suitcases that Walter, good friend, offered to help by carrying and checking the Lucerne bag in question. It wasn't his bag and he didn't know it was full of heroin and neither did she.

So, anyway, Walter got sick in Capreol and went home to Montreal. And when Liz reached Vancouver, she couldn't claim the green Lucerne suitcase because Walter had checked it through for her. He had the baggage tag. Which meant she had to wait for Walter to get to Vancouver, and then he went down to the train station for her and claimed the suitcase from the baggage room.

Everyone in the courtroom, lawyers and judge and especially Walter Guay, listened in fascination to the tale that Liz and Rolly recounted. Did anyone besides Guay believe the testimony? Hell, no, but it made terrific theatre.

"Tell us exactly what happened," Arthur MacLennan said

to Liz at one point in his cross-examination, trying to wrest from her a few details about the cross-country journey with the Lucerne suitcase.

"It's really hard for me to recall, you know, *exactly*," Liz said. "I was drinking a lot the whole two weeks I was in Montreal."

"Well, what time did you board the train to go to Vancouver?"

"I was three-quarters drunk," Liz said. "So I don't remember."

"But you saw Mr. Guay on the train?"

"We had a couple of drinks. And then I think I went back to my car."

"You went to bed feeling three-quarters drunk?"

"By the time I got to bed," Liz said, "I think I was about all the way drunk."

Hey, the other defence counsel thought, with an alibi witness like Liz, Walter Guay's goose is cooked for sure.

There goes Larry again.

When all the witnesses had been heard from and accounted for, there remained only the counsel's arguments before the trial ended. Counsel began the arguments on the morning of February 24 and nattered through most of the next three days.

Harry Walsh led off for the two Palmer brothers. He argued the lines he'd developed in his cross-examinations of the crown witnesses and in his examination-in-chief of Doug Palmer. That the Mounties' observations in the Polynesian Lounge revealed nothing more sinister than a series of social gatherings. That the crown had established no connection between either Palmer brother and drugs. And that Fred Ford, the witness who purported to link Doug Palmer to the heroin trade, had plenty of reason to lie, partly to save his own neck and partly to reap the benefits dangled before him by the RCMP. Walsh quoted to Mr. Justice Macfarlane dozens of cases on the law of conspiracy and wound up his argument, in mid-afternoon of the twenty-fourth, with a small flourish:

"Under all the circumstances, my lord, and especially having regard for the testimony of Douglas Palmer, there is, on the evidence raised, at least a reasonable doubt, the benefit of which must go to the accused."

The other defence counsel followed in like fashion, hammering with particular emphasis on the prinicple of reasonable doubt.

Joe Wood, speaking eloquently on behalf of Tommy Duncan, said, on the crown's evidence, there existed a *reasonable doubt* that the drugs in the back of Doug Manuel's crew-cab truck were really the same drugs the Mounties picked out of the big garbage pail at the back of the Ladner Hotel. With such a break in continuity in the trail of the drugs, Wood argued, the heroin couldn't be pinned to Duncan and he should be acquitted. For Wood's other client, Cliff Luhtala, he contended that the crown hadn't advanced evidence from which Mr. Justice Macfarlane could properly infer that Luhtala had joined in a drug conspiracy.

David Gibbons, next up for Johnny Smith and Bobby Porter, did a similarly concise job in arguing that, even with the mother lode of RCMP evidence, all those hours of surveillance, there still remained a *reasonable doubt* that Smith and Porter had conspired to carry out any sort of illegal drug-dealing. And as for the apparently damning identification that Corporals John Paterson and Karl Richert, the inside men on the bus depot stake-out, made of Smith as the man in the long sideburns who strolled away with the suitcase of heroin, er, flour, Gibbons said piffle. The identification had to be mistaken. For one thing, Smith was taller than the guy with the sideburns. Besides, Johnny Smith kept his sideburns trimmed to normal length. *Reasonable doubt.*

Larry Hill, for Walter Guay, performed a reprise of the Liz and Rolly Show in a try at persuading Macfarlane that Guay

313

was only a pawn in the works, a kindly gent doing a good turn for a lady that, alas, got him in the soup. Unlucky Walter, Hill said to the judge, was no worse than "a sucker twice removed".

The last defence counsel to argue, Russ Chamberlain for Bill De Ruiter, worked different territory from that of the other lawyers. Chamberlain pointed out, forcibly as usual, that a jury had already acquitted De Ruiter at his earlier trial on the substantive charge of possession of heroin for the purposes of trafficking. The acquittal meant, apart from many other things, that the crown in the conspiracy case could not rely on the presence of the heroin in De Ruiter's attic as evidence against De Ruiter. Nor could the crown depend on the rest of the paraphernalia — the weigh-scales, condoms, and so on — as evidence to yank De Ruiter into the conspiracy. And what other evidence existed to tie De Ruiter to Doug Palmer and the other alleged conspirators? None — apart from Fred Ford's story about supplying Sergeant Jim Locker with the licence number of an aged white Chrysler that turned out to be registered to De Ruiter. But was that enough to convict De Ruiter of conspiracy? Not, Chamberlain answered, on your life.

Russ Chamberlain finished his argument at two-thirty in the afternoon of February 25. But Chamberlain had plenty more to get off his chest. Once again his temper was at the boil, controlled — Chamberlain was, after all, a pro — but simmering at about one hundred degrees Celsius. He was upset with Macfarlane — who else? — and he'd been fuming over a grievance that reached back to February 17.

On that day, immediately before the noon break, Macfarlane had shot a bolt from the blue. He announced to the courtroom that he was revoking the bail of the accused and remanding them into custody for the rest of the trial. The ruling didn't bother Cliff Luhtala: he was already in prison

314

serving time on an earlier drug conviction. But the other seven had been free on bail, living at home, driving down to the courthouse for each day of the trial. Now, with Macfarlane's sudden zap, the Palmer brothers and the others were confined to the slamer. It was hard to tell who was more surprised, the seven accused men or their lawyers.

Arthur MacLennan was delighted. Much earlier, on January 28, he had *asked* Macfarlane to put the seven loose accused in custody. January 28 was the day after Doug Palmer approached MacLennan at the end of court and wondered about a small favour. When Palmer had been first arrested in 1972, one of the conditions of his bail was that he surrender his passport to the court. By January 27, 1976, the passport had expired, and Palmer asked MacLennan to retrieve it. MacLennan obliged, but Palmer's request winked MacLennan's suspicion light-bulb. Sure enough, swift investigation revealed that Palmer, his wife, and brother Donald had recently, *very* recently, applied for new passports. MacLennan jammed up whatever plan for flight Palmer might have had in mind by instructing the Vancouver passport office to stall on documents in the Palmer name. And next day in court, January 28, MacLennan made his appeal that Macfarlane revoke all the accused men's bail.

Curiously, MacLennan didn't peg his argument on the passport applications. For reasons he kept to himself, he never *mentioned* the passports. Maybe he thought it would be dirty pool to bring up the matter after Doug Palmer had come to him, whether out of naivety or foolishness, for the favour. Instead, MacLennan talked to Macfarlane about the relatively low bail that had been set for the accused men, about the seriousness of the charges against them, about the increasingly obvious strength of the crown's case, and, given all of the above, about the temptation that the accused were bound to feel to skip out on the trial. The defence counsel, when Macfarlane gave them a chance to reply to MacLennan's arguments, pooh-poohed the notion that their clients, innocent and reliable chaps, wouldn't see the trial through to the end from their seats in the prisoners' box. Macfarlane, apparently agreeing with the defence, left the bail in place and the accused, apart from Luhtala, on the street.

Nothing more about bail or custody came up during the following few days. Except that MacLennan, in his cross-examination of Doug Palmer, made a point of asking about the applications for new passports. Palmer acknowledged that, sure, so what, he and the wife and Donnie had put in for the passports. The exchange between MacLennan and Palmer seemed to pass without raising Macfarlane's antennae. But exactly one week after the exchange, at noon on February 17, from out of left field, without any warning preliminaries, most conspicuously without permitting defence counsel to argue the matter, the judge slapped the accused men into prison. The seven had been expecting to nosh on their usual lunch of hamburgers and draft beer at a restaurant around the corner from the courthouse. But that noon and thereafter, they joined Cliff Luhtala on the prison luncheon diet of baloney on white and milk.

After the noon recess on the seventeenth, Harry Walsh went through the motions of objecting to Macfarlane's action. The judge turned aside the objections, and Walsh, in truth, wasn't terribly steamed over the incident. In prison or out, Palmer would, Walsh figured, be acquitted.

"The passport applications, supposing they were what Macfarlane based his ruling on, were nothing to get excited about," Walsh said. "If Douglas and his wife were going to flee, the lack of passports would never have stopped them."

But Russ Chamberlain couldn't so casually brush off Macfarlane's ruling.

"I was furious," he later recalled. "When we broke for lunch that day, the seventeenth, I told the other counsel Macfarlane had showed he wasn't applying the presumption of innocence any more. I said Macfarlane was out to convict everybody in the case. I wanted to go back in the courtroom and stir up the dust. But the other guys talked me into just letting Harry Walsh make his weak objections. I had a hell of a time keeping my mouth shut."

What especially rankled for Chamberlain was that he could see his man, De Ruiter, going all the way down the tubes with the other accused. First, he'd had his bail revoked, next he'd get convicted. And all the while, as far as Chamberlain was concerned, De Ruiter belonged in a different category of innocence from the others. He had *nothing* to do with the conspiracy, and the whole damned mess galled Chamberlain.

On the afternoon of February 25, after Chamberlain finished his argument, he at last let loose his views — and his venom — on Macfarlane.

"I would like to draw your lordship's attention to the case of *Regina v. Kelly*," he began mildly enough. The Kelly case was a 1966 appeal to the British Columbia Court of Appeal in a narcotics case, and Chamberlain quoted to Macfarlane a short passage from the decision:

"The depths to which people engaged in the nefarious business of drug trafficking will sink is well known to the law courts, and the courts will be ever vigilant to do all within their power to punish the guilty offenders. But, while people accused of crimes may in some minds be entitled to very little consideration, the law courts must guard the rights of such accused people as sacredly as possible and be mindful of the fact that society is not well served by the conviction of any man" — here Chamberlain's voice took on emphasis — "*unless by adherence to the due process of law.*"

Uh-oh, the other defence lawyers thought, this was going to get heavy.

"Now," Chamberlain went on, "I have in mind when I bring this quotation to your lordship's attention the fact that my client, William De Ruiter, was ruled summarily into custody without any submission from counsel, and at the time of the ruling there wasn't one more scintilla of evidence against my client than there had ever been."

Macfarlane, in Chamberlain's later description, "went grey with fury." Small wonder. Chamberlain had just accused him of tromping over De Ruiter's rights, of ignoring the principles of due process of law. There could be no more black-and-white challenge to a jurist's integrity.

"I must say those last remarks disturb me," Macfarlane said, keeping his civility intact. "Counsel are entitled to say what they want on behalf of their clients and I must sit here patiently and listen."

"I have said very little," Chamberlain snapped, sending up a signal that he had more hand grenades to lob in Macfarlane's direction.

That crack opened the floodgates. For the next ten minutes Macfarlane talked steadily. He offered his justification for remanding the accused men into custody. He said it initially had nothing to do with the Palmer passport applications. He said that as he listened to the evidence, as he appreciated the great seriousness of the charges and the enormous value of the drug transactions in the alleged conspiracy — millions and millions of dollars in profits — it dawned on him that "it would be less than human to expect that each of the eight accused in these circumstances could be relied on to continue in attendance." In other words, the trial had reached the stage where, in Macfarlane's view, one or two or more of the accused men might decide it was smart to do a Bill Turner and go into hiding. But, Macfarlane rapped on, aiming his remarks at Russ Chamberlain, his fury turning a deeper shade of grey, "to suggest that because I made that decision in the public interest to revoke bail, I'm not going to judge the accused on the evidence in the case, that is an affront to the court!"

Chamberlain stood his ground, and the argument over Macfarlane's ruling whipped back and forth until Joe Wood put in his two cents' worth. His money was on Russ Chamberlain's side.

"All I wish to say," Wood said to Macfarlane, "is that I have searched diligently for some precedent where this kind of ruling has been taken without counsel being afforded the opportunity of speaking to the matter before the order was made. I have found no such precedent, and it is my view that the step which was taken is contrary to the whole notion of British justice since the time of the Magna Carta."

That powerful declaration got Larry Hill to his feet in a hurry.

"My lord," he said in a burst, "I want to disassociate myself from those last remarks."

There goes Larry again.

When the dust that Russ Chamberlain had stirred settled thirty minutes later, it wasn't clear what had been gained. The accused, including Bill De Ruiter, were still in custody. No change there. But Chamberlain had unburdened himself of a passionately held belief. So had Joe Wood. And just maybe Chamberlain had scored a very significant point for his client. Maybe, after the explosion of that afternoon, Chamberlain had influenced Mr. Justice Macfarlane to look at Bill De Ruiter in a different light. Maybe, from then on, in the dying hours of the long trial, Macfarlane would separate De Ruiter from the rest of the pack of accused.

There was a coda to the argument over the bail revocation that was ironic, comic, and perhaps incredible.

"Just after the trial ended," Arthur MacLennan said years later, "Larry Hill went to Macfarlane and told him he was absolutely right to put the men in custody. Larry said Walter Guay had tipped him that two of the accused had been planning to skip. The two, Larry said, were the Palmer brothers."

MacLennan chuckled.

"But," he said, "could you believe Walter Guay? Or, for that matter, Larry?"

MacLennan went last in his argument to Macfarlane, and needed the rest of the afternoon of February 25 and all of the morning of the twenty-sixth. He trudged through a review of the crown's case, punching up the highlights, and he asked Macfarlane, mincing no words, to find all the accused guilty on all the charges. Macfarlane allowed defence counsel to speak brief rebuttals to MacLennan's argument, and when they'd run out of things to say, he told everyone to return to the courtroom on March 11. That day, he'd have his judgment for them.

Mr. Justice Macfarlane missed his scheduled decision date by twelve days. It wasn't until March 23 that the accused men, still of course in custody, gathered with their lawyers and Arthur MacLennan and his crew to hear Macfarlane read his judgment in the courtroom. The twelve-day delay was understandable. Macfarlane's painstakingly thought-out judgment ran to ninety-three pages and was thick with recitation of evidence, analysis of law, and conclusions about the accused.

The largest and most crucial chunk of the ninety-three pages necessarily dealt with the conflicting stories that Fred Ford and Doug Palmer told from the witness stand. Palmer's fate turned on Macfarlane's dissection of the two men's evidence, and while neither witness, Macfarlane said, was exactly an angel, one of them, he believed, had told the truth. The other had lied.

But who was the liar? And who was the man of truth?

To sort out who was who and which was which, Macfarlane started with his own blunt assessment of Ford and of Palmer.

Ford: "He is obviously a most disreputable character. I pause to note, however, that one ought not to be surprised that a person involved in the type of activity under consideration here is of that character."

Palmer: "Although he says he only has a grade eight education, he appears knowledgeable and quite intelligent. He struck me as a shrewd and calculating witness. He gave his evidence carefully and deliberately. He was prepared to give detailed explanations of events, which struck me as unusual in view of the fact that such events would have little or no importance to him at the time they happened."

Then, as a stick by which to measure the two men's approach to the truth, Macfarlane homed in on Ford's note of August 10, 1974, the note that his brother Billy took to Palmer at the Waldorf.

Macfarlane on Ford's version of the note's origins: "He says he cannot recall the circumstances in which he wrote the note because he had been drinking a lot and was scared. He said there had been pressure on him from both sides about his testimony, that he knew he had broken the code, and thought he would be shot. The note was written after the charges had been laid against Douglas Palmer and the others, and about a month before Ford was scheduled to give evidence at the preliminary hearing, from which he subsequently absented himself. It seems reasonable to conclude that Ford probably wrote the note to relieve pressure upon himself."

Macfarlane on Palmer's version: "He testifies that he received the note from Ford's brother after having requested a meeting with Ford when he noticed that Ford was one of the co-conspirators named in the indictment. One has to ask why Palmer's attention was directed so specifically to Ford if he had no questionable association with him but rather just an innocent 'nodding' relationship. One also has to ask why Ford, if he was not involved with Palmer, rather than coming to see Palmer as requested, would write such a note."

321

As Macfarlane weaved through the evidence, he was relishing his role as a kind of Sherlock Holmes of the bench, separating out the clues, weighing them against one another, drawing deductions. Thus, he went on, as long as the subject of notes was in the air, my dear Watson, what about the second note? The note that someone named Rick Bezanson was supposed to have delivered to Palmer at the Waldorf? The note signed "FF" and asking for ten grand in return for silence at the trial?

"Palmer says he immediately ripped up this note," Macfarlane said. "He did this despite the fact he had carefully kept the earlier note. I do not believe that a man of his obvious intelligence and quick wit would fail to keep the second note, the blackmail note.

"Palmer is not the type of man who would have preserved one note and thrown the other away," Macfarlane continued, mixing a dash of Freud with his Holmes. "Palmer's version of the almost non-existent relationship with Ford is out of harmony with the receipt from Ford of a note denying a relationship for which no denial was required if, in fact, they had nothing to do with each other."

Let's see. If Ford and Palmer had no relationship, as Palmer maintained, there'd be no call for Ford to dispatch a note of any sort to Palmer. But if Palmer and Ford were employer-employee in the heroin business, as Ford insisted, then Ford would have plenty of reason for bombarding Palmer with notes of reassurance. Or of blackmail. Got it.

"The receipt of the first note," Macfarlane said, "and the importance which Palmer obviously placed on it by keeping it, seems inconsistent with the theory that Palmer was not involved in any way in the traffic of narcotics. One would almost think that Palmer suspected Ford might try to implicate him. Palmer is unable to give any reason why Ford would want to implicate an innocent man in his story."

Macfarlane was leaning to the Ford version of the note of

August 10, 1974. Not just leaning. Macfarlane had almost embraced Ford's story. But first, in his Sherlockian mode, he had to eliminate one last possible interpretation of Ford's testimony. Was it conceivable that Ford was out to hoodwink everyone from the Mounties to the lawyers to the judge himself? Could it be that his evidence was a mountain of lies? Was he a teller of tall tales on a massive scale? The Baron Munchausen of the East End? Macfarlane had to remind himself that Ford had the motivation to concoct magnificent fibs that would ensnare Doug Palmer. As Harry Walsh had brought out in his cross-examination of Ford, there was the RCMP's guarantee to protect, support, and relocate Ford and his family. There was the apparent hold that the Mounties had put on the jewellery-store charges against Ford, and, again, the blind eye that the RCMP may have turned to Ford's post-Palmer drug-dealing. As motivations went, weren't these awfully convincing?

Ah, well, Macfarlane said, they could be explained.

"The benefits which may accrue to such an individual as Ford by giving evidence against the accused in this case," he said, "must be weighed against the extreme danger to himself and perhaps to his family, in doing so. To use his own words" — though, as Harry Walsh later pointed out, in proceeding to talk about the "code", Macfarlane was using *his* own words and nothing that Ford had said on the witness stand — "he had 'broken the code,' and he knew the consequences. I was of the impression, as he gave his evidence, that he fully realized that he had as much, if not more, to lose by giving his evidence as he had to gain. The conclusion I reached after he had finished giving his evidence was that it had the ring of truth to it."

Macfarlane had finally and diligently sleuthed his way to a solution.

"I have concluded," he said, "that the relationship between Ford and Palmer was as Ford testified rather than as

Palmer would have me believe."

Ford, at least for the purposes of the trial, was the witness who spoke the truth.

Doug Palmer was the liar.

And from that conclusion, everything that damned Palmer fell into place. The Palmer drug network — back-end men, cap-up operations, burials, maps on cigarette paper, huge profits — had functioned in just the way Ford had described in his testimony. That was what Macfarlane held. And he held that the gatherings at the Polynesian Lounge were occasions when Palmer and the others plotted heroin transactions, that Palmer's meetings with Conrad Gunn and other convicted drug offenders were in furtherance of the narcotics conspiracy, that the money-changing and all the other events which the Mounties said they observed were part and parcel of the single objective of making a profit on the drug market.

"Even aside from the Ford matter," Macfarlane said, "it seems inconceivable, on a fair view of the evidence in this case, that Douglas Palmer had never had any dealings in narcotics. I do not believe him when he testifies that he was not part of the alleged conspiracy."

Macfarlane had put his stamp on the case: Doug Palmer was guilty of the charge of conspiring to traffic in narcotics. And so were the others in the gang who congregated at the Waldorf, took instructions from Doug, and went about the clandestine business of capping, burying, and selling. Tommy Duncan, Cliff Luhtala, Johnny Smith, Bobby Porter, Donald Palmer — all were guilty as charged.

What about Walter Guay?

He got a break on the conspiracy charge. Macfarlane held that the crown hadn't proved it was Johnny Smith who picked up Walter's green Lucerne suitcase at the bus depot. The identification evidence of John Paterson and Karl Richert, the corporals who fingered Smith as the guy with the long sideburns who got into locker 610, wasn't good enough, and since Smith was the only conspirator who might link Walter Guay into the Palmer gang, with no other evidence against Guay of association with Palmer people, he walked on the conspiracy charge.

But he wasn't so lucky on the other charge against him, the count of possessing heroin — the thirty-four ounces in the suitcase — for the purposes of trafficking. Macfarlane ruled that the crown had established Guay had possession of the drugs. The alibi evidence of Liz Harnois and Rolly Trudell, he said, was nonsense. The drugs were Guay's. Guay knew they were in the suitcase. It didn't matter that the crown had not proved the heroin was intended for the Palmer operation. It had proved enough to convict Walter Guay of possession of the drugs, and, given the large quantity, it could be for only one purpose. Trafficking.

Tommy Duncan went down the same way. On the count against him of trafficking, Macfarlane said he was satisfied with the crown's evidence about the events in Ladner on the night in January 1971 when Tommy got careless with his stash of heroin. Maybe the heroin ended up in the back of Doug Manuel's truck and in the garbage pails behind the hotel, but the crown established that Tommy had possession of it long enough to be convicted of trafficking.

That left Bill De Ruiter.

In the part of the judgment that dealt with De Ruiter, it seemed almost possible for the counsel in the courtroom to hear Macfarlane's brain ticking over. He was meticulous, sedulous, and assiduous in dissecting the case against De Ruiter. A gnat couldn't have found space to squeeze between the lines of Macfarlane's fine reasoning. He considered two main claims against De Ruiter: that he had allowed his aged Chrysler to be used for the transportation of heroin ("Couple of nights, more than a couple actually," Fred Ford told Sergeant Jim Locker, "I went with Dougie and he picked up packages of heroin from the white Chrysler"), and that De Ruiter was aware that the Palmer gang, through De Ruiter's occasional tenant Tommy Duncan, was operating a cap-up centre in his house.

And this is the decision that Macfarlane reached:

"Although the evidence relating to De Ruiter is a basis for grave suspicion about the man, I have come to the conclusion, after anxious consideration, that the crown has failed to proved beyond a reasonable doubt, on the admissible evidence, that he was a member of the conspiracy."

At the end of the trial that began nine weeks earlier, only one of the eight accused left the courtroom a free man.

He was Bill De Ruiter.

He was Russ Chamberlain's client.

On the morning of March 30, seven days after the trial finished, Fred Ford went by appointment to the office of Inspector Lawson Eyman at the RCMP headquarters on Heather Street. Ford had made up his mind once and for all that he wanted money, not relocation. For the Mounties' part, with the trial over and the Palmer gang shot down, they weren't fussy where Ford took himself or how he got there. They agreed to cash over relocation, and Inspector Eyman was waiting for Ford with a cheque.

"You must be the famous Fred Ford," Eyman said when Ford arrived.

"Don't know about famous," Ford said. "But I better be a hell of a lot richer when I leave here."

"The cheque's signed and countersigned," Eyman said, handing it to Ford. "There you go, and I have a receipt I'd like you to sign."

Ford looked at the cheque he held in his hand, and for an instant it seemed his piggy little eyes might fall out of his fat round face.

"For chrissake!"

Ford's voice was close to a scream.

"Something the matter?" Eyman asked mildly.

"Plenty's the matter, man," Ford shouted. "This thing's for twenty-five thousand!"

"Lot of money, Mr. Ford," Eyman said.

"Sixty!" Ford was still shouting. "*Sixty's* what I'm supposed to get!"

"I wouldn't know about that," Eyman said. "And would you mind just keeping your voice down, Mr. Ford."

"What am I gonna do on twenty-five grand?" Ford said. "The plan was I take me and the family off you guys' hands. We might go to England, some place like that. Jeez, on twenty-five, I can't get us to Tacoma."

"You going to accept the twenty-five thousand or not?" Eyman asked.

"You think I'm crazy?" Ford said. "Of course I'm gonna accept it. But I'm coming after you people for the other thirty-five thousand."

"That's something you'll have to take up with Neil MacKay," Eyman said. "Or maybe further up. Jack White."

"White, yeah, I remember he was by once over at the Plaza 500," Ford said. "Where's he at now?"

"Inspector White's on holidays."

"What about MacKay?"

"Holidays."

"Shit."

"Look, Mr. Ford, would you sign this receipt for me?"

Ford examined the receipt. It was in the form of an affidavit acknowledging payment of the twenty-five thousand dollars.

"'Paid in full for services rendered,'" Ford read from the affidavit. "You ain't paid me in *full* yet."

Inspector Eyman crossed out "in full". Ford signed the affidavit, and it was sworn by a notary public in the RCMP offices. Ford kept a copy of the affidavit for himself.

"Tell you absolutely positive," Ford said to Eyman. "I'm

gonna be over this place like a blanket till I get the rest of my money."

"Sergeant MacKay'll be back in the office two weeks from now," Eyman said. "Inspector White the same."

"Guys really fucked me."

On April 7, the seven convicted members of the Palmer outfit and their lawyers — all the regulars except De Ruiter and Chamberlain — assembled once again before Mr. Justice Macfarlane. It was sentencing day, and the lawyers were prepared to put their clients' best feet forward.

Harry Walsh called character witnesses who said Doug Palmer ran a kids' hockey program in the East End. Everybody, the witnesses said, considered Doug a real straight-shooter. Donald Palmer, Walsh told Macfarlane, had had it rough ever since the childhood accident that left him a touch addled. Larry Hill asked Macfarlane to take into account Walter Guay's age. He was fifty-nine, and a long sentence, Hill argued, might mean Guay would never again see the outside world. Joe Wood pointed out that Tommy Duncan had never been in trouble with the law before the conspiracy case and that Cliff Luhtala, while in prison on the earlier conviction, had showed true grit by finishing his Grade 12 and by being active in a rehabilitation program called the Seven Steps. David Gibbons submitted a letter from an officer of the Ladner Legion that called Gibbons's client Bobby Porter "honest and sincere in the time I have known him". For Johnny Smith, Gibbons told Macfarlane that, in the bad-news department, Smith had a severe drinking problem, but that, good news, he was almost cured.

All of the lawyers, no matter what specific words of praise or excuse they spoke, sounded one common theme for all of the accused. Their clients, they said, had always lived in humble circumstances and were, as far as the lawyers could tell, flat broke.

328

Macfarlane had a comeback for this recurring claim.

"One of the obvious things," he said in court, at that point interrupting Gibbons's tale of penniless woe on behalf of Bobby Porter, "is that a person who is involved in this sort of drug business where the sentences are so severe is that he is not going to live in a lifestyle which is out of keeping with his training and background. He doesn't drive a fifty-foot yacht or a Lincoln Continental or live in a big house. Where he puts his money, I'm not going to speculate on, but the courts have found that this sort of person keeps a low profile."

When the defence lawyers heard Macfarlane's words, they had the sinking feeling that the judge was about to go tough in his sentencing. They were right. Macfarlane announced to the courtroom that the least he could do for the public was to put the Palmer gang away for as long as he could "to prevent them from plying their miserable trade".

Then he pronounced sentence.

For Doug Palmer, life in prison.

For Donald Palmer — though everyone else considered him to be under Doug's thumb, Macfarlane thought Donnie's close association with his twin made him a co-leader of the operation — life in prison.

For Tommy Duncan, twenty years on the conspiracy conviction and twenty years concurrent on the trafficking conviction.

For Johnny Smith and Bobby Porter, twenty years.

For Walter Guay, twenty years on the trafficking conviction.

For Cliff Luhtala — "I take into account," Macfarlane said, "the time you have served and the prospects of your rehabilitation and what you have already done along that line in prison" — five years.

"I wish you luck in your future," Macfarlane said to Luhtala.

"As I do the others," he added as an afterthought.

Macfarlane tidied the papers in front of him.

"That deals with everything in this unhappy matter," he said to the courtroom. "We will now adjourn."

Fred Ford was a busy beaver in the weeks after the visit to Inspector Lawson Eyman that left him so devastated.

He hired a lawyer to bring an action against the RCMP for thirty-five thousand dollars.

He phoned Inspector Neil MacKay.

"I'm sorry about the money, Fred," MacKay said.

"Sorry, shit," Ford said. "How do you think I feel?"

"I know we talked sixty thousand," MacKay said. "But you remember yourself that was just a recommendation."

"What happened to the recommendation?"

"The people in Ottawa must've thought it was excessive."

"After all I done for you at the trial."

"Fred," MacKay said, "we're not going to budge Ottawa on this."

Ford phoned Inspector Jack White.

"It's the Department of Justice in Ottawa, Mr. Ford," White said. "They won't go higher than twenty-five thousand. My hands are tied."

"I heard that already," Ford said.

He phoned Arthur MacLennan.

"I know about your problem, Fred," MacLennan said.

"Everybody knows but nobody's doing anything."

"I tried," MacLennan said. "I went through channels to get you more money."

"Yeah? So?"

"The superintendent refused to approve more in your case."

"Superintendent of what?"

"RCMP," MacLennan said. "You see, Fred, you accepted the twenty-five thousand, and the superintendent feels your insistence on more money comes close to blackmail."

"I'm not trying to blackmail nobody," Ford said. "I gave

my evidence. Now all I asking is fair payment to take care of me and the family."

"I'm on your side there, Fred," MacLennan said. "Twenty-five thousand isn't the right amount to get yourself established somewhere else."

"This hassle ain't over," Ford said.

He visited Harry Walsh, who happened to be in Vancouver on other legal business.

"When Ford phoned me at the Bayshore Inn and asked to come over," Walsh recalled some years later, "I was wary. I didn't expect him to be friendly after the vigorous way I cross-examined him at the trial. And I thought, for another thing, he might be wired with a tape-recorder when he talked to me. With a person like Ford, there was no telling in whose interests he might be acting."

Walsh insisted that his meeting with Ford take place in the coffee shop at the Bayshore. A safe and noisy public place. Ford told Walsh his story about the promised sixty thousand and the delivered twenty-five thousand. He said he'd retained a lawyer to sue for the difference, but the lawyer was pushing too slowly to suit Ford. He asked Walsh to take over the collection job. Walsh declined. Ford grumped on for several more minutes.

"At the end of his rambles," Walsh recalled, "I told Ford if he was serious to call on Joe Wood."

That turned out to be a very significant piece of advice.

Ford eventually reached Joe Wood's office, but he travelled by way of a round-about route. Something was stirring in Ford's wily mind. He wanted to come out ahead in the whole deal. He hadn't given his testimony at the Palmer trial for free, and twenty-five thousand wasn't his price. But what was the best plan? How could he emerge a bigger winner? Things hadn't shaken clear in his head. He'd hang in for the other thirty-five thousand from the government, but that was looking like a lost cause. Maybe he should work the other side. The Palmer side. Something dangerous might be happening there. The Palmers would be pissed off at him. Naturally. But what if they'd put a contract on the street to have him hit? Shit, if they had, he was really up the creek. It'd mean there was maybe some guy waiting to take a shot at him and he didn't have enough cash to clear the hell out of the city. He had to plan things cautious and smart.

As a first unformed, tentative step, Ford dropped around to the Polynesian Lounge. He had with him his copy of the affidavit he'd sworn when he picked up the cheque from Inspector Lawson Eyman. The signed and sworn affidavit was one sentence long: "I hereby acknowledge receipt of the sum of twenty-five thousand dollars cash payment from the RCMP in the month of April 1976 for services rendered in regards to Palmer Drug Conspiracy Trial, to wit re Testifying at said Trial." Ford left the affidavit with a Waldorf waiter named Jim Fouts. Later that day, May 14, Fouts passed on the affidavit to another customer in the lounge. The second customer was Ray Palmer, Doug's older brother.

Son of a *bitch*, Ray thought, reading the affidavit, the fat bastard got *paid* for the bunch of bullshit he said at the trial.

Ray knocked back his drink and drove to the offices of Deverell, Harrop & Company in their slicked-up Gastown building. He left the affidavit with the receptionist, for the immediate attention of Joe Wood.

Seven days later, May 21, Fred Ford arrived unannounced at Deverell, Harrop. No appointment, but he wanted to see Joe Wood. He was shown past the greenery and Canadian Indian artifacts to Wood's office.

"Ray Palmer stopped by last week, Fred," Wood said to Ford, no beating around the bush. "But I expect you know that."

Ford said, "I gave this waiter over at the Waldorf my receipt from the Mounties."

Wood nodded.

Ford said, "The idea was more or less the waiter'd give it to Ray and he'd come here."

"He did," Wood said.

"So now you and Ray know where everything's at," Ford said. "I got money for testifying."

"What do you have in mind as a next step?" Wood asked.

"You want the truth?"

"I'm always interested in the truth, Fred," Wood said. He held up his hand. "Hold on a minute."

Wood dialled his telephone and asked another of the firm's lawyers, Jay Clarke, to step into the office. Wood had no sure idea what Ford was going to say, but discretion told him he ought to have a witness to the conversation.

"Shoot, Fred," Wood said when Clarke had joined them.

Ford was his usual darty-eyed, flat-toned, glum-faced self. Nothing was out of the ordinary in his looks or voice, and he sent out no signals to Wood or Clarke that he was about to throw the Palmer case into reverse gear.

"Doug Palmer," Ford said. "Him and me weren't in the drug business together."

"That's not what you said in court, Fred," Wood said.

Ford said, "Same with Don Palmer, Tommy Duncan, those other guys. I didn't operate with them."

Wood, silent, waited for Ford to go on.

"It was the Mounties," Ford said. "Like I showed you in the receipt, they made me tell that story for the trial."

Ford stopped talking.

"That's it?" Wood said.

Joe Wood had a deep voice, a take-charge voice, and a style to match the voice. He didn't flap, not even when someone — Fred Ford, for an immediate example — dropped a bomb on the rug in his office.

"That's it, Fred?" Joe Wood asked again.

"That's plenty, right?" Ford said.

Wood said, "Like to put it in writing, Fred?"

"I don't mind," Ford said. "Dictate it to a girl, you want, a secretary."

"No dictation, Fred," Wood said. "This is in your own handwriting. Your own words."

Ford, in Wood's office, wrote the date at the top of a sheet of paper and began the note with his favourite salutation, "To whom it may concern". His handwriting had a schoolboy's curls and loops and leaned about seventy-five degrees to the right. He wrote: "Any evidence I gave at the Douglas Palmer trial in 1976 was not of my own free will. I was pressured into saying what I said and also promised payment of $60,000. I never had any drug dealings with Doug Palmer, Don Palmer, Tom Duncan or John Smith. Any drug dealings were on my own and had nothing whatsoever to do with the above mentioned names. In April 1976 I rec. $25,000 cash from the RCMP."

Ford put his signature to the note. Wood and Jay Clarke signed as witnesses. And Ford left the offices of Deverell, Harrop & Company.

Ford lay low for most of the summer of 1976. He was sweating and thinking and calculating. The way he figured, he'd given the Palmers enough to keep them off his back. Temporarily anyway. They wouldn't want to see him rubbed out if they thought he'd come up with more of the kind of stuff he'd already delivered to Joe Wood. That was a taste of what he could produce. He'd said the Mounties had paid and pressured him into testifying. He could go further. He could take back the whole testimony and get Dougie Palmer off the hook.

Ford realized he had to balance his interests.

First, the thirty-five grand. He might as well kiss it goodbye. No matter what route he went, sticking to the story he told in court or telling everybody it was all bull, the Mounties were never going to pay him more than twenty-five thousand anyway.

Second, his future. He didn't really want to split from Vancouver. Not when he thought about it. Forget England. His whole life, his and his wife's and his kids', was in the East End.

Third, his safety. The Palmers, even with Doug and Don in the Pen, were guys to be scared of. The contacts they had, the money, Ray stirring up trouble — they could snap him out whenever they wanted. Whenever he wasn't any use to them. As far as the Palmers went, it was better to be useful.

Fourth, the truth. Who gave a shit about it? What he said in court, what he wrote in that statement for Joe Wood — it was all the same to him when you got right down to things. The truth might as well be whatever worked out to be the best deal.

On October 7, Ford showed up at Deverell, Harrop. He had another statement he'd written in his own curls and slants. Joe Wood wasn't in the office. Another Deverell, Harrop partner named Wayne Powell spoke to Ford. Powell took the statement and said he'd give it to Wood as soon as Wood came back from court.

In part, the statement said this:

"My name is Frederick Thomas Ford of Vancouver, British Columbia. Everything I am about to write in this statement is the truth and I am writing it of my own free will without any threats or inducements. I started dealing in heroin (drugs) in 1972. My nephew worked for me burying drugs and got caught. I went to the police and made a deal to turn someone in if they gave him a stay of proceedings (which they did). I talked to RCMP Staff Sgt. Jim Locker. He asked me if I knew a person named Doug Palmer. I said yes and he said we want him for dealing in drugs and we will let you deal in drugs without getting caught if you can help us nail Doug

Palmer. I didn't really know a thing about Doug Palmer but I saw an easy way for me to stay on the street and make money. I kept telling them different stories about Palmer, none of them true. In January 1975 I was shot in front of my home, 3475 Triumph Street. The RCMP (Neil MacKay) came and saw me at the hospital and told me all kinds of stories on who shot me. He said it was a hired killer paid for by Doug Palmer. I knew this was not so but in order for me to get their protection I played along with what they said. In February or March 1975 I went to a preliminary hearing concerning a drug case against Doug Palmer and some associates. I got up on the stand and made up a bunch of lies only because I didn't want to go to jail, also I was promised a large cash settlement, new ID and transportation to anywhere I wanted to go. Naturally I could not turn this down. The RCMP kept me and provided myself and family with $1200.00 per month to live on. In January 1976 they took me to the Plaza 500 Hotel on 12th Avenue, Vancouver. There Staff Sgt. Almrud, Neil MacKay and other RCMP officers kept harrassing me and threatening me to get on the stand and say the same things about Doug Palmer. By then I was in so deep I had to go along. Neil MacKay said he could not tell me personally how much I would get but he told Corp. Hoivik to tell me I would get $60,000.00. The Prosecutor Art MacLennan and Neil MacKay came to see me and threatened me with all kinds of charges if I did not give evidence at the trial of Doug Palmer. They said make sure I brought up Doug Palmer's name every chance I got. So I gave the same evidence as before (all lies). . . ."

A few days after Mr. Justice Alan Macfarlane handed down his judgment on March 23, Harry Walsh had made up his mind to bring an appeal of the judgment on behalf of Doug Palmer. Walsh thought Macfarlane had committed several appealable errors. For example, in Walsh's view, Macfarlane erred in not accepting Doug Palmer's testimony, which, also in Walsh's view, hadn't been shaken or rebutted by any of the crown witnesses. Again, Walsh would argue, Macfarlane was mistaken in adopting Fred Ford's testimony when it was without corroboration from other witnesses or documents. Walsh thought he had solid grounds for asking the British Columbia Court of Appeal to overturn Macfarlane's judgment and direct a new trial.

That was what was on Harry Walsh's mind back home in Winnipeg *before* he heard about the extraordinary events in Vancouver. With Fred Ford's astounding about-face, Walsh knew he could put a brand-new spin on his plans for appeal. He could now bring into play a section of the Canadian Criminal Code that permitted an appeal court to issue an order admitting fresh evidence in a case. The kind of statements that Ford was tossing off were fresh evidence of the knockout variety. Ford was taking back everything he'd testified to in court, and his retractions turned the Palmer case upside down. The way was open, Walsh felt convinced, to ask the appeal court to admit the Ford statements as evidence, and from there, a new trial would be just about inevitable.

Walsh had no doubt that the material Ford was feeding into Joe Wood's office amounted to the real goods. To Walsh, Ford wasn't writing revisionist history; he was at last telling the truth. All through the trial, Walsh had remained certain that Ford was lying on the witness stand. The thrust of his cross-examination of Ford had been to unmask him as a diabolical prevaricator, and Walsh was frustrated that Mr. Justice Macfarlane chose to accept Ford's word over Doug Palmer's. But with Ford finally coming clean, the frustration was over, and the pivotal matter of veracity — Ford or Palmer? — could be thrashed over from a much different and far more favourable perspective in the appeal courts.

Still, as Harry Walsh read over the statement Ford left for Joe Wood on October 7, he knew something else was needed.

Details. What exactly did Sergeant Neil MacKay say to Ford when he badgered Ford to testify against Doug Palmer? And how was the figure of sixty thousand dollars arrived at? Who brought up the numbers? And what about Art MacLennan? How many times did he visit Ford at the Plaza 500 and what did MacLennan lay out for Ford in the way of promises or threats? By the time Walsh thought his way through Ford's October 7 statement, he had jotted down twenty-three areas that called for elaboration. The only person who could provide the elaboration was of course Fred Ford, and Walsh relayed his notes with the twenty-three areas to Joe Wood in Vancouver. Call in Ford, he instructed, and get the details.

Harry Walsh's list of queries brought out the creative side in Ford. He picked up the notes with the twenty-three points from Joe Wood's office in the second week in October and spent three or four days scribbling his answers over four sheets of notepaper.

Some of the answers showed an influence of old *Untouchables* TV shows. Asked for specifics about "threats" from MacKay and MacLennan, Ford wrote: "Neil MacKay and Art Mclennan [*sic*] came to the Plaza 500 in January 1976 and told me I better testify or I would never see daylight. Also they said you'll be killed as soon as you get in the Pen. Also they said to use Doug P. name every chance I got!"

Ford fell in love with the exclamation point.

"It was 1975 Jan. I was shot!" he wrote in answer to a question about the promise of RCMP money. "They put me in protective custody. I was really scared! They said they would pay me $25,000 and relocate me. I agreed!"

Ford's answers suggested a new variation on the financial arrangements. According to his fresh version, from the beginning he was to receive twenty-five thousand *plus* relocation, rather than, as he'd earlier claimed, an overall sum of sixty thousand *in lieu of* relocation.

"While at Plaza 500," he wrote, "I told Staff Sgt. Almrud I

would not testify for $25,000. He said how much do you want? I said $60,000. He said I do not have authority to authorize it. I'll be back with an answer. He came back a couple of hours later and said okay you can have sixty thousand if you give evidence. Art Hoivik was there at the time. He also told me Neil MacKay said $60,000 but for me not to mention money on stand."

No matter what changes Ford worked on past history, the consistent theme in his answers to Harry Walsh's demand for details was that he'd testified only after awful and unremitting pressure from the Mounties. "Neil MacKay," Ford wrote, "kept on insisting I testify or I would be charged with many charges!" Walsh was delighted with this response. It opened the way for him to take two general lines of argument to the appeal courts.

One, Ford's testimony at the trial was, by his own admission, a pack of lies.

Two, the *reason* for the lies was that Ford, as a crown witness, had been held incommunicado by the crown and its agent, the RCMP, who exercised dire threats and dangled monied promises to squeeze false testimony out of the witness.

With Ford's statements in hand — the first that he'd written in Joe Wood's office on May 21, the second that he'd delivered to the office on October 7, and the third in reply to the twenty-three points — Harry Walsh was on his way to the B.C. Court of Appeal to ask that new evidence, namely the three statements, be received in the Palmer case.

As the wording of section 610 in the Criminal Code put it, new evidence could be admitted in a case where the admission was "in the interests of justice".

In the interests of justice.

What precisely did that loaded phrase mean?

The bureaucrats and politicians who stuck the phrase in the Code left it to the courts to figure out its implications. And over the years, in the course of hundreds of applications under section 610, the courts hit on a set of guidelines. It would be "in the interests of justice" to admit new evidence in a case, they held, where the evidence measured up to all of — meaning no fewer than — three general principles:

Where the new evidence couldn't have been deduced by due diligence at the original trial.

Where the new evidence was the kind that might reasonably affect the verdict at trial.

And where the new evidence was reasonably capable of belief.

Harry Walsh checked the facts in the Palmer appeal against the three principles.

"Deduced by due diligence at trial?"

Walsh was certain he was okay on that one. There was no way he could have known for sure Ford was lying when he testified. He *thought* Ford lied. But with all the due diligence in the world, it would have been impossible to prove to Macfarlane that Ford was making up his story under pressure from the RCMP.

"Might reasonably affect the verdict?"

Well, of course, Doug Palmer would surely have been acquitted if Ford had told the truth about his non-dealings with Palmer. Walsh would call that a prize example of reasonably affecting a verdict. So, no problem on the second principle.

"Reasonably capable of belief?"

This might be the sticking-point. Ford's volte-face could be too much for the appeal court to accept, and it could very well decide that Ford's second-time-around story, which was diametrically the opposite to the tale he told on the witness stand, wasn't reasonably capable of belief. *Reasonably*. That was the troublesome word.

Still, Harry Walsh liked his chances, and he set in motion the process of appeal.

Fred Ford backslid.

On January 11, 1977, he phoned his old companion from the Plaza 500, Staff Sergeant Harold Almrud, and asked for a meeting. Almrud told Ford to come on down to the Mountie offices, but he warned Ford that Almrud's boss, Inspector Jack White, would have to sit in on the meeting. Ford showed up within an hour.

Ford said, "That stuff I gave the lawyers about me lying at Dougie Palmer's trial, I heard it on the radio. Bannerman, you know, the news guy, he read practically the whole thing."

"Spooked you, did it, Fred?" Almrud said.

"I didn't know they were gonna use what I wrote, the lawyers I mean," Ford said. "Now it's on the fucking radio."

"If you think you're in a spot, Fred," Inspector Jack White said, "you know who put you there. You did it to yourself."

"Well, shit . . ."

"I want to make something clear before anything else is said in this office, Fred," White said. "You don't have to tell us anything, Sergeant Almrud or myself, but if you do, it could be used in evidence."

"Evidence?" Ford said. "What're you talking about anyway?"

"Come on, Fred," Almrud said. "Those statements you gave weren't for nothing. There could be another trial. The whole thing's started up again."

"They don't count, the statements don't," Ford said. "They only count if I get up in front of a judge and say what's in the statements in court."

What Ford was forgetting or leaving out — or what he didn't grasp — was that, besides writing his three statements, he'd willingly gone to a lawyer's office later, to a firm other than Deverell, Harrop & Company, and sworn all three statements in affidavit form. They had become legal documents, and after Ford returned them to Joe Wood, Harry Walsh filed the affidavits in the B.C. Court of Appeal as part of his appeal package.

"Let me ask you this, Fred," Inspector White said. "Why did you give those statements in the first place?"

"I had a good reason," Ford said. "I wanted to stay alive."

"Who said anything about staying alive?" White asked.

"I got a message."

"From whom?"

"Can't tell you who."

"Fred," Almrud said, "you want to level here? Did someone *force* you to make those statements?"

"I got threatened."

"Who by?"

"I'm still getting threatened," Ford said. "That's what I'm talking about. Threats. What I wanta know, you think you guys can protect me?"

"Protection?" Almrud said. "It'd help if we knew who we were supposed to be protecting you from?"

"I don't know how much I oughta say," Ford said.

"For God's sake, man!" Almrud said. "You're the one who called this meeting. What'd you expect when you came down here?"

"I thought, well, like, we might see what the solution is for everything that's going on."

"Okay," Almrud said. "One possibility of what might happen next is there'll be another trial for Palmer and you'll be called as a witness. Except this time, Fred, it'll be Palmer's lawyers that call you. Not the crown."

"There's a second option open to you, Fred," Inspector White said. "You could give one more statement if you think that'd clear up any misunderstanding. I'm talking about a statement to our people."

"What about protection?" Ford asked.

White said, "We can't keep going back and forth on this protection business when you're not telling us any facts we can put our teeth into."

Silence came from Ford's side of the meeting.

"All right, Fred," White said. "My proposal is that Sergeant Almrud and I discuss your matter with the crown's office and get right back to you."

"Don't you guys phone me," Ford said.

"Whatever you want," White said. "It won't take more than a few hours."

"I'll phone you," Ford said.

The next day, January 12, Ford got Sergeant Almrud on the line.

"I changed my mind," he said to Almrud.

"Hold it, Fred," Almrud said. "A lawyer's ready for you over at the Department of Justice."

"Forget it."

"All you do, Fred, is make out another statement," Almrud said. "An affidavit."

"Don't think so."

"Say in this affidavit what's really been happening."

"Probably what I'll do," Ford said, "is get my own lawyer, some guy to look after the whole thing."

Ford hung up, and neither Almrud nor White nor anyone else at the Heather Street RCMP offices heard again from him.

Ford had backslid, but not far enough to suit the Mounties.

Arthur MacLennan was hopping mad.

When Harry Walsh filed his appeal documents, with Fred Ford's affidavits as the centrepiece, the crown was obliged to file its own affidavits to counter Ford's retractions, revelations, charges, and other finger-pointing claims against the RCMP. Since Ford included MacLennan among the list of villains who harried him, MacLennan had to fire back with an affidavit placing on the record his side of the story.

"Art Mclennan [*sic*] came to see me 2 or 3 times at Plaza 500," Ford wrote in answer to one of Harry Walsh's twenty-three queries. "He said I had no choice but to testify at Doug P trial. He said you will make money and be clear of all charges."

MacLennan's affidavit in rebuttal covered nine long paragraphs. He swore that he visited Ford at the Plaza 500 only a single time for three or four minutes, that he said nothing to Ford about charges against him, that the subject of money never came up, that, in fact, he was "not aware, prior to Ford's testimony at trial with respect to his present allegations, that he had been promised money apart from maintenance for relocation to which he testified at the trial."

MacLennan was annoyed that he was put in a position of dignifying Ford's charges with an answer. "A lot of silly fancy" he called them. The necessity for his own affidavit was demeaning. But that wasn't MacLennan's basic complaint. What really cheesed him off was that the act of filing the affidavit took him out of the case.

"I couldn't argue the appeal," he said years later, still steamed at the unfairness. "As soon as an affidavit went into the Court of Appeal in my name, I was barred from appearing in court on the same case."

Sometimes, in his darker moments, MacLennan sensed a conspiracy at work against him.

"The very fact that all those nonsensical claims were included in Ford's affidavit about me threatening him, one thing and another like that," he said, not chuckling at all. "Maybe the defence counsel did it just to get me out of the way."

In addition to MacLennan's affidavit, the crown — now in

the person of Frank Haar, who assisted MacLennan at the trial and took over from his boss for the appeal — also filed affidavits from seven Mounties who contradicted Fred Ford every step of the way.

Sergeant Jim Locker swore that, way back at the beginning, when he interviewed Ford at the RCMP detachment in Burnaby on the morning in October 1972 after the Mounties busted Jimmy Mortimer, it was Ford who brought up Doug Palmer's name on his own initiative and identified Palmer as the big mover-and-shaker in the heroin operation that employed Ford as a back-up man.

Sergeant Neil MacKay, in the longest affidavit of all, covered the whole ground in his hectic dealings with Ford. For starters, MacKay was adamant that he hadn't frightened Ford with stories about Doug Palmer's hit man gunning him down in front of 3475 Triumph Street. "I did not tell Ford he was shot by a hired killer paid for by Doug Palmer." MacKay said. "That was the conclusion Ford himself had drawn." And MacKay reviewed the financial promises to Ford. He was guaranteed relocation, down payment on a house, twelve hundred dollars a month while he was in protective custody, and, oh yeah, the removal of those dratted tattoos. When Ford went for money over relocation, the sum fixed on was sixty thousand dollars but — can't anyone get this straight? — that was just a *recommendation*.

So it went, seven RCMP affidavits. Corporal Hoivik and Sergeant Almrud backed up MacKay's story about the ways in which the sixty-thousand figure evolved. And Inspector Lawson Eyman described the unhappy day in March 1976 when Ford arrived at his office to pick up what Ford thought was sixty thousand and Eyman knew was twenty-five thousand. Eyman said he drove Ford to the main branch of the Bank of Commerce and helped him cash the cheque. When Ford left the bank, according to Eyman's affidavit, "Ford said the RCMP would be hearing from him concerning the balance of the money he wanted."

Ford had that part right.

The British Columbia Court of Appeal gave Harry Walsh astonishingly short shrift.

Walsh's appeal of Doug Palmer's conviction, his request that the Ford affidavits be permitted as new evidence in the case, was heard on a single day, May 17, 1977, by a panel of three judges, Messrs Bull, McFarlane, and Seaton, and it was disposed of in a short judgment, perfunctory even, that Mr. Justice McFarlane wrote on behalf of the court dismissing the appeal. The judgment was seven pages long, and most of the seven were taken up with matters raised by Walsh that he regarded as rather peripheral to his main point, and with the reasons for rejecting the appeals of Smith, Duncan, Luhtala, and Porter, which a lawyer named Banks unsuccessfully argued the same day.

The explanation for the swift brush-off of Walsh's case wasn't hard to locate. It was that the three judges weren't biting on the arguments Walsh raised under section 610. Was it "in the interests of justice" to accept the new affidavit evidence of Fred Ford? The moon would turn blue before Bull, McFarlane, and Seaton answered yes to that proposition.

"In my opinion," McFarlane wrote in the court's judgment, "it would not serve the interests of justice to receive the tendered evidence of Ford because it is simply not capable of belief. I am satisfied that it is untrue and that any intelligent adult would reject it as wholly untrustworthy."

Walsh had expected that the third principle in the guidelines that defined "in the interests of justice" would give him his toughest hurdle. Was the new evidence "reasonably capable of belief"? As hurdles went, in the opinion of the B.C. Court of Appeal this one was made of cement, and Harry Walsh crashed into it head on.

346

Ah well, back to the drawing-board and on to the Supreme Court of Canada.

In contrast to the licking he got in the British Columbia court, the naked scepticism of its judges, Walsh's experience on the day he argued Doug Palmer's appeal before the Supreme Court in Ottawa was the stuff to warm his lawyerly heart. The day actually stretched over parts of two days, most of June 26 and 27, 1979. All of the time was devoted to Doug Palmer issues — the appeals of Smith, Duncan, Luhtala, and Porter were effective abandoned — and Walsh and the crown counsel, a senior lawyer named Mark de Weerdt, were permitted plenty of space to explore the thorny terrain of section 610 and new evidence and "interests of justice". What's more, the court sat the full complement of nine judges, not a mere seven as it did on lesser appeals. Clearly the Palmer case was regarded as serious business, and Justices Laskin, Martland, Ritchie, Pigeon, Dickson, Beetz, Estey, Pratte, and McIntyre were all on hand. They gave Walsh and de Weerdt their concentrated attention, breaking in now and then to ask clarifying questions. Walsh, since he carried the burden of making the case for the appellant, took most of the questioning, and Chief Justice Bora Laskin did most of the asking. He peppered Walsh with questions. Politely of course. The court was nothing if not decorous, and it was keen to make sure it had the law and Walsh's points straight. For Walsh, the occasion, though he'd been through it many times before in Ottawa, was a counsel's equivalent of dwelling in seventh heaven.

At the end of argument on June 27, the nine judges, as was their custom, left the courtroom by the double doors behind their long elevated bench and gathered in the conference room directly across the corridor. They sat around a circular oak table and entered the ritual of discussion in the Palmer appeal. Each judge, beginning with the most junior, William

347

McIntyre, and working through to the Chief Justice, spoke his piece. Opinion shook down rapidly, smoothly, and unanimously. There would be no dissent in *Douglas Garnet Palmer v. Her Majesty The Queen*. The nine judges were in agreement on the case, and all that remained was for Laskin to assign one of the justices to write the court's opinion. He chose McIntyre.

Bill McIntyre, appointed to the court the previous January, came from British Columbia. That was one reason why Laskin picked him for the Palmer judgment. Where possible and politic, it was the custom to match up judge and province in judgment-writing. But in this instance, McIntyre had at least one other qualification. When he practised in Victoria, he was active in criminal law. He knew his way around the Criminal Code. Bill McIntyre was a heavy, jowly man and had a military air that he earned as an officer fighting a tough war from Sicily up the length of Italy in 1944. In his later years on the court, he was to write a handful of decisions that could fairly be described as refereshing. The Palmer judgment, though it didn't quite reach the refreshing class, was McIntyre's first notable bit of writing for the Supreme Court of Canada.

He was thorough. The judgment, which he issued on December 21, 1979, in time for Harry Walsh's Christmas reading, covered twenty-five pages and touched all the bases. Should the later affidavits of Fred Ford be admitted into evidence in the Palmer case? McIntyre was going to give the old and critical question a good thrashing. He reviewed the evidence as it came out at the trial as well as the later illumination — or confusion — that emerged from the affidavits filed by Ford and the RCMP officers on the appeal. And along the way, McIntyre singled out events that he thought shone a small beam of light on the truth. "I considered it significant," he interrupted his recital of the facts at one point, "that moments after the shooting [in front of 3475 Triumph in January 1975] Ford identified Palmer as either his assailant or the instigator of the attack." That, McIntyre figured, showed what was really going on in Ford's head. And a few other episodes had in his view a similarly revealing quality.

Once McIntyre had the facts organized in what appeared to him to be manageable order, he took a look at past cases that dealt with applications under section 610 of the Criminal Code. He went over the principles in the cases and he got the law down as fine as he could. He stated it in the form of two questions:

"Firstly, is the new evidence possessed of sufficient credibility that it might reasonably have been believed by the trier of fact? If the answer is no, that ends the matter, but if yes, the second question presents itself in this form. If presented to the trier of fact and believed, would the evidence possess such strength or probative force that it might, taken with the other evidence adduced, have affected the result? If the answer to the second question is yes, the motion to adduce new evidence would have to succeed and a new trial be directed at which the evidence could be introduced."

McIntyre's style in getting his thoughts on paper wouldn't have won cheers from E. B. White. "Trier of fact" was the long way round of saying "the judge" or, more specifically in the Palmer case, "Mr. Justice Alan B. Macfarlane". And such words as "probative force" and "adduce" got in the way of clear thinking, though lawyers are accustomed to language that might bog down other reasonably literate readers. Still, no matter how thick and gluey McIntyre's prose was, the double proposition he posed had the great merit — especially since there was no appeal from *his* decision — of pinning for all time the ultimate question: did Fred Ford tell the truth in his first story from the witness stand or in his second story in the affidavits?

Bill McIntyre's answer: the first time in court.

In fact, *two* times in court.

To McIntyre, the key giveaway was that Ford testified with the same recital of facts and in essentially the same wording on two different occasions. The first was at the preliminary hearing in the Palmer case and the second was at the trial. The two court appearances were separated by almost a year, February 1975 for the preliminary and January 1976 for the trial. And for Ford, as he later swore in his affidavits, to make up the identical "bunch of lies" both times out and to stick to the "lies" under Harry Walsh's determined cross-examination, well, in Bill McIntyre's opinion that would amount to an unbelievably virtuoso feat of false testimony.

"The accurate repetition of extemporaneous invention after such a long interval," he wrote, as E. B. White winced, "would be a remarkable performance on Ford's part under any circumstances, But when one adds the fact that the trial judge considered that his evidence was in harmony with the general picture of events which emerged from the evidence of many other witnesses, it becomes impossible to believe that the evidence was fabricated on the spur of the moment."

And that wasn't all.

McIntyre thought the timing of certain events likewise pulled the rug from under Ford when he insisted he lied at the trial. The sequence went this way: testimony at the preliminary hearing; Ford's claim of promise of money from the RCMP; testimony at the trial. Ford said the prime motivating force — or one of them — behind his improvisations on the witness stand at the trial was the Mounties' guarantee of cash for lies. But, wait a minute, McIntyre said, if that were so, how come Ford's story was the same at the preliminary hearing, *before* he was supposedly promised money, as it was at the trial *after* the alleged money bribe?

"It is impossible to believe," McIntyre wrote, "that the nature of his evidence given at trial was affected by the payment or promise of money." And, McIntyre went on, "the suggestion that this [money] arrangement was undisclosed and that the trial judge could therefore have been misled in his assessment of Ford's credibility" just didn't wash.

As a clincher, McIntyre held that wherever there was a

difference in the explanation of events as it appeared in the Ford affidavits and in the RCMP affidavits — not so much a difference as a chasm — he accepted the Mountie version every time. McIntyre said his preference applied to the stories about the pressure on Ford to testify, about Ford's fear he'd be charged with the jewellery-store robbery and the drug-dealing if he didn't deliver on the deal to lie in court, and about the compensation in cash for the fake testimony. In each instance, McIntyre believed the Mounties and disbelieved Ford, especially when the talk got around to money, which McIntyre regarded as fundamental to everything about Ford and his evidence.

Ford swore the money, whether it was twenty-five thousand (which he ultimately received) or fifty thousand (which he first asked for) or sixty thousand (which the Mounties, beginning with Neil MacKay, thought was a fair figure), came as recompense for the lies he told about Doug Palmer. The RCMP said it was payment in place of the cost of relocating Ford and family. McIntyre had no doubts on that one. It *had* to be the way the Mounties described. Why, McIntyre said, just consider the above-board way the RCMP in the person of Inspector Lawson Eyman made payment to Ford a week after the end of the trial. If the arrangement with Ford had been tainted and corrupt, the pay-off would more likely have been by cash in some back alley, not by cheque in the RCMP Heather Street offices.

McIntyre wrote: "The manner of payment of the twenty-five thousand dollars, which involved no secrecy and was done openly by cheque, negates improper motives on the part of the police. And the use of the words 'services rendered' and 'services' on the receipt has, in my opinion, no sinister significance. It is evident that these words were employed to describe the arrangement for payment in lieu of travel and relocation expenses."

The matter was ended for McIntyre.

Ford's affidavits would not be admitted as new evidence,

and there would be no second trial for Doug Palmer.

Appeal dismissed.

To this day, Harry Walsh is convinced that Mr. Justice McIntyre missed the boat and the point in his judgment. Walsh sticks to his contention that Ford's recitation of the same story — rather, the same *lies*, as Walsh insists — at both the preliminary and the trial was no big deal. It's the liar, he repeats, who's the wizard at consistency. The liar, Ford in this instance, gets a story fixed in his head and hangs on to it through thick and thin.

And Walsh thinks he should have won the appeal on another ground that also has to do with truth and falsehood. At one moment in Walsh's cross-examination of Fred Ford, he asked Ford about money. He was pumping Ford for his motivations in testifying on the crown's side and he'd raised the matters of the jewellery-store charge that the RCMP hadn't pursued and of the guarantee by the Mounties that Ford and his wife and children would be relocated. Then Walsh asked another question.

"Were you also promised money?" he said to Ford.

"No," Ford answered. "They promised to look after me and relocate me."

But Walsh points out that the answer, on the afternoon of January 28, 1976, came just after the round-robin of conversations among Ford and various Mounties which led Ford to believe he'd receive sixty thousand dollars in cash.

"It didn't matter whether the money was or wasn't in place of relocation costs," Walsh says. "It was still a promise of money, and Ford's answer meant he was lying to me. He *was* promised money. He perjured himself, and just his lack of credibility on that answer should have been sufficient to allow my appeal and order a new trial.

"However," Walsh goes on, the sound of a small shrug in

352

his voice, "there is the popular expression about the opera not being over until the fat lady has sung. After Mr. Justice McIntyre's judgment, the fat lady had sung for Douglas Palmer."

In the late 1980s, in his mid-seventies, Harry Walsh thrives in the law. For almost a half-century he practised out of the Childs Building, an ancient stone semi-skyscraper at Winnipeg's definitive corner, Portage and Main. In 1985 he moved across the corner, diagonally and upscale, to the spiffy new glass-and-steel Richardson Building. His firm, Walsh, Micay and Company, occupies a whole floor and employs two dozen lawyers. Walsh has a corner office, and he works at the kind of cases you'd expect a senior counsel to pass up.

"I like acting for the fellow who's supposed to be a rogue," he says. "I suppose I should prefer cases where there's some fine legal point involved. But when you've been around as long as I have, the legal complexities all begin to seem the same. The cases that satisfy me most are the cases with human drama. Which is probably why I think often of Doug Palmer. Maybe there are a dozen cases of the hundreds and hundreds I've argued in my career that keep coming back to me. The Palmer case is one of the dozen."

For Russ Chamberlain, there's a puzzle about the Palmer case that won't go away.

In the early 1980s, Chamberlain left the firm of his mentor, Harry Rankin, and opened his own partnership, Giusti and Chamberlain. It's one of the hot Vancouver criminal-law practices. Why not? Everyone in the profession thinks Russ Chamberlain is one hell of a counsel.

What stays in Chamberlain's mind about the Palmer trial isn't the fate of his own client. Bill De Ruiter died in 1985 of

353

natural causes. Chamberlain is still saddened by De Ruiter's death, but he's baffled by Doug Palmer's conduct — or, more accurately, his failure to act — before the trial.

"It's amazing to me Palmer didn't have Fred Ford blown away," Chamberlain says. "From the moment De Ruiter got raided by the Mounties, Palmer must have known Ford was a fink. If he'd been more hard-nosed, he'd have killed Ford and never got convicted."

David Gibbons, who defended Johnny Smith and Bobby Porter, took a three-year break from the law not long after the Palmer trial ended. He sailed his own boat through the South Pacific for a year and studied art in Quebec for another two years. When he returned to Vancouver and the law, he joined Deverell, Harrop & Company. His reputation as a smart cookie spread. He acted for the parents of the victims of Clifford Olsen who were suing for the one hundred thousand dollars the police paid him to point out the burying-places of the children he murdered — and lost. He acted for the Canadian Sikhs who were charged with plotting to blow up the Parliament Buildings in India — and won. Gibbons still sails, usually with his young son on excursions near his summer home on an island off the west coast of Vancouver Island.

On July 18, 1983, Joe Wood, who defended Tommy Duncan and Cliff Luhtala, was appointed to the trial division of the British Columbia Supreme Court. Before Wood left Deverell, Harrop & Company for the bench, Bill Deverell had also departed to live on the nearby Gulf Islands and write novels. The firm is now called Harrop, Phillips, Powell & Gibbons.

Larry Hill, Walter Guay's counsel, died five years after the Palmer trial, done in by booze and a career of scrambling around the criminal courts.

Arthur MacLennan retired from the Department of Justice in 1978. Two years later he was summoned back to act as legal adviser to the federal government on Indian land claims on the west coast. He found things in a mess and worked at straightening them out until 1984, when he retired again. He still lives in the townhouse across from the golf course in Burnaby and he still chuckles.

On April 29, 1983, Mr. Justice Alan Macfarlane was elevated from the trial division of the B.C. Supreme Court to its Court of Appeal.

Francis Rattenbury, the architect who designed Vancouver's courthouse, would probably have been appalled if he'd lived to see what happened to his pride and joy. It was turned into an art gallery. In fact, the Vancouver Art Gallery.

When the British Columbia government, prodded by Sonny Nemetz, the province's Chief Justice, finally realized that the Rattenbury courthouse was too old, small, dusty, and drafty to handle B.C.'s trial business, it commissioned a local architect with an international reputation to design a new courthouse. The architect was Arthur Erickson, and his courthouse, just to the south of Rattenbury's, is an asymmetrical building of glass, air, calm, concrete, and trailing green plants.

With the new courthouse opened in 1979, Erickson turned his hand and twenty million dollars to remodelling the original courthouse. The Vancouver Art Gallery is now a bright, stark, mostly modernist place, but here and there, especially on the exterior, Francis Rattenbury's fussy, affectionate neoclassism shows through.

When Doug Palmer and the rest of his crew went to prison in 1976, there was a scramble in the East End to take charge of the heroin trade Palmer left behind. A man named Gordon Pawliw emerged as top dog. But he had plenty of angry competition. Much of it came from Conrad Gunn, the old hand in drug-wholesaling, and perhaps from a man named Dennis Vandooren.

According to Pawliw, Vandooren owed him $120,000 as a result of a misfired drug transaction. Vandooren lived in a lovely old farmhouse on the shore of Quamichan Lake on Vancouver Island, and in May 1984 Pawliw dispatched two hit men to Vandooren's farmhouse. The hit men were a pair of East Enders named Rod Camphaug and Rod Schnob, and their instructions were to rub out Vandooren the welsher.

Camphaug and Schnob let themselves into Vandooren's farmhouse at three in the morning. But Vandooren heard them and, nude, he dived through the glass of an upstairs window and flattened himself against the roof. That left Vandooren's wife as the only target in sight, and Schnob, armed with a .357 magnum and a .44 magnum, pumped bullets from both into her. The two men beat it, but the police weren't far behind. They arrested Schnob, Camphaug, and Pawliw, and, after a thirteen-week trial, the three were convicted of Mrs. Vandooren's murder and sentenced to life in prison with no parole for twenty-five years.

And what of Conrad Gunn?

He, too, went to prison, convicted of conspiring to murder two men. One of the two was Gordon Pawliw, and the second intended victim was none other than Cliff Luhtala, the former Palmer gang member who did his time, won parole, and got back to the drug business.

The RCMP thought the eldest Palmer brother, Ray, might have been active in the heroin trade, but they never caught him at it. Ray was slick — and a bright man too. While he was in the B.C. Pen he earned a Bachelor of Arts degree, and after his parole he took a teacher's diploma at Simon Fraser University. He never went into teaching or any other business that the police could figure out. But Ray seemed to have plenty of money, enough to dabble profitably in real estate in the New Westminster area south of Vancouver.

On January 21, 1983, Ray dropped around to the New Westminster Courthouse to check the title to one of his properties. He talked business with a lawyer and left for another appointment. He didn't make the second date. Ray vanished, and a few weeks later a man walking his dog in New Westminster spotted a decomposed body in a small woods near the corner of 72nd Avenue and 144th Street. The body was Ray's. He had been shot with a single bullet in the back of the head. The killing was in the classic hit-man technique, but no one, in or out of the drug trade, has ever been charged with Ray's murder.

On the day that Ray Palmer was tending to his land business at the New Westminster Courthouse, January 21, 1983, a man named Lorne Wenn was standing trial in one of the courtrooms on a charge of attempted murder. Ray had a personal interest in the case, but decided against stopping by the courtroom. Too many cops in the neighbourhood, he told the lawyer he had been meeting with. The chief witness against Lorne Wenn in the trial, the man whom Wenn was supposed to have tried to kill, was the Palmer family nemesis, the one and only Fred Ford.

Wenn's alleged attempt on Ford's life went back to December 8, 1981. Ford was living in Port Moody, a municipality

357

along the Burrard Inlet east from Vancouver. On the morning of the eighth, Ford noticed a loose wire dangling under his car. The wire was attached to a home-made bomb. Ford called the cops, and much later, after clever sleuthing, they charged Lorne Wenn with the attempted murder.

At the trial, Ford testified that he was now certain Wenn was the guy who took the shots at him in front of 3475 Triumph Street in January 1975. He said he thought Wenn was trying to get into the Palmer brothers' good books by making another try at his life. Everyone, Ford told the court, knew the Palmers had put out a contract on his life. Wenn was convicted and sentenced to life in prison.

Fred Ford disappeared from the Vancouver area after the Wenn trial. But by the mid-1980s he was back in town, alive and healthy but, according to the Mounties, looking over his shoulder.

Donald Palmer served his jail time quietly. For the early part of his sentence, he was taken out of the B.C. prison system. The people who administered the system thought the Palmers had too many connections among other prisoners, and shipped Donald to Dorchester Penitentiary in New Brunswick. A few safe years later, Donald was brought back to the medium-security prison at Mission, B.C., then transferred to the low-security Sumas Correctional Centre at Abbotsford. Everybody in the system looked on Donald as a model prisoner. He got day parole in February 1983 and full parole in February 1984. Donald was happy to be on the street, though someone wrote in his record that he was "having trouble finding support in the community". Six months after his release, Donald felt low. He thought it was depression brought on by his failure to land a steady job. The doctors said it wasn't depression. It was cancer. Donald died a few weeks later.

After the Palmer trial, the British Columbia prison officials were especially keen to hustle Doug Palmer out of the province to serve his sentence. They decided on Millhaven Penitentiary in Ontario. On the day in the spring of 1977 when Doug was to be transferred to Millhaven, a posse of guards escorted him to Vancouver Airport. In the Air Canada waiting-area, Doug tore off his clothes and screamed at the other passengers, "There's a fucking bomb on that plane!" Air Canada decided it didn't wish to fly Doug Palmer on its aircraft, and the posse returned him to the Kent maximum-security prison at Agassiz, B.C., where he spent the next three years.

Doug kept his nose clean at Kent and comported himself in such gentlemanly fashion that he won transfer to the more accommodating medium-security prison at Matsqui near the American border. That was an error on the part of the people who made decisions about prisoners, because on August 28, 1980, Doug hunkered down in a garbage truck and rode out of Matsqui. Someone — Ray Palmer, the police were certain — met Doug down the road with a car and a change of clothes. Doug took off over the border.

Someone in the California office of the FBI got smart. When the RCMP routinely notified the FBI of Doug's escape and his undoubted presence in the United States, the unknown wise man at the Bureau put together two known facts about Doug: his love of golf and his preference for the Los Angeles area. There are 350 public and private golf courses in and around Los Angeles, and FBI agents set themselves the job of showing Doug's photograph at all 350. By the time they reached the Santa Anita course close to the race-track of the same name in the town of Arcadia, it was May 1982 and the agents had covered slightly more than one hundred courses.

At Santa Anita, everyone recognized the photograph. It

was of Arnold Ross, a quiet guy who showed up at the course three or four time a week, always by himself, and usually picked up a game with the older gents who were Santa Anita regulars. Didn't shoot much of a game, Arnold Ross, lucky if he broke into the 90s, but he was a nice fella. The FBI arrested Doug Palmer — or Arnold Ross or, as he was also known in town, Vern Parkes — on the back nine at Santa Anita. They extradited him home to British Columbia, where he sat out the rest of his sentence, together with something extra for the escape, in the Kent maximum-security pen.

Doug got out of prison the honest way, on parole, in January 1986. For a few months he lived in Prince George, but eventually he moved back to Burnaby close to his old East End stamping-grounds.

"On the surface he's clean," an RCMP officer named George Mackay said in the spring of 1987. "But with Doug Palmer, the surface tells you nothing."